T0271935

Innovation and Economic Crisis

The recent financial and economic crisis has spurred a lot of interest among scholars and the public audience. Strangely enough, the impact of the crisis on innovation has been largely underestimated. This book can be regarded as complementary reading for those interested in the effect of the crisis, with a particular focus on innovation in Europe.

The book is divided into three main parts. The first part briefly summarizes the origin of the crisis and the three main explanations for it: the financial explanation, the global imbalances explanation, and the technological explanation. It then sets the scene, reviewing the longstanding tradition regarding innovation, technical change and economic development. The second part empirically explores the impact of the crisis, with a focus on national-specific factors such as the National System of Innovation and labour market institutions. Finally, the third part investigates what is happening as a result of the crisis at the level of the firm in terms of patterns of creative destruction, innovation strategies, and types of innovation activity.

This book shows that there are still several firms continuing to innovate despite the crisis. However, creative destruction is also at work. In terms of national characteristics, countries with a stronger national system of innovation are better off. The crisis seems to put the convergence of innovation at risk in Europe, as the new EU Member States appear to be those heavily affected by the crisis. Regarding differences in labour market institutions, countries coupling a security system for workers with high provision of skills are performing better. Concerning firms' behaviour, the identikit of the innovator seems to be changing as a result of the crisis. Those who dare to swim against the stream are small and recent firms, with innovation capacity and internal financial resources.

Daniele Archibugi is a Research Director at the Italian National Research Council in Rome, and Professor of Innovation, Governance and Public Policy at the University of London, Birkbeck College.

Andrea Filippetti is a researcher at the Italian National Research Council, and visiting researcher at the University of London, Birkbeck College.

Routledge studies in global competition

Edited by John Cantwell
Rutgers, the State University of New Jersey, USA
and
David Mowery
University of California, Berkeley, USA

Innovation and Economic Crisis

Lessons and prospects from the economic downturn

Daniele Archibugi and Andrea Filippetti

Routledge
Taylor & Francis Group

LONDON AND NEW YORK

First published 2012
by Routledge
2 Park Square, Milton Park, Abingdon, Oxon OX14 4RN

Simultaneously published in the USA and Canada
by Routledge
711 Third Avenue, New York, NY 10017 (8th Floor)

Routledge is an imprint of the Taylor & Francis Group, an informa business

British Library Cataloguing in Publication Data
A catalogue record for this book is available from the British Library

Library of Congress Cataloging in Publication Data
Archibugi, Daniele.
 Innovation and economic crisis: lessons and prospects from the
 economic downturn/Daniele Archibugi and Andrea Filippetti.
 p. cm.
 1. Global Financial Crisis, 2008–2009. 2. Technological innovations–
 Economic aspects–Europe. 3. Economic development–Europe. 4. Labor
 market–Europe–Case studies. 5. Organizational behavior–Europe.
 I. Filippetti, Andrea, 1977– II. Title.
 HB37172008 .A73 2011
 338'.064094–dc22

                                                            2011008984

ISBN: 978-0-415-60228-0 (hbk)
ISBN: 978-0-203-80451-3 (ebk)

Typeset in Times
by Wearset Ltd, Boldon, Tyne and Wear

Contents

Figures

Tables

Preface and acknowledgements

This book is the result of an initial disappointment regarding the fierce debate on the 2008–09 economic crisis. Why were scholars involved in innovation studies not participating in this debate? After all, the relationship between innovation, technology and economic change has been widely explored since the seminal contribution of Joseph Alois Schumpeter.

This led us to start thinking about innovation and the economic crisis, with a specific focus on the effects of the crisis on the innovation investment of the firm. The question is fundamental, and still deserves some attention, possibly grounded on empirical analysis. Economic crises are periods of big change. Recent and less recent history is full of breakthrough innovations that were introduced during periods of great turbulence and recession.

Yet the recent crisis has led to uncertainty on both demand and supply sides. This specific crisis has severely hit the financial side of the economy, which is a central propeller of risky projects such as those associated with innovation activity. Furthermore, countries differ in terms of patterns of innovation, types of institutions, and several other characteristics. These can influence the behaviour of firms during a major economic downturn. Thus, there are several key questions, both fascinating and interesting, that spur the interest to investigate what happens to innovation in times of crisis. Finally, there are substantial policy questions at stake.

During the writing of the book we have benefited from several suggestions and comments from two categories of colleagues. The first category pertains to those people who we regularly bother, in various circumstances. Among them we would particularly like to mention Grazia Ietto-Gillies, Simona Iammarino, Mario Pianta, Giorgio Sirilli, Francesco Crespi, Mario Denni, Cristiano Antonelli, Rinaldo Evangelista and Giovanni Cerulli. The second category includes those who have provided valuable insights and comments during conferences, seminars and talks. Here, we remember Andrew Taylecote, Maria Savona, Ed Steinmueller, Valentina Meliciani, Keld Laursen, all the participants in the FIRB Conference held at the University Bocconi of Milan, and at a seminar at SPRU, University of Sussex, October 2009. We are doubly indebted to Marion Frenz and Frederick Guy, who participated in the writing of two preliminary versions of two chapters in this book. We would also like to express our gratitude to Hugo Hollanders and Keith Sequeira, and to the DG Enterprises and Industry of the European Commission for allowing us to use data from the Innobarometer and of the European Innovation Scoreboard.

Finally, putting a book together always involves other hands besides those who write it. In our case, these hands belong to Paola and Renata. This book is dedicated to them, together with Clara, Orlando, Gabriele, Aurora and Valerio.

Rome, 17 May 2011

Introduction

Major events have unpredictable consequences.

Notre-Dame de Paris (V. Hugo), 1831

Aim and research questions

Strangely enough, scholars of innovation are not participating in the debate on the current economic crisis. This is surprising, as a long-lasting tradition of economists of innovation, specifically within the so-called neo-Schumpeterian strand of research, emphasizes that the instable nature of the capitalistic system and innovation are two faces of the same coin. The upswings and downswings of economic activity are closely intertwined with science, technological change, and the way innovation takes place over time and diffuses throughout the entire economic system. This book analyses the effects of the 2008–09 economic crisis on the innovation activity of the firm in European countries.

The economic landscape we have been witnessing since the burst of the financial crisis in 2008 is a peculiar one. It is characterized by a huge plunge in demand and international trade, a generalized worsening of credit conditions on financial markets, an unprecedented intervention of the states and central banks, as well as a growing uncertainty about the future direction of technical change and profit opportunities. Within this unique scene, a number of questions can be raised that are relevant for both economic theory and policy: *How does the firm behave in terms of innovation? To what extent is innovation cyclical, as opposed to persistent? Which countries are most affected by the crisis in terms of innovation performance? What factors can explain the different impact across countries? Which strategies are more conducive to innovating during a recession? What are the most suitable innovation policies in this situation?* This book seeks to answer these questions empirically, by employing data at the level of the country and at the level of the firm.

Why write a book about innovation and economic crisis? Rationale and limitations

The production of books regarding the crisis is itself counter-cyclical. Notable examples of this include *The Great Crash 1929*, by John Kenneth Galbraith (1954), and *Maniacs, Panics, and Crashes*, by Charles Kindleberger and Robert Aliber (2005; first edition 1978), as well as the current *Crisis Economics: A Crash Course in the Future of Finance* (Roubini and Mihm, 2010) and *The Ascent of Money* (Ferguson, 2008), among several others. We cannot even claim the original idea of writing a book about innovation during a crisis, as we have been pre-empted by Keller and Samuels' (2003) *Crisis and Innovation in Asian Technology*, which explores the impact of the 1997 crisis in South-East Asia on technology. Having said that, we believe there are still good reasons to investigate what happens to innovation during a major recession.[1]

First, major recessions are unique situations in the economic and social life of modern capitalistic systems. They have been shown to be detrimental for both social and economic systems. They are associated with higher suicide and homicide rates, higher crime rates, higher divorce rates, and declines in other measure of societal well-being (Knoop, 2008). Regarding the economic system, recessions can exert persistent effects on state budgets, companies' profits, workers' skills, and long-term levels of unemployment.

Second, a wealth of empirical evidence has convincingly demonstrated the close relationship between the innovation performance of a country and its long-term rate of economic growth, productivity and wealth.

Third, as explained in the following chapters, innovation activity is closely intertwined with economic change and recession. A better understanding of the innovation behaviour of the firm during a major recession is therefore doubly relevant: (1) it will contribute to the branch of economic theory that addresses the patterns of change and economic development over time; and (2) it can be useful in designing appropriate policies for recovery.

The empirical analysis of this volume is confined to European countries. There are pros and cons of this choice. Starting with the latter, the analysis provides insights into what is happening in a particular part of the world, in a period in which economies are increasingly intertwined at the global level. In this respect we are able to tell only a part of the story, but we illustrate these circumstances with a great deal of empirical inductive research.

Regarding the former, there are good reasons for doing this. First, the countries under scrutiny here do not show huge differences in terms of their stage of development, as they include the European advanced countries along with the transition economies that have become increasingly integrated as a result of the European enlargement process that has occurred over the past decade. As such, firms belonging to these countries operate in the same markets.

These countries also show a sufficient degree of homogeneity in terms of institutional arrangements, even though there are still important differences that can play a role, as shown in Chapter 6. These differences are less than they would be in the case of countries belonging to areas that differ greatly across a wide spectrum of institutional aspects, such as the US, Europe and Asia. Moreover, even if countries have adopted different public policies in response to the crisis, coordination at the European level has taken place to some extent. Overall, the sample considered here allows us to investigate the phenomenon we are concerned about within a context in which countries do not differ too much. This permits us to make assumptions about factors that could have exerted an effect on the behaviour of the firm but would have been hard to capture in an empirical analysis, such as the political system, stages of development, culture, and so on.

A further two limitations of this book must be briefly pointed out. The first has to do with the role played by new firms and entry-and-exit dynamics. While this is a key point within our theoretical context, we are not yet able to take it fully into account, due to lack of data at this stage. The second regards the importance of the industrial dynamic. As we will explain, this is also at the centre of neo-Schumpeterian theorizing, specifically as recessions and major technological breaks are often associated with the rise of new industrial sectors and structural change. The latter point pertains to long-term analysis, which is outside the scope of this book. This volume should instead be interpreted as a fresh snapshot of what is happening in terms of innovation behaviour of firms during the current economic crisis. Further in-depth and comprehensive analysis will be possible in the coming years, as more accurate data will be available.

The patterns of innovation and technological change

The role of technical change and innovation in relation to economic change has been a central concern of the fascinating debate about the presence of *long waves* (Tylecote, 1992; Van Duijn, 1983). The concept started gaining popularity in the 1920s, thanks to the statistical studies carried out by Nikolai Dmitrievich Kondratieff at that time in the Moscow Business Conjuncture Institute (Kondratiev, 1979). The crucial role played by innovation was pointed out by and large by Joseph Schumpeter in his *Theory of Economic Development* (Schumpeter, 1911 (1934)), where he argues that 'innovation is the engine of change and economic development in modern capitalistic systems'. This debate underwent a passionate revival during the 1970s and 1980s, thanks to the studies by Gerard Mensch and scholars of the Science and Policy Research Unit (SPRU) at the University of Sussex, such as Freeman, Clarke, Soete, Dosi and Perez, among others.

A central argument addressed in this field of research is the role played by innovation during a crisis driven by a major technological discontinuity. On the one hand, the *creative destruction* model portrayed by Schumpeter in his *Theory of Economic Development* has proved to be a very powerful argument. On the other, Schumpeter himself later observed, in *Capitalism, Socialism and Democracy*, that innovation tends to be persistent and structural, as it takes place in a cumulative fashion (Schumpeter, 1942). This is regarded as the *creative accumulation* model. The differences between the two are far-reaching. In the former, new entrepreneurs and new firms are responsible for introducing radical innovation, and displace the old firms. In the latter, innovations are introduced mostly by existing large firms, which also manage to survive major technological breakthroughs thanks to their wide competences, organizational structure and financial resources. As a consequence, the creative destruction model leads to strong competitive market structures, while creative accumulation is mostly associated with oligopolistic markets.

The reality has proved to be more complex than is depicted in the two ideal types. True, major recessions come with intense turbulence in the markets, and new swarms of firms tend to appear, mainly in the emerging industries. However, many existing firms (although not all of them) manage to survive major transitions by adapting themselves over time, even in an extreme manner. Thus, today we find what was previously the largest typewriter company in the world, IBM, operating in the market of business service software, along with more recent companies such as Microsoft, and a vast array of very young open source-based companies, such as Red Hat.

There is little doubt that major recessions heavily shape the patterns of economic change and bring about structural change. However, even though the long-wave theory is based on the assumption that there are regularities in the way economic systems develop over time, it is also true that each big transition is different from previous ones.

Innovation activity has profoundly changed over time since the First Industrial Revolution, from the ascent of the railways industry and mass production of automobiles to the development of information and communication technology (ICT). These days, the service sector is more prominent than ever. Thus, innovation in the service sector and its relationship with the manufacturing sector are key for the competitiveness of economic system. This has led to a change in the nature of innovation that is no longer solely based on technological development and science. Also, the importance of sources of innovation external to the firm has risen, along with the establishment of networks (or ecosystems) of firms that continuously innovate (Langlois, 2003; Pavitt, 2005).

Finally, research has demonstrated the presence of a substantial heterogeneity across firms in terms of innovation strategies. Exploring the extent to which these differences matter when it comes to innovation investment during a crisis is worth exploring. Furthermore, countries differ significantly along different dimensions, such as the structure of National Systems of Innovation (NSI), labour market institutions, financial market arrangements, and the skills and competences of the labour force. It is therefore reasonable to assume that these factors can play a role in affecting the firms' innovation decisions during a depression.

To sum up, major recessions have three characteristics that make their investigation extremely attractive. The first is the unique macroeconomic environment, as characterized by a deep plunge in demand and great difficulties in the credit and financial markets, as well as major discontinuities in technology and markets. Second, they are quite rare, and thus it is not always possible to 'observe' them occurring. Third, they tend to profoundly change the direction of modern economic systems, as they greatly affect the long-term patterns of economic growth, technical change and employment opportunities. A better understanding of how major crises shape the economic system still represents a challenge for the theory of innovation, and is key for policy recommendations. Within such a challenging and fascinating context, this volume seeks to make a contribution in shedding some light by investigating investment in innovation during the current economic crisis.

An overview of the book

The book is divided into three parts. Part I sets the scene for the empirical analysis carried out in Parts II and III. Chapter 1 discusses three main explanations that have been put forward to explain the current economic and financial crisis. Chapter 2 reviews the contribution of the neo-Schumpeterian stream of research on the patterns of innovation, focusing on the relationship between innovation and economic change, and innovation during economic downturns. Chapter 3 discusses two streams of literature that put institutions at the centre of the understanding of the functioning of economic systems: the National Systems of Innovation (NSI) research, and the Varieties of Capitalism (VoC) research.

The second part of the book includes three chapters that explore empirically the effect of the crisis on innovation investment at the country level. Chapter 4 explores the effects of the economic downturn on innovation in light of the process of enlargement undertaken by the European Union (EU) over the past decade. The role played by the structure of the NSI vis-à-vis the role of the drop in the demand is investigated in Chapter 5, while Chapter 6 analyses how differences in labour market institutions and skills map into different patterns of innovation investment of the firm during the crisis.

In Part III, the scope of the analysis shifts to the level of the firm. Chapter 7 examines whether the economic downturn is bringing about major changes in the innovation landscape. Specifically, we compare two customary ideal types in the Schumpeterian literature: *creative accumulation* versus *creative destruction*. Chapter 8 explores the strategies of the firm in terms of innovation investment, highlighting differences between the manufacturing and service sectors. Chapter 9 employs the concept of *slack*, which has been defined as the pool of resources in an organization that is in excess of the minimum necessary to produce a given level of organizational output. It has been argued that slack is necessary for firms to innovate, and the chapter addresses this issue in relation to the economic downturn. Finally, the concluding section discusses the main findings of the book and some policy suggestions for recovery.

PART I
Setting the scene

1 At the root of the crisis

Some proposed explanations

The way in which money and finance affect the behaviour of the system can be perceived only within a theory that allows money and finance to affect what happens.

(Minsky, 1986, p. 4)

The 'Minsky moment'

In September 2008, for the first time since 1866 in the United Kingdom, several people were neatly queuing in front of the entrance of a bank – Northern Rock – to claim their money back, as they were frightened that the bank could go bankrupt. This episode followed quite a hectic summer in which the sub-prime mortgage market in the US had shown the first signals of tension. This was the side effect of a slowing down in the real estate market after an impressive boom in the 2002–2007 period.

Very soon the tension spread to the entire financial market, and eventually the interbank market was almost stuck. Simply put, banks had lost confidence (the basic engine of finance) in one anothers' solvency. Bear Stearns was the first giant investment bank to go bankrupt, followed by the largest provider of mortgages in the US, Countywide Financial. After the bankruptcy of one of the most prestigious American investment banks, Lehman Brothers, in September 2008, it became very clear that what was happening was an extraordinary crisis across the entire financial market.

It took just a few months for the crisis to spread from Wall Street to Main Street, with huge effects on the real side of the economy. In OECD countries (Figure 1.1), the change in gross domestic product (GDP) shows a modest 0.31 per cent rise in 2008 and a fall equal to –3.41 per cent in 2009; similarly, industrial production plunged by –11.46 per cent in 2009 while unemployment rose considerably, with a 43 per cent increase in the harmonised unemployment rate in the three-year period from 2007 to 2009.

Every great crisis has its hero: these days are, by all accounts, the 'Minsky moment' (Cassidy, 2008)[1] (see Figure 1.2, which appeared on *The New Yorker* in February 2008). Hyman Philip Minsky (1919–1996) was above all a Keynesian economist who believed that the neoclassical school was the reduction of

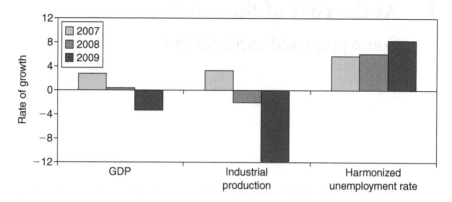

Figure 1.1 Real gross domestic product, industrial production, unemployment rates, total OECD countries (source: authors' elaboration on OECD.stat database).

Figure 1.2 The Minsky moment (source: *The New Yorker*, February 2008).

the Keynesian revolution to banality (Minsky, 1975). His scientific programme, as illustrated in his major text *Stabilizing an Unstable Economy* (Minsky, 1986), was basically to replace the equilibrium theory with an economic theory based on a business cycle associated with a financial instability view of how economy operates.

By emphasizing the Keynes key lessons of the *General Theory*, Minsky insisted upon the intrinsic instability of the capitalistic system due to the growing prominence played by the financial side of the economy. Investment, he claimed, is basically a financial decision. With the upswing of the business cycle, investment tends to grow along with the financial assets that support it. For reasons that he explains (Minsky, 1986), he concludes that the liability structures that support investments tend to deteriorate over time. This natural tendency of the economic system to move from robust to fragile finance is at the heart of the *financial instability hypothesis* advanced by Minsky.

According to many observers and scholars, this is exactly what has happened again in 2008–09. The financial market had deteriorated so far that it was no longer sustainable. The slowdown of the real-estate market and the following tension in the mortgage sector were only the incidental cause that led to the burst of the bubble; deeper causes should be looked for in the way the financial system had grown and transformed over the past decade along an unsustainable path. This, then, was the Minsky moment. But since economists are overwhelmingly apt to seek causes, soon the question became: what caused the crisis in the financial sector? This chapter reviews three main explanations that have been proposed.

Three possible explanations of the causes of the crisis

We have already made it clear that the main concern of this volume is not that of analysing the causes of this crisis. However, in this section we discuss three main explanations that could be at the root of one of the deepest depressions since that of 1929: (1) the financial explanation; (2) the global economic imbalances explanation; and (3) the technological explanation.

The financial explanation and the 'credit crunch'

According to several scholars, the current crisis originated with the creation of a financial bubble that was the result of an excessive accumulation of debt (see, among many others, Brunnermeier, 2009; Crotty, 2009; Roubini and Mihm, 2010). This was associated with a dramatic surge in the supply of credit made possible by both regulatory arrangements and an expansive monetary policy, primarily driven by the Federal Reserve. Innovation in the financial sector also made a substantial contribution, as it allowed the detachment of credit from risk,[2] as well as increasing the *leveraging* (the ratio between assets and liabilities) of the banking system. This had led to a dramatic increase in the supply of credit. Between 1981 and 2008, the debt of financial institutes in the US grew from 22 per cent to 117 per cent of the gross domestic product (Roubini and Mihm, 2010). Minsky himself had already stressed the increasing role played by financial innovation aimed to create new money during periods of expansion. A similar argument regarding the importance of financial innovation in the 1929 Great Depression was made by Galbraith (1954), who stated that 'the most notable piece of speculative architecture of the late twenties [...] was the investment trust' (p. 72), which by 1929 had marketed a third of all new capital issued in that year.

In a thought-provoking book, Johnson and Kwak (2010) make their case against the 'ideology of finance' that pervaded the American political and economic system in the last decades. They claim that the dramatic financialization of the economy was the result of an impressive increase in power of the large banks in the US. Some figures reported in their book are worth reiterating.

In 1978, the financial sector borrowed thirteen dollars in the credit markets for every 100 dollars borrowed in the real economy; by 2007, this had grown to fifty-one dollars. In support of the 'too big too fail' argument, they show that from 1995 to 2009 the value of the six larger banks in the US grew from less than 20 per cent to around 60 per cent of US GDP. A brief look at Figure 1.3, reporting the corporate profits in the US in the financial and non-financial sectors over the past two decades, gives an indication of the dramatic expansion of the financial sector compared to that of the non-financial sector.

Those who advocate that the crisis originated in the financial system argue that it spread to the real sector of the economy as a result of a credit crunch. The credit crunch reflects a situation in which the financial and banking system reduces the availability of credit for internal reasons that do not directly depend upon demand conditions and monetary policy. Figure 1.4 shows the total value of loans to non-financial corporations, for the period 2006–2010, aggregated for the Eurozone. Across the Eurozone, a generalized reduction in loans has occurred in the business sector, equal to a –3.8 per cent drop from the peak of January 2009. Figure 1.5 displays the rate of growth of loans to non-financial companies for different periods of maturity. It reveals that short-term loans have been the most affected, followed by mid-term loans, while the rates of growth of long-term loans have been positive following a substantial plunge. In order to support the financial nature of the current crisis, the key question is whether these trends are the causes or the results of the depression.

One way to seek to corroborate this hypothesis is to look at qualitative data on the relationship between the banking system and the business sector concerning

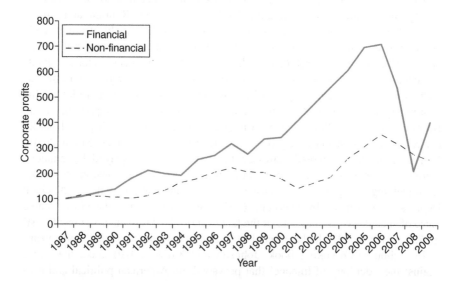

Figure 1.3 Corporate profits, financial and non-financial corporations, 1987–2009 (base year=1987), US (source: authors' elaboration on Bureau of Economic Analysis *National Income and Product Account*).

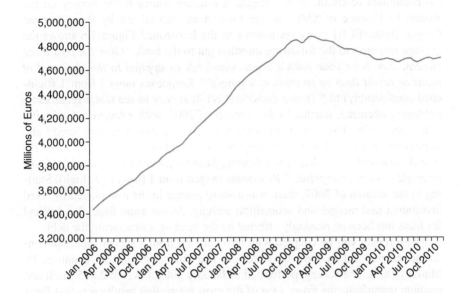

Figure 1.4 Loans to non-financial corporations: outstanding amounts at the end of each period (stocks), Eurozone, 2006–2010 (millions of euros) (source: European Central Bank).

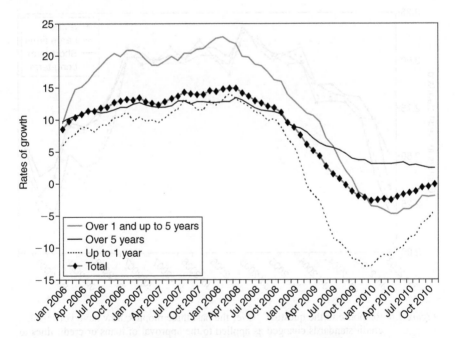

Figure 1.5 Loans to non-financial corporations for different periods of maturity (annual rates of growth), Eurozone (source: European Central Bank).

the conditions of credit. In this regard, a relevant source is the Survey on the Access to Finance of SMEs in the Euro Area, carried out by the European Central Bank (ECB) every six months in the Eurozone.[3] Figure 1.6 shows the average response to the following question put to the bank: '*Over the past three months, how have your bank's credit standards as applied to the approval of loans or credit lines to enterprises changed?*' Responses ranged from 1 (tightened considerably) to 5 (eased considerably). It is easy to see that a remarkable tightening occurred, starting in the summer of 2007, with a recovery beginning at the start 2009. This was particularly the case regarding long-term credit and large firms. Figure 1.7 shows the response to the following question: '*Over the past three months, how have the following factors affected the demand for loans or credit lines to enterprises?*' Responses ranged from 1 (low) to 5 (high). Starting in the autumn of 2007, there was a sharp plunge in the role played by fixed investment and merger and acquisition activity. At the same time, the demand for loans has been increasingly affected by the need of restructuring the debt.

These results can be coupled with those arising from a survey on credit conditions carried out in fourteen European and emerging markets countries by Markit (2009). The survey, performed in January 2009, covered 2,875 small and medium manufacturing firms. One of the most interesting results was that firms reported that their net demand for credit had increased (apart from the case of Poland).

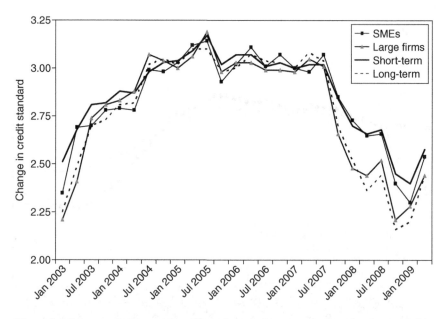

Figure 1.6 Response to the question: 'Over the past three months, how have your bank's credit standards changed as applied to the approval of loans or credit lines to enterprises?' (source: *Survey on the Access to Finance of SMEs in the Euro Area*, European Central Bank, 2010).

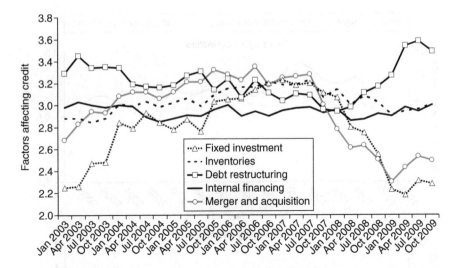

Figure 1.7 Response to the question: 'Over the past three months, how have the following factors affected the demand for loans or credit lines to enterprises?'
(source: *Survey on the Access to Finance of SMEs in the Euro Area*, European
Central Bank, 2010).

Overall, the reduction of credit and tightening of the credit standard by the
banking system, along with high demand for credit and an extremely loose monetary policy, seems to lend some support to the credit crunch hypothesis.

Global economic imbalances

The financial explanation put forward above is sometimes referred to as the
'easy credit and lax regulation' argument. Some scholars argue that the dramatic
expansion of credit and debt is only the manifestation of more profound imbalances. They contend that the savings glut in Asia led to a major part of these
savings flowing into the US, with the result that there was too much money in
the US financial system chasing too few opportunities, leading to a 'Global
Savings Glut' (Dooley *et al.*, 2005).

The route of the global imbalances can be tracked in Figure 1.8, which highlights the mirroring dynamic in investment, savings and current accounts in
developed and emerging countries. The dramatic growth of the emerging economies and oil exporters (thanks to the surge of the price of natural resources) led
to an excess of savings and a large surplus in the current accounts of these countries. On the other hand, developed countries experienced larger increases in the
current account deficit (Faruqee *et al.*, 2009).

To balance this deficit in the current account, massive capital inflows took
place, initially into US government debt, and later into the more attractive
financial products. Almost the entire increase in current account balances from

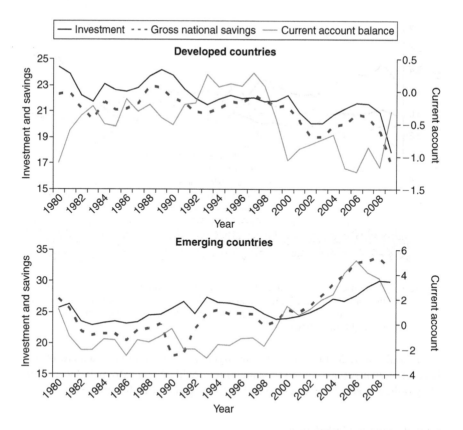

Figure 1.8 Investment, gross national savings and current account balance (rates of growth), 1980–2008: developed and emerging countries (source: authors' elaboration on IMF, World Economic Outlook database).

emerging economies has been matched by the increase in current account deficit in a single country, the US (see Figure 1.9). Thus, for the first time in centuries, the direction of capital flow is not from West to East, but from East to West. As Ferguson (2008) put it, 'China has become the banker to the US'.

Further, a not insignificant role in this financial flow from emerging to developed countries has been that played by sovereign wealth funds, which are state-owned investment funds comprising financial assets such as stocks, bonds, property, precious metals or other financial instruments. The amount of these financial assets has risen spectacularly over the past decade as a result of the increase in the price of natural resources, primarily oil and gas (*The Economist*, 2008).

Advanced countries have managed to sustain high levels of consumption and house market prices thanks to capital inflows, financial innovation and an expansion of credit. The presence of these large amounts of savings – or the Asian 'savings glut' – has been argued to be the reason for the dramatic increase in the

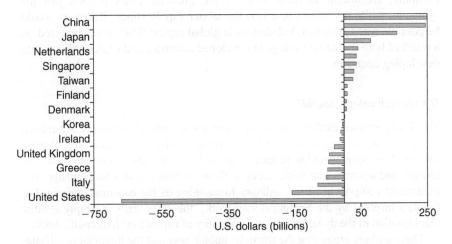

Figure 1.9 Current account in billions of US dollars, 2008 (selected countries) (source: authors' elaboration on IMF World Economic Outlook database).

US mortgage market, in which 100 per cent mortgages could be obtained by people with no income, no job and no assets (Ferguson, 2008). This generated the bubble in the housing and financial markets, which eventually burst. According to this line of argument, the solution lies in a process of reduction of global imbalances. In this regard, scholars have called for global financial reform and global governance reform, in which international institutions such as the International Monetary Fund and the World Bank should play an increasing role (Adam and Vines, 2009; Crotty, 2009; Wade, 2009).

Along similar lines of reasoning, another interesting explanation for the origin of global imbalances is that put forward by Jagannathan and colleagues (2009). They maintain that these imbalances have their root in a labour supply shock that occurred in developing countries, particularly China. They explain that the urban population in China increased by nearly 300 million from 1990 to 2007. A major part of those who migrated to urban areas have become part of the Western world's workforce through working for industries that export to the West. The effect on the developed world's labour supply is of similar magnitude to that of the Western world's increased access to land and natural resources following the discovery of the Americas. The sudden increase in labour supply from workers in developing countries because of globalization should have resulted in significant sections of the population in developed countries experiencing a decline in their living standards as more and more manufacturing and service jobs were outsourced.

This process was mitigated by the flow of cheap liquidity from abroad during this period, which brought about the housing bubble and created the illusion of wealth among households sustaining high levels of consumption. This had the effect of masking the real structural changes that were taking place in the world economy. According to these authors, the financial crisis is thus just the symptom, while the main cause was the labour supply shock. Recovery would be possible when structural imbalances in global capital flows were corrected, as a result of both increased savings in developed countries and capital inflows into developing countries.

It's the technology, stupid!

The third proposed explanation for the current economic downturn is that related to the presence of long waves in the economy driven by major technological innovations. Neo-Schumpeterian research puts at its centre innovation and structural change, and assumes that crisis, along with innovation and structural change, is a constituent component of the ordinary functioning of the economic system. For scholars inspired by the Schumpeterian work, 'the 2008 crisis is simply another manifestation of the dynamic intrinsic instability of capitalism' (Antonelli, 2009).

These authors argue that the financial bubble was just the financial manifestation of the dot.com bubble of 2000. In turn, the latter was rooted in the ending of a long wave characterized by the rise of the information and communication technology (ICT) industry since the 1980s (Antonelli, 2009; Perez, 2009a). Following the burst of the dot.com bubble, and also as a consequence of the 9/11 terrorist attacks, governments and central banks tried to avoid a big recession mainly by means of a dramatic expansion of credit in the economic system, led by real interest rates of around zero (Figure 1.10). This had the temporary effect of avoiding a big depression, but paved the way for the creation of the big financial bubble that eventually burst a decade later.

According to this thesis, in order to understand the causes of the current turmoil we should look at those at the root of the dot-com bubble. The latter was the natural result of a progressive decrease in technological opportunities and profit opportunities following an excess of investment and production capacity in the ICT industry, which was at the core of the fifth technological wave that started around the 1980s. Within this context, the crisis has long-term roots in the real side of the economy.

Perez (2009a) refers to these phenomena as a major technology bubble; that is, 'a special class of bubbles that constitute a recurring endogenous phenomenon, caused by the way the market economy absorbs successive technological revolutions' (p. 780). The two boom and bust episodes – the Internet mania and crash of the 1990s, and the easy liquidity boom and bust of the 2000s – are, then, two distinct components of a single structural phenomenon. The first was basically driven by technological change and large investment, and the second by financial innovation and monetary factors. Like the advocates of the global imbalances explanation, the belief here is that the financial crisis is just a manifestation of a more profound structural phenomenon.

Figure 1.11 shows the corporate profits before taxes in the US for some industries in the period 1987–2009. Over this period, the communications industry has shown the best performance, reaching its peak in 1994. From 1994 it underwent

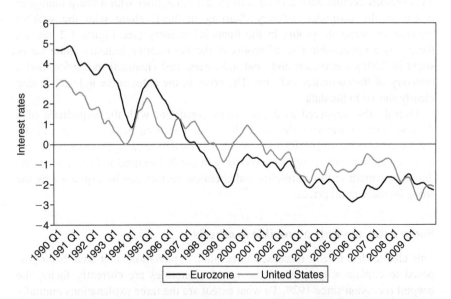

Figure 1.10 Long-term interest rates (ten-year bond) measured as devition from 1990–2009 average, United States and Eurozone (source: authors' elaboration on 'Enhanced Principal Global Indicators (PGI)', IMF, released December 21, 2009).

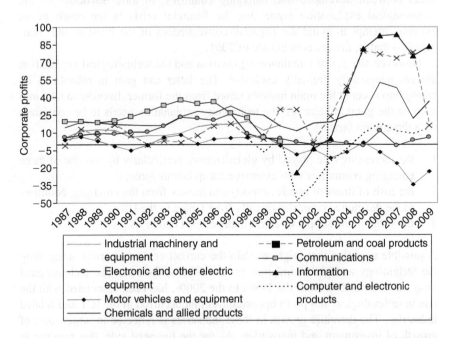

Figure 1.11 Corporate profits before taxes in the US for some industries, 1987–2009 (source: authors' elaboration on US National Bureau of Economic Research data).

a continuous decline until around zero by 2000, together with a sharp plunge in profits in the computer industry. Starting in 2001, along with the striking increase in corporate profits in the financial industry (see Figure 1.2 above), there was a remarkable rise of profits in the information industry (time series starts in 2001), petroleum and coal industries, and chemical industries, and a recovery of the computer industry. The crisis in the automotive industry is also clearly shown in the data.

Overall, this scattered evidence seems consistent with the hypothesis of a decline in profit opportunities in the ICT sector starting before the burst of the 2001 bubble. The surge of profits in the information industry, and the recovery in the computer sector, suggest a recovery in the ICT-related industry, while the dramatic growth in the petroleum and chemical sectors can be explained by the sharp increase in oil prices.

Some notes towards a possible synthesis

This chapter has briefly discussed three main explanations that have been proposed to explain why most of the world economies are currently facing the deepest recession since 1929. To what extent are the three explanations mutually exclusive? In fact, those supporting the global imbalances explanation claim that the financial crisis is a natural consequence of the rise of unsustainable imbalances between developed and emerging countries. In turn, advocates of the technological explanation argue that the financial crisis is the result of an extreme attempt to avoid the negative consequences of the burst of the 'real' bubble – that is, the dot.com bubble of 2001.

However, the global imbalance explanation and the technological explanation are not necessarily mutually exclusive. The latter can gain in robustness by taking into account the main insights raised from the former. In order to take into account the great imbalances, the technology explanation needs to be consistent with three main facts:

1   the increasing role played by globalization, particularly by the rise of large emerging economies with extensive cheap labour force;
2   the rush of flows of goods (import) and money from the emerging countries to the developed countries (mostly from China to the US);
3   the surge in the supply of credit in developed countries.

A possible narrative that might explain the current economic crisis, integrating the technology and global imbalances, could be as follows. The technological long wave, extending from the 1980s to the 2000s, has been associated with the rise in technological and profit opportunities that occurred in the ICT and related industries. The dramatic growth in these industries is reflected in larger rates of growth of investment and innovation. As for the financial side, this resulted in the surge in credit, venture capital and stock market values.[4] The overall effect on the rest of the economy was that of 'crowding out' the other industries.

However, the opportunity to import goods from emerging countries at very cheap cost made this process viable. In turn, the large amounts of money that were transferred to the emerging countries for imports got back in the financial markets of developed countries, which in turn reinvested the money in the ICT and ICT-related sectors. This has led to an excess of investment and capacity in this industry, as well as a reduction in profit opportunities. According to the technological explanation argument, the burst of the financial bubble was therefore the result of an excess of investment and production capacity in the ICT and ICT-related industries. Crucially, that was made possible, and even amplified, by the growth of global imbalances between developed and emerging countries, in terms of constant flows of cheap goods and financial resources.

Though this book is not an enquiry into the causes of the current crisis, this chapter is intended to frame the analysis in the general macroeconomic situation. The synthesis proposed in this previous section should be further developed and tested against empirical evidence, but this is outside the scope of this volume. Instead, in the next chapter we focus on the neo-Schumpeterian stream of research, which is more in tune with the role by played technology and innovation in the current economic crisis.

2 Technological change, patterns of innovation, and economic development
The contribution of neo-Schumpeterian research

The most impressive characteristic of modern economic systems since the First Industrial Revolution has been the relentless pace of change. The way in which firms organize their activities and manage their production processes has evolved dramatically, together with the impressive steps forward in the production techniques and technical knowledge applied. Alongside this process, the contribution of the scientific discoveries and technical advancement applied to production processes has been recognized as the key factor in driving economic growth (Kuznets, 1969). It comes as no surprise that the relationships between science, technological change and economic development have always fascinated economists and sociologists no less than the public at large.

This chapter, together with Chapter 3, sets the scene for the empirical analysis carried out in Parts II and III of the book. It does so by reviewing the contribution of the so-called neo-Schumpeterian strand of literature to the understanding of these central issues in the economic theory.[1] Our concern is that of establishing a theoretical framework in order to investigate what happens to innovation during a major recession such as the current global economic downturn. To this end, a strand of research which puts at the core of its analysis the idea that innovation is the engine of economic development and economic fluctuations is a very suitable candidate.

Even if our analysis is not concerned with the effects of the crisis on long-term trends of economic activity, this chapter's review touches upon the debate about the *long waves*. This began with the seminal studies by Nikolai Dmitrievich Kondratieff and Joseph Schumpeter during the 1920s and 1930s, and had a passionate revival in the late 1970s and 1980s. In fact, even though this research focuses mostly on the relationship between innovation and economic fluctuations in the long term, a crucial issue addressed is what happens to innovation during a crisis, which is the core interest of this volume.

Behind this debate there is also the central issue about the very nature of innovation activity and its relationship with economic activity. That is, is innovation cyclical or persistent? The chapter then examines the most recent developments of neo-Schumpeterian research by focusing on the different patterns of innovation, namely those of creative destruction and creative accumulation, as well as the evolution of innovation activity and the role of finance in funding innovation over time.

The 'discovery' of long waves

Those who first approached the issue of economic development were captured by a basic observated fact: economic development does not occur smoothly, but tends to proceed in jerks and leaps. Periods of growth and prosperity were interrupted by depressions. This led to continuous oscillations of aggregate production, prices and levels of employment. These periods of downswing were previously attributed to major events and exceptional circumstances – for instance, wars. However, in the course of the nineteenth century economists were not satisfied with the 'exceptional' explanation, and started considering the idea that periods of prosperity and depression were the 'heart-beat' of modern economic systems.

Malthus had already proposed a theory for cyclical movements by pointing at the interplay between the rate of growth of population and the rate of growth of food. Among others, Marx himself emphasized the presence of industrial cycles related to the reproduction of fixed capital with important effects on the rate of unemployment. In the twentieth century, other scholars interpreted cyclical movements as characteristic of economic system that reacts to and absorbs external shocks (e.g. Pigou).

As Reijnders (1990) argued, the first systematic references to the existence of long waves were as a by-product of business-cycle theory emerging in the second half of the nineteenth century, and mainly from the development of business-cycle theory at the beginning of the twentieth century. By simple observation of long time-series, economists started speculating about the existence of different types of business cycles characterized by different durations. Specifically, along with short-term cycles, scholars traced the presence of longer cyclical movements of about fifty years ... they 'discovered' long waves. The 'discovery' of long waves occurred along with the development of more refined statistical methodologies for the assessment of time series, of which Juglar was an important pioneer.

The main representative of early long-wave analysis was Nikolai Dmitrievich Kondratieff.[2] He was the founder of the Moscow Business Conjuncture Institute, of which he was director from 1920 to 1928, before being removed from his position, accused of subversion and deported to Siberia in 1930. According to Kondratieff, cycles are 'organically inherent in the capitalistic system' (Kondratieff and Stolper, 1935). He was also persuaded that there are different cycles overlapping in the working of economic systems. According to Kondratieff, on the grounds of available data, the existence of major cycles (lasting between forty-eight and sixty-nine years) was very likely.

In his dynamic theory there were already some factors regarding the role of technical change and scientific advancements that would be further developed by the neo-Schumpeterian school. First, he pointed out that the rate and direction of these inventions would be contingent on previous developments and accumulation of knowledge (the path-dependent argument), and driven by practical needs (the inducement argument). Second, he stated that inventions would not have an effect on the economic system until the economic conditions necessary for their application were met. Third, he raised the issue of the financial dynamic linked to the pattern of investment in the economy. Finally, Kondratieff also argued that

> during the recession of the long wave, an especially number of important discoveries and inventions in the technique of production and communication are made, which, however, are usually applied on a large scale only at the beginning of the next long upswing.
>
> (Kondratiev, 1979, p. 535).

This issue was taken up by Schumpeter, and was at the core of the dispute in the late 1970s. Crucially, it raises one of the major questions of this debate (and this book): *are depressions a fertile environment for major innovation?*

The process of economic development according to Schumpeter: innovation, the entrepreneur and the banker

Joseph Alois Schumpeter designed the very ambitious project to develop a comprehensive theory of the process of economic development and technical change. He produced at least three main books – *The Theory of Economic Development* (TEC) (Schumpeter, 1911 (1934)), *Business Cycle* (BC) (Schumpeter, 1939), and *Capitalism, Socialism and Democracy* (CSD) (Schumpeter, 1942) – in which he explored a large number of arguments linked to economic development and technical change. This section is not meant to review all his contributions; rather, it discusses some points that are key for the central concern of this volume and the further development of the neo-Schumpeterian school.

Schumpeter was well aware of the work of Kondratieff, and two points are also central to his analysis. First, like the Russian scholar, he was convinced that all the elements of capitalistic system are organically related. Second, he too was persuaded that cycles are an inherent feature of modern capitalistic systems. Therefore, he attempted to develop an *endogenous* theory of economic development – in other words, the causes of change and fluctuations need to be found within the working of capitalistic systems, rather than in external shocks or casual accidents.

The solution proposed by Schumpeter in his works is that *innovations[3] are at the heart of economic change and development.* The specific nature of innovation activity is the key element of the Schumpeterian theory of economic change. First, innovation is the outcome of economic decisions taken by the business community that, by definition, act within the economic system. Thus the entrepreneur, with his or her intuitions and incentives, is a central figure in his theory. Second, innovation does not occur smoothly over time, but rather tends to occur '*in swarms*'. Third, innovations are not uniformly distributed across the industries, but on the contrary tend to group around specific industries. When innovations are introduced in a specific sector, the latter is profoundly modified in terms of processes, costs, productivity and organization of the economic activity. This leads to a dynamic of structural change that does not occur in a uniform and tidy way. On the contrary, each wave is characterized by the rise of a specific industry (e.g. textiles, the railways, electronics and so on).

In his book specifically devoted to business cycle analysis (BC), the Austrian economist put forward a theory that associates innovation with economic development and business cycles. Here, Schumpeter reinforces his idea of capitalism as a process whose evolution is inherently tortuous, discontinuous and disharmonic. This depends on the forces that drive economic and technical progress. Thus, progress, change and cycles are all faces of the same coin: modern capitalism at work.

In Chapter 4 of his BC book, Schumpeter outlines the process of economic evolution as he conceives it. He envisages four main phases: prosperity, recession, depression and recovery. Economic systems usually work 'in the neighborhood' of Walrasian equilibrium.[4] The effect of the introduction of an innovation is that of moving the system away from its equilibrium into a surge of capital investment, leading to the prosperity phase of the cycle. Those entrepreneurs that introduce innovations receive a prize, in the form of extra profits. This is the prize, in capitalistic systems, for the introduction of innovations, and is temporary by nature, as profits tend to disappear in the following process of imitation and increasing competition.[5]

In fact, other firms will follow the pioneer innovator in the industry in which the innovation is first introduced, being attracted by higher profit opportunities. This gives rise to a wide process of imitation and further innovations and improvements in and around that industry. Schumpeter defines this process as the 'secondary wave'. In terms of effects on the economic system, he emphasized that this is more important than the initial introduction of innovation. It should also be observed that this process leads to a reallocation of resources between industries, because it is associated with structural change as a result of the uneven rate of technical change across industries (see also Freeman *et al.*, 1982).

Eventually, an excess of investment and productive capacity, fuelled by credit, will bring about a progressive reduction of profit opportunities – a recession. Then the system will tend to overshoot into the 'depression excursion'. From here, the forces at work will bring the system back to (the neighborhood of) equilibrium. This new equilibrium differs from the previous one, as it is characterized by a higher level of productivity followed by the introduction and the diffusion of innovations. The new equilibrium will eventually breed innovation, which in turn will breed a new cycle. In this manner, innovation and cycles are strictly associated.[6]

In a subsequent section, Schumpeter complicated his model by adding minor fluctuations alongside the major one. Following his line of reasoning, it is plausible that innovation activity, along with further improvements, imitation and adaptation, can give rise to a number of fluctuations that overlap and interfere with each other. Secondary waves are more likely to occur during the phase of prosperity, when innovation activity builds on the major innovation (this is the central point raised by Freeman and colleagues, as discussed below). However, he argues that all types of cycles can be explained by his model. Innovations are the underlying cause of each (major and minor) wave, even though different types of innovation play a different role in each type of wave.

In what follows we discuss three main points that are central in the Schumpeterian stream of studies: (1) the central role of the process of imitation, creative adoption and diffusion of innovation; (2) the centrality of entrepreneurs among economic agents; and (3) the importance of the financial system.

1   *The central role of the process of imitation, creative adoption and diffusion of innovation.* A feature of innovation activities that is fundamental for the Schumpeterian model is its tendency to occur 'in swarms'; that is, to cluster in particular periods. In his argument, the introduction of a clear-cut innovation is soon followed by an intense process of imitation, which leads firms to apply similar solutions to similar problems across different industries through creative adoption and imitation. This brings about a process of diffusion of innovation throughout the entire economic system, characterized by cumulative innovative activities and a substantial rise in the aggregate levels of productivity. This cumulative and self-reinforcing process continues along with the new profit opportunities opened up by the introduction of innovation. Eventually, profit opportunities, along with the exhaustion of technological opportunities, will decrease, leading to lower rates of innovative efforts.

2   *The centrality of entrepreneurs among economic agents.* In the Schumpeterian theory of economic development, the role of entrepreneur is far from being a rational calculator that responds to external stimulus. By contrast, the entrepreneur resembles a romantic character animated by a willingness to break up the *status quo.* Entrepreneurs are responsible for both the introduction of innovation and the following process of imitation and diffusion. The entrepreneur that first introduces an innovation, if successful, will be able to reap the fruits of her initiative by gaining real profit. She will be soon followed by other entrepreneurs attracted by new profit opportunities. Thus, within this context, *new firms* that are established by these kinds of entrepreneurs play a major role in establishing new sectors characterized by growing profit opportunities and technological opportunities. A side effect is the destruction of old sectors that now use production techniques with an inferior level of productivity. This is the familiar *creative destruction* process.[7] Hence, a few entrepreneurs are responsible for moving the system away from its equilibrium, but a crucial aspect is that, as they are outside of the economic system, they need to find resources to invest from somewhere. In Schumpeter's CSD, the emphasis is shifted from the entrepreneur and the new firm to the role played by large corporations in introducing innovation, as discussed below.

3   *The importance of the financial system.* Schumpeter defined capitalism as 'that form of private property economy in which innovations are carried out by means of borrowed money' (1939, p. 223). Together with the entrepreneur, the banker – 'the ephor of the exchange economy' – makes a substantial contribution, as she provides the financial resources necessary to the *new* entrepreneur to establish the *new* company and invest in innovative activities. Two points are key emphasizing here. First, the banks play a central role in modern capitalism as they create money by providing credit. Second, this function is essential as innovation are carried out by *new firms*. Schumpeter notes that the role of banks would be irrelevant if innovations were undertaken by existing firms. By providing credit, banks allow new players to make innovations by taking control of the productive resources away from existing firms. In his later CSD the focus is shifted towards the major role played by large established firms in the 'trustified capitalism'. This led him to downplay the role of external finance and the banking system in favour of internal finance for innovation investment.

Since his Schumpeter's contribution, interest in the role of finance has been rather scattered. The mainstream economists have disregarded it for a very long time, as the real side of the economy is regarded as the only one that plays a role in their models (e.g. the real business-cycle literature). Also, neo-Schumpeterian research has devoted limited attention to the role of finance, at both micro and macro levels (O'Sullivan, 2005). Later in this chapter we discuss the notable attempt made by Carlota Perez to reintroduce the role of the financial sector within a comprehensive model of long waves. In this volume, the importance attached to the financial sector for innovation during a crisis is explored both at the country level (Chapter 5) and at the level of the firm (Chapter 9).

Schumpeter was a careful observer of the economic reality surrounding him. He witnessed the rise of giant firms and oligopolistic markets, as well-described by Chandler's (1977, 1990) works. Accordingly, Schumpeter made some substantial changes from the 'competitive capitalism' described in the TEC to the 'trustified capitalism' described in CSD. In the former, he portrayed an economic environment characterized by fierce competition, in which the new firm is the driver of innovation activity supported by the creation of new credit by the banking system. In the trustified capitalism described in the latter, he instead emphasized the role of well-established large firms in which innovation has become a routine activity. Here, market structure has shifted into oligopolistic competition, and an internal source of financing is the most relevant source of innovation activity. In the former scenario, the dynamic of innovation is characterized by a process of 'creative destruction' in which the new, innovative firms give rise to new industries displacing the old ones. In the latter, the pattern of innovation resembles a process of 'creative accumulation', where the emphasis is on the cumulative nature of innovation that takes place within large existing firms. These two ideal types have been further developed in the neo-Schumpeterian literature, as discussed below (see also Chapter 7).

In the Schumpeterian wake: Mensch, the SPRU school, and the Perez synthesis

Innovations overcome depression: the Mensch provocation

In Schumpeterian theory, the central point is the fact that major innovations tend to appear in swarms and give rise to a major upswing of the economy. But why do major innovations tend to cluster in this way over time? Several authors have raised this issue as an important 'bug' in Schumpeter's theory (Mensch, 1979; Tylecote, 1992). In his review of Schumpeter's *Business Cycle*, Simon Kuznets (1940) claims that, according to Schumpeter, the grouping of innovation depends on entrepreneurs' behaviour. However, he argues that the association between the innovation cycle and the distribution of entrepreneurs' capabilities needs to be better defined, and requires further evidence. It is easy to see that this point is central to this argument. Business cycles are said to be driven by an endogenous force that, according to Schumpeter, resides in innovation activity. It follows that (at some point) during the downswing one has to observe those economic, technical and social factors that set the opportunity for a new swarm of innovations to appear, leading to the next phase of prosperity.

This conceptual and empirical challenge was taken up by Gerard Mensch at the end of the 1970s, in his *Stalemate in Technology* (Mensch, 1979). He put forward a thought-provoking hypothesis that would spark the debate on long waves after many years of scarce attention – characterized, incidentally, by prosperity. The Mensch theory can be summarized as follows. First, fundamental (basic) innovations tend to occur during depressions, giving rise to new industrial branches and economic recovery. Second, basic innovations are followed by a series of improvement innovations. This process is characterized by a diminishing return on investment and demand that will eventually lead to stagnation.

The main concern of Mensch was to develop a comprehensive theory of innovations during recessions. He wrote in a period in which, after decades of sustained growth, low unemployment and low rates of inflation, advanced countries were facing *stagflation* (that is, stagnation of the aggregate production coupled with high rates of inflation). In his book he argued that the West was facing, in the early 1970s, a typical situation that characterizes recessions – that is, a *stalemate of technology* – and that the recovery would eventually be brought about by new basic innovations and new branches of industry.

The 'upswing side' of his theory was in tune with the Schumpeterian one. Periods of prosperity are spurred by basic innovation that gives rise to new branches of industry, followed by several improved innovations of new firms attracted by a higher rate of investment return. In this phase, demand is able to absorb the whole production, and also induce further developments and innovation. Eventually, demand becomes saturated, return on investment starts to decline, and innovation is substituted by pseudo-innovation. According to Mensch, competition in formerly highly dynamic industries tends to be substituted by increasing concentration, large firms, and high barriers to entry. Those firms are less inclined to invest in risky activity, and start investing their capital away from production and towards monetary markets. Stagnation is then the result of a lack of innovation activity. In addition, firms tend to overcome decreasing profits by increasing prices in their protected markets. In this way, Mensch seeks to explain *stagflation* as the result of the same phenomenon: a lack of innovation activity in concentrated markets.

The main controversial argument of Mensch theory regards the mechanism through which the economy will recover. In his view, stagnation and innovation coexist. His model is not one of long waves in which each phase comes after the previous one; on the contrary, stagnation and innovation for recovery overlap. His main claim is that stagnation is at the same time a period of crisis and of opportunity. In his words, 'at the same time that wide areas of current economic interests are gripped by stagnation, creative progress is building in new areas of activity [...] in the technological stalemate, the economy becomes structurally ready for basic innovations' (Mensch, 1979, p. 74). A fundamental point is the different roles that different branches of industry play during stagnation. His model allows stagnant industries to be kept separated by new industries that basic innovations have brought into being.

In a period in which the debate about which policy to adopt was a fierce one, the Mensch hypothesis had a bearing on policy for recovery. Mensch was against Keynesian policies, in which policy finds are distributed according to the watering can principle. Public funds should not be directed towards projects in a mature industry; rather, they must be directed towards emerging sectors.[8]

The SPRU response

It is innovation diffusion that matters!

Schumpeter had relatively little to say about unemployment and wages. In their book *Unemployment and Technical Innovation*, Freeman, Clark and Soete (1982) develop a theory of unemployment on the basis of the Schumpeterian theory of the business cycle and technical change. They make a strong criticism of the central argument put forward by Mensch. The objective of their critique is the Mensch *depression-induced* hypothesis of basic innovations. In their words:

> Innovations are pushed forward in expectations of profits associated with expanding prospects. To suggest that this would be more likely to occur during depression flies in the face of all economic theory, whatever description ... It also contradicts the evidence of case histories of innovations, and the general consensus that high risk is one of the main factors inhibiting innovations.

They agree with Mensch (and Schumpeter) that fundamental or basic inventions exhibit a clustering behaviour. However, they disagree with the proposition that these types of innovation tend to cluster during recessions, and that there is evidence of any depression-induced mechanism at work.

By contrast, they provide a theory of technological change which has some points of interest here. First, fundamental innovations seem to be better explained by advances in scientific knowledge, along with demand factors (including booms and wars). Thus, they are not in favour of a pure 'science-push' theory of innovation. However, they claim that scientific research advancements are key to spurring fundamental innovations. They add that demand does play an important role. Namely, they suggest that the effects of demand as a driver of innovation (the so-called 'Schmookler-type', as we will see below) are more prominent at a later stage of growth of industries.

Their *pars costruens* of the theory revolves around the concept of the *new technology system*. In response to Mensch, they maintain that the 'swarming process' that counts in terms of economic aggregate effect is not a mere clustering of major innovations during a specific period. The very effect of radical innovation can be delayed for a decade or more, until there are the profitable conditions, as well as a receptive social environment (we will return to this point when discussing Perez's contribution). When these conditions are met, a process of diffusion takes place, as described by Schumpeter using the bandwagon analogy. This is the right 'swarm' to look at if, according to Freeman and colleagues, one wants to understand how innovation can give rise to significant economy-wide effects on the patterns of investment and output. This can occur only in the presence of two possibilities: first, if these radical innovations are considerably large and have long-term effects (e.g. railways); alternatively, and here the new technology systems are introduced, if 'some of them were interdependent and interconnected for technological and social reasons if general economic conditions favoured their simultaneous growth' (p. 67). Thus, *technology systems* have a major effect on different industries and, in general, a wide effect on the economy. Examples of technology systems include the cluster of synthetic materials innovation, petrochemical innovations, and innovations in injection moulding and extrusion machinery. In a way, they establish the central link between innovation activity and economic change.

The controversy between these two positions is a key one, and can be summarized as follows. Is it primarily the dynamic of the new industries led by the introduction of major innovations that overcomes depression, as suggested by Mensch? Or can the diffusion process of innovation occur only in a climate of prosperity and profit expectations, as proposed by Freeman and colleagues?

Technological paradigms and technological trajectories

Another contribution in a similar line of reasoning comes from Giovanni Dosi's studies on the concepts of *technological paradigms* and *technological trajectories* (Dosi, 1982, 1984a). Dosi's argument consists of an indirect response to the Mensch's argument, as it deals with the patterns of technological change, and the continuity and discontinuity in technical change. Recalling Kuhn's model of revolution in scientific research (Kuhn, 1962), Dosi puts forward the concept of a *technological paradigm*. It is broadly defined as a model and a pattern of solutions to selected problems, based on principles derived from natural sciences and on selected material technologies. As such, similarly to the research programmes, technological paradigms define the boundaries and opportunities within which technical change would proceed. The latter process, analogous to the 'normal science', is named a *technological trajectory*, and can be defined as the pattern of 'normal' problem-solving activity on the ground of a technological paradigm (Dosi, 1984a, p. 83).

In relation to the issues discussed here, we can think of the technological paradigm as the Schumpeter's radical innovations or Mensch's basic innovations. Crucially, according to Dosi, the emergence of new technological paradigms is a rather autonomous phenomenon with respect to economic variables such as the level of output, demand and relative prices. In his view, scientific and technical advancements play the major role in bringing about the rise of new technological paradigms. He also maintains that these are only necessary conditions, but not sufficient, as the emergence of new technological paradigms is not independent from the evolution of the socio-economic system. However, the emphasis here is on the implausibility of the depression-inducement mechanism suggested by Mensch. According to Dosi, the state variables of the economy system (demand, relative prices, level of output) can exert an inducement effect only on 'normal' innovation activity. In other terms, market conditions are likely to affect innovation activities within an already established technological paradigm and within an existing industry. This contradicts the Mensch idea, according to which depressions induce basic innovations and lead to the rise of new branches of industry.

The Carlota Perez synthesis: technological revolution and financial capital

As stated above, one of the pillars of the Schumpeterian model is the financial and banking system. Despite this, neo-Schumpeterian research has mostly focused on the science and technological aspect. The most prominent attempt to reconcile the two sides of the economy has been made by Carlota Perez in her *Technological Revolutions and Financial Capital* (Perez, 2002). The cornerstone of her model is the dynamic structural linkage between production and technology on the one hand, and financial capital on the other. The dynamic of production ('productivity explosion') and the dynamic of the financial capital ('burst of financial excitement') are interrelated phenomena. They share the same root cause and are in the nature of the system and its workings, as '*they originate in the way technologies evolve by revolution [...]*' (Perez, 2002; our emphasis). The model revolves around the following central arguments:

1   the basic fact that technological change tends to occur in clusters of radical technical innovations that profoundly affect the whole economic system in terms of organization of economic activity and productivity;
2   the functional separation between production capital and financial capital;

3   the role played by the socio-institutional framework during major technical
     breakthroughs.

Very much in the spirit of the Schumpeter's vision, augmented by the technological paradigm and technological system concepts, technological revolution is
defined as a cluster of new products, technologies and industries that lead to
major changes in the overall economic system in terms of technological and
organizational principles, levels of productivity, and social 'common sense'.
Following Freeman and colleagues (1982), Perez identified five technological
revolutions in the period 1770–2000: the First Industrial Revolution (starting in
1771), the Age of Steam and Railways (1829), the Age of Steel, Electricity and
Heavy Engineering (1875), the Age of Oil, the Automobile and Mass Production
(1908), and the Age of Information and Telecommunications (1971).

The initial phase of a technological revolution, through the introduction of a
new techno-economic paradigm, brings about a period of mismatch between
'the economic and the social and regulatory system'. It is wide recognized that
institutions have a natural rate of inertia over time (North, 1990, 2005).
According to Perez, it takes some time (20–30 years) for the economic and
social system to absorb the major changes caused by the new techno-economic
paradigm and for a 'recoupling' of the system. It is this different rhythm of
change between the techno-economic sphere and the social-institutional sphere
that explains the turbulence that follows each surge of a technological
revolution.

The third pillar of the Perez's model is financial capital. As she emphasizes,
there is a division of labour between the production system and the credit
system. The latter makes it possible for the former to enter into new ventures
along with new technological opportunities. The separation between productive
and financial capital is central at the onset of technological revolutions. In her
words, 'it is because there is available money looking for profits in the hands of
non-producers that the new entrepreneurs can bring their ideas into commercial
reality' (p. 33).

These three main phenomena interplay closely in technological revolutions.
Each technological revolution evolves along four distinct phases grouped into
two major periods: 'installation' and 'deployment'. In the installation period, the
new technologies enter the economic system and spread across it. This brings
about a process of creative destruction as old products, technologies, firms and
industries are threatened by the new technological systems. The new technological system then attracts increasing flows of investment attracted by greater
profit opportunities, leading to diminishing profits and productivity in older
industries' markets. In the deployment period, the new technology becomes the
established paradigm. This is the 'recoupling' phase, in which new networks,
suppliers, distribution channels and services are developed around the new technologies. At the same time, there is a cultural adaptation process going on in
which the logic of the new technologies becomes accepted in terms of organization of economic and social activities.

Innovation in technological revolutions

Technology, industry and market structure

The theory on long waves revolves around two main arguments. First, it predicts the presence of long cycles, over the process of economic development, that occur in a regular fashion. Second, these regularities have been associated with the rise of the techno-economic paradigm that characterizes each of these period. However, throughout these phases there have been remarkable changes in terms of: (1) the main innovators; (2) the characteristics of the innovative activity; and (3) the role of finance.

Table 2.1 seeks to sketch the main characteristics of successive techno-economic paradigms by building on the contributions by Freeman (1987), Freeman and Soete (1997) and Archibugi (2001). Five major techno-economic paradigm shifts (or technological revolutions) have been identified, and with each one we have associated several characteristics. To begin with, as already explained, each techno-economic paradigm is associated with a specific industry (or set of interrelated industries). The First Industrial Revolution occurred mainly in the cotton industry, driven by small, individual manufacturing firms. In this period, innovation was mostly the result of continuous technical improvements that occurred within the firm itself, with a negligible role for the application of science (Freeman and Soete, 1997; Mokyr, 1992).

The next techno-economic paradigm, of steam power and railways, was characterized by the rise of small specialized firms along with the creation of the large modern business enterprise, which became possible thanks to the introduction of several organizational innovations that led to the establishment of a managerial hierarchy and bureaucracy (Chandler, 1988, 1990). While before the middle of the nineteenth century technical progress was mostly independent of scientific progress, after 1850 science started playing a role – for instance, in the steel industry. Steel became a fundamental source of innovation in several sectors characterized by high-volume production, such as railways, construction, bicycles and so on. Another example of numerous 'specialized suppliers' in the development of innovation is the electricity industry, in which many applications of electric power were opened up. However, in this industry the first giants also started to appear, as a result of progressive mergers and vertical integration (as in the case of General Electric) in response to the fact that technological development was becoming more complex and expensive (Freeman and Soete, 1997). However, innovation was still mostly the result of tinkerer and inventor-entrepreneur, and trial-and-error activity within the firm itself.

The chemical and oil techno-economic paradigm is of paramount importance for modern innovation for two main reasons: (1) the introduction of internal professional large-scale R&D laboratories in firms; and (2) the systematic application of science to technical advancements. As for the latter, the development of the new discipline of chemical engineering also played a role. Thus, for the very first time, this period witnessed the rise of 'science-based' firms. In this industry the size of the innovators tends to grow substantially, as both production and innovation are characterized by high fixed capital costs. The shift from the inventor-entrepreneur of the nineteenth century towards large-scale corporate R&D is clearly evident here (Freeman and Soete, 1997; Mokyr, 1992).

The next wave was represented by new complex products for mass consumption, based on cost-cutting trajectories. Taylorism and Fordism are associated to large and heavily organized firms whose competitive advantage is based on economies of scale. We then associate innovators with the 'scale-intensive' category of the Pavitt's taxonomy. Technological innovation is mostly based upon R&D activity, which is highly concentrated in large firms (Cohen, 1995), even though there are significant differences across industries. Overall, while small firms seem, in some industries, to have a comparative advantage in the earlier stages of invention, large firms are better equipped in later stages of scaling-up and development (Freeman and Soete, 1997).

The last paradigm has been associated with the dramatic development of Information and Communication Technology (ICT). It corresponds to the rise of information-intensive firms active in both the manufacturing and the service industries, and based on the intensive analysis and use of data-processing. This period witnessed a radical shift in the industrial organization, named 'the second industrial divide' by Piore and Sabel (1984), that occurred in response to the crisis of mass production and consumption. The introduction of 'new manufacturing systems' and 'flexible specialization' gave rise to a new organization of the firm, more able to continuously adapt and innovate. The response to giant firms, vertical integration and internal sources of innovation has been remarkable in terms of organizational change towards more flexibility (through modularization), vertical disintegration, extensive use of sources of innovation external to the firm, and the rise of networks (or the ecosystem) of firms as a new way to manage technical change and innovation activity.[9] Innovation here is the result of a continuous process of learning through internal R&D activity, interaction with users and suppliers, and collaboration with universities and research labs (Chesbrough, 2003; Chesbrough *et al.*, 2008; Edquist, 1997; von Hippel, 1998).

The evolution of innovation activity

In *The Theory of the Economic Development*, Schumpeter (1911) put forward his classic taxonomy of innovations. This taxonomy includes the introduction of a new product or production process, a new market, a new source of supply, and organizational innovations. This reflects a broad vision of what can be defined as innovation activity. After Schumpeter, for a very long time the economics of innovation has been focused solely on *technological innovation*. This approach postulates that innovation is based on *technological change* and *scientific knowledge* advances. Accordingly, R&D has been regarded as the most prominent source of innovation, and scholars have devoted their attention to the manufacturing sector (Freeman, 1994).

However, the major changes occurring in recent decades have made the technological definition of innovation far too wide for a comprehensive understanding of innovation activity. The rise of the ICT sector has dramatically amplified the opportunities for innovation in the organizational structure, distribution systems and business models. The shift from manufacturing to services has also contributed to a change in innovation towards a less technology-based activity. As recently claimed by Freeman and Soete (2007), 'alongside the process of de-industrialization there has also been a process of *deR&Dization*'. This is reflected in the last edition of the *Oslo Manual* (OECD, 2005a), in which the definition of innovation was considerably widened to include service innovation, marketing innovation and organizational innovation, along with technological innovation.

We believe that there is today the need for a broadening of innovation activity. With regard to this, firm-specific strategies and business models are central to innovation activity. This is not meant to deny the role played by science and R&D labs. On the contrary, we are among those who claim that the 'linear model' has been declared dead too soon (Balconi and Brusoni, 2010). However, we argue that these categories are no longer enough to explain how innovation takes place in key sectors such as, for instance, the business service sector, the Internet sector and creative sector. A suitable approach could be that of starting, by the broader category of *change*, to address the several forms in which innovation occurs today. While it raises the obvious risk of including too many factors in the realm of innovation, we believe that this could be a more reliable starting point to apply the concept of change to more specific areas of innovation activity.

Financing innovation

Entrepreneurs are constantly in need of external financial resources to support their activity. In this respect, the development of the financial system and banking system has been a key factor for economic growth in modern capitalistic systems. However, financing innovative activities presents some differences, depending upon the specific nature of the innovative activity. The latter is inherently a *risky* activity, characterized by high uncertainty and long-term returns. Table 2.1 also summarizes the evolution in the innovation-related financing activity. As previously stated, the First Industrial Revolution was characterized by a low ratio of fixed costs and 'low-cost' innovation activity. The problem of financing innovation arose with the establishment of large-scale R&D labs within big firms. Schumpeter (1942) argued that the increasingly scientific basis of economic activities had caused innovation to require substantial financial resources, as a result of indivisibilities and significant economies of scale and scope. As a result, innovation occurred in large firms characterized by large profits and healthy cash flows.

One of the implications of the well-known Modigliani-Miller (1958) arguments is that a firm choosing the optimal level of investment should be

Table 2.1 Successive techno-economic paradigms

Period	Techno-economic paradigm	Industries	Industrial organization	Innovation activity	Typology of innovative firm (Pavitt's taxonomy)	Financing of innovation
1770–1830	Early mechanization	Textile, potteries, machinery	Growing importance of small manufacturing firms	Incremental improvements in processes and organization (not science-based)	Specialized suppliers in capital goods and machinery	
1840–1880	Steam power, steel and railway	Mechanical engineering, steel and coal, electricity, gas	Separation between producers of capital and consumption goods	More complex and expensive technological innovation; inventor-entrepreneur innovation; managerial innovation	Specialized suppliers and scale-and-scope intensive	Stock market; and internal financing
1890–1930	Chemical and oil	Chemical, synthetic materials	Emergence of large firms	Growth of internal professional large-scale R&D; science-based technological development; opportunities associated with scientific discoveries	Science-based	Internal funding to finance R&D in large firms through cash flows stemming from profits
1940–1980	Fordist and Taylorist revolution	Automotive, synthetic products, consumer durables	Oligopolistic competition for mass consumption	R&D is highly concentrated in large firms, with significant industry differences	Scale-intensive	Internal funding to finance R&D in large firms through cash flows stemming from profits, banking system
1980–(2000?)	Information and communications technology (ICT)	Microelectronics, Telecoms, Software, biotechnologies, nanotechnologies	Networks (ecosystem) of firms, strong user–producer interactions	Modularity and system integration, coordinating internal and external factors, 'system of innovation' approach	Information intensive	Venture capital and business angels; public investment funds; high-tech dedicated stock market (e.g. the Nasdaq)

indifferent to its capital structure, and should face the same price for investment and R&D investment on the margin. On the base of theory and empirical evidence, Hall and Lerner (2010) drew two conclusions regarding this issue. First, small and start-up firms in R&D-intensive industries face a higher cost of capital than do their larger competitors and firms in other industries. Second, large R&D firms prefer to use internally generated funds for financing investment. These arguments parallel those made in a survey on finance and innovation by O'Sullivan (2005), where she too claims that R&D-intensive firms are more inclined to rely on internal funds to finance their investment.

By the beginning of the 1980s, a key source of external funding had started to grow in importance: venture capitalism (VC) (Cornelius, 2005).[10] VC is a high-risk, potentially high-return investment to support business creation and growth. As such, it was intended as more suitable for financing innovative projects than credit provided from the banking sector. Venture capitalists (VCs) provide the firm with funding in exchange for firm equity, and invest with a view toward an exit and the ensuing capital gains. The most spread forms of exit are typically IPO (initial public offering) and acquisitions (Gompers and Lerner, 1999). It has been argued that VCs are at the centre of the explosion of the high-tech cluster at Silicon Valley, along with entrepreneurship and the role of universities (Ibrahim, 2010; Wonglimpiyarat, 2006).

Alongside the rise of VC in the private sector, the public sector also put in place policies to encourage innovation through VC. Reduction in capital gains taxes is recognized as being an important legal instrument for stimulating venture capital markets (Gompers and Lerner, 1999). Another more direct form of support is via direct government-created venture capital funds (Lerner, 1999). The rationale for establishing the public form of VC is that of making it active in areas characterized by market failure. For example, private VCs tend to take on an insufficient number of projects at an early stage of development or start-up firms. This is a typical case where a public innovation investment fund can step in.

Another source of entrepreneur finance that has grown in importance over recent decades is *business angels* (Kerr *et al.*, 2010). An angel investor is an affluent individual who provides capital for a business start-up, usually in exchange for convertible debt or ownership equity. Business angels typically invest their own funds, unlike venture capitalists, who manage the pooled money of others in a professionally-managed fund. In the US, the business angel market is almost as large as that of the VC, but tends to finance a larger number of companies with smaller amount of money. Similarly to the VC, business angels support high-risk ventures and high-tech start-up companies

Patterns of innovation and technological discontinuities: creative destruction or creative accumulation?

There is little doubt that technological revolution as a result of the shift to the techno-economic paradigm has brought about major changes in the economy.

The rise of new technology systems, new industries and new firms is the result of the Schumpeterian 'gales of creative destruction'. However, this powerful argument has been challenged by that of 'creative accumulation'. The latter is based upon the premise that technological change is cumulative and path-dependent. The concepts of technological accumulation and creative destruction are at the very core of Schumpeter and Schumpeterian economics. As illustrated above, the young Schumpeter looked at innovation as an event that could revolutionize economic life by bringing to the fore new entrepreneurs, new companies and new industries. The mature Schumpeter, on the contrary, observed and described the activities of large oligopolistic corporations, able to perform R&D and innovation routinely by building on their previous competences.

On the basis of these insights, the Schumpeterian tradition has further investigated the relative importance of the two processes (Breschi *et al.*, 2000; Malerba and Orsenigo, 1995; Nelson and Winter, 1982; Patel and Pavitt, 1994). Creative destruction is described as a result of a regime characterized by low cumulativeness and high technological opportunities, leading to an environment with greater dynamism in terms of technological ease of entry and exit, as well as a major role for entrepreneurs, new firms, and fierce competition. Creative accumulation is associated with a technological regime that is characterized by high cumulativeness and low technological opportunities, bringing about more stable environments in which the bulk of innovation is carried out incrementally by large and established firms, leading to a market structure with high entry barriers and oligopolistic competition (see Chapter 7 for an in-depth discussion).

The advocates of the 'creative accumulation' argument have some important points to raise: (1) empirical evidence reveals the survival of large firms over long periods of time; (2) established firms *know* more than they *do*; (3) established firms have enough organizational capabilities and financial resources to adapt to and survive major technological discontinuities. Van Duijn (1983) argues that the leading sector can survive major depressions and resume expansion again during the next upswing (as seems to be the case for the ICT sector in the current crisis). Dosi (1984b) discusses the relative role of established firms vis-à-vis new firms in relation to breakthrough innovations during technological discontinuities. He maintains that

> breakthrough innovations do not need to be developed by Schumpeterian companies themselves. There is evidence that often in this century the production of major technological advances has been the result of organized R and D effort as opposed to the 'inventiveness' of individuals.
>
> (Dosi, 1984a, p. 89)

He adds that these periods are usually characterized by new emerging firms, even when the major technological advances were produced in the old firms.

Pavitt and colleagues suggest that incumbents might have the resilience to survive and to adapt to major changes (Grandstrand *et al.*, 1997; Patel and

Pavitt, 1994). He states that large firms 'know more than they do' – that is to say, their competences are spread over a wider range of fields than those associated with their core products, and they have learnt how to assimilate new fields of knowledge through their internal competences in order to manage technological discontinuities. Methé *et al.* (1996) present empirical evidence showing that established firms are often sources of major innovations, for example in telecommunications and medical instruments. In a similar vein, Iansiti and Levien (2004) suggest that, despite the many predictions about incumbents' failures, technological transitions in the computer industry are survived by the overwhelming majority of firms. Among the supporters of the 'continuity' thesis we should also include Chandler (1977), who observes that the population of incumbent large firms has remained stable over the last decades.

This position has been challenged by several studies. In different studies, Simonetti (1996), Louca and Mendonca (1999) and Freeman and Louca (2001) have found that a stream of new firms joins incumbent firms during periods of radical discontinuities. Tushman and Anderson (1986) suggest that in an environment with technological discontinuities where new capabilities and skills are required, existing firms could be disadvantaged by a lack of relevant competence. This is referred to as 'competence-destroying discontinuities' (Henderson and Clark, 1990). Similarly, Leonard-Barton (1992) argues that each firm builds a knowledge set based on core capabilities, systems and values, and that the 'core competencies' can turn into 'core rigidities' in the sense that they can create inertia to change and innovation that is driven from outside the core competencies of the firm.

March (1991) and Levinthal and March (1993), who investigated the issue from an organizational and learning perspective, suggest that the likelihood of firms' survival is linked to their capacity to put forward effective processes of organizational adaptation; that firms are able to exploit their current knowledge while at the same time exploring future technologies (see also Tushman *et al.*, 2004). Moreover, Christensen and Rosenbloom (1995) and Christensen (1997) emphasize the fact that the advantage of the 'attacker' – the new firm establishing itself alongside the incumbent firm – relies on the fact that the latter's business is nested in a value network, defined as the context within which a firm competes and solves customers' problems. In the case of innovations that change the structure of the relevant value network, large firms fail to keep up – not because of a lack of technological competences, but rather because they are stuck in their old contexts and tied to existing customers.

In their book, Freeman and colleagues (1982) discuss the role of small firms vis-à-vis that of large established firms in taking the risk of entering new and uncertain markets. As they claim, 'while the large multi-product firm will no doubt diversify into new areas, most of its output will be into relative mature industries' (p. 145). Later, they add that 'there is little doubt that [small dynamic firms] will move quickly into uncertain new markets'.

As demonstrated by this great wealth of empirical study, the reality is more complicated than that described in the two stylized models of creative destruction and creative accumulation. What really happens during a major technological discontinuity can in fact depend on several factors that are technological- and industry-specific. For instance, industries at different stages of development can react in different ways.

One point of interest would be to investigate what really is 'destroyed' during a recession as a result of the creative destruction process. In fact, creative destruction can work at different levels: (1) technological competences, (2) industry, and (3) firm. A major recession bringing about a substantial technological discontinuity might lead to the destruction of mature technologies and competences, but not of the industry and the existing firm, which may be able to survive by adapting to the new technological system (think of the shift from typewriter to computer). Of course, it is very likely that not all the existing firms can manage to survive, and new firms will join the renovated industry. Similarly, a recession driven by a major technological discontinuity might lead to the rise of a new industry with new technological competences and types of knowledge. This does not imply that existing firms belonging to the old sector would not be able to adapt and enter the new sector along with new firms. Studying the effects of the current recession across these different levels could lead to a better understanding of how creative destruction really works.

Some learned lessons and key questions

This book is concerned with the innovation behaviour of the firm during a major recession. From the discussion in this chapter, there are some key lessons that can be drawn in order to frame the results of the empirical analysis of Parts II and III of the book. Two main points are discussed here: (1) the cyclical versus the persistent nature of innovation; and (2) innovators during a crisis.

Behind the debate there is a crucial question about the relationship between innovation and economic activity. *Is innovation cyclical or persistent over the business cycle?* We have explained that innovation, namely technological innovation, takes place along established technological trajectories in a cumulative and path-dependent fashion. This lends some support to the *persistency* of innovation, as also confirmed by empirical research (Cefis and Orsenigo, 2001; Geroski *et al.*, 1997; Geroski and Walters, 1995).

However, there are also good reasons to believe that innovation is cyclical to some extent. Demand and finance play a part here. It has been argued that demand can affect innovation (Freeman, 1994; Schmookler, 1966). We have also illustrated that innovation is usually financed by the flow of internal resources of the firm, and thus depends on the dynamic of the profit. Also, venture capitalism, an important source of external funding for innovation, has been demonstrated to be cyclical. The importance of all these factors – demand, profit, finance – is largely amplified during a major recession like the current one, characterized by a sharp drop in demand and profits, and worsening of credit conditions. This is explored empirically in the remainder of the book.

The neo-Schumpeterian stream of studies has pointed out that on the one hand technological discontinuities are a source of creative destruction through the rise of new firms, industries and technologies. On the other hand, it has also been argued that existing firms are able to survive technological revolution and manage to remain key innovators by adapting to the new environment and mastering technologies in new knowledge-domains. It is very likely that a recession spurs a great wealth of new firms, along with the survival and adaptation of incumbent firms. Also, firms that were not innovators in the period prior to the crisis might make the decision to take advantage of the peculiar situation by becoming innovators.

Thus, *who are the innovators during a major crisis*? Such a crisis potentially represents a good opportunity for firms to gain advantage by innovating. However, the specific situation makes this statement true only in principle. Several factors can play a role here, both at the country level and the firm level. Country-specific factors can pertain to the macroeconomic condition in terms of a drop in internal or foreign demand. Also, different structures of the National System of Innovation – technological specialization, knowledge base, education – can play a role. Finally, differences in the organization of labour markets can also influence the firm's decision to invest in innovation during an economic downturn.

Regarding the firm, large firms can be better equipped to face a drop in demand, as they are more diversified, operate in different markets and have larger financial resources. Uncertainty can also play a part. Small firms, characterized by quicker decision-making processes, can be more able to adapt in a fast-changing environment. Other firm-specific characteristics can affect the opportunity for firms to innovate – for instance, the availability of financial resources, or a flexible and searching-oriented organizational structure. Finally, different types of innovation (i.e. product innovation, process innovation, service innovation, organizational innovation) and different innovation strategies can affect the decision of the firm to respond to a crisis by innovating. These are all central questions in this book, and will be investigated in the empirical chapters.

3 The role of the rules

National Systems of Innovation and labour market institutions

Increasing attention has been devoted to exploring the part that institutions – broadly defined as the rules of the game of a socio-economic system – make in affecting the behaviour of economic agents, technical change, and the patterns of economic growth (Hodgson, 2006; Mokyr, 2002; Nelson, 2001; North, 1990, 2005; Rodrik, 2007). This chapter is concerned with the role played by institutions in innovation and labour market functioning. It first discusses critically the contribution of the neo-Schumpeterian strand of research presented in the previous chapter. Second, it reviews the most comprehensive attempt to establish a link between innovation and institutions; that is, the theoretical framework of the National System of Innovation. Finally, it proposes an attempt to link innovation to labour market institutions. Both these frameworks are addressed empirically in Chapters 5 and 6 respectively.

Too much science and technology?

The neo-Schumpeterian stream of literature has been particularly concerned with the role of science and technology in economic change and innovation (see, among many others, Freeman and Soete, 1997; Mowery and Rosenberg, 1989; Nelson and Winter, 1982; Rosenberg, 1982). This is perfectly understandable, as this research developed in a period characterized by major scientific advancements and technological breakthroughs occurring in the manufacturing sector. However, there are at least three lines of research that have been underdeveloped but are relevant when it comes to innovation, and particularly innovation activity during economic crisis: the role of finance, demand, and labour markets.

The importance of finance and the banking system has been emphasized by Schumpeter himself, and represents a fundamental pillar of the Perez model described in Chapter 2 (see also the more recent Perez, 2009b, 2010). The role of credit creation to support innovation has been emphasized in Schumpeter's (1911 (1934)) first book, *The Theory of Economic Development*, while the last Schumpeter (1942), *Capitalism, Socialism and Democracy*, is more concerned with the self-financing of innovative investment in large firms. This is also reflected in the evolutionary research, starting with Nelson and Winter (1982), in which the relationship between innovation and economic performance at the level of the firm is conceptualized as being two-way and cumulative (Dosi, 1988; Nelson and Winter, 2002).

A recent stream of literature has addressed the microeconomics of enterprise finance; that is, the way firms finance their innovation activity. This research focuses on the different sources of finance for innovation, and particularly on the differences between internal and external sources (Hall, 2002; Hall and Lerner, 2010). However, systematic research about the relationship between finance and innovation along economic change has been quite scarce. As O'Sullivan (2005) effectively put it,

> contemporary economists of innovation have largely neglected the relation-ship between finance and innovation. Though there are a few exceptions to this rule, they are too recent and too few to suggest that we are on a brink of any systematic change in this regard

(for a valuable exception see Santarelli, 1995).

The second point that might have suffered from the prominence of the science and technology approach of the Schumpeterian school is that of demand. The hypothesis that technical change is mainly 'demand-pulled' was proposed by Schmookler (1962, 1966). This hypothesis was empirically supported by the positive correlation found between cycles of inventive effort (proxied by patents) and cycles of output across industries producing capital goods. This idea sparked a lot of interest, and was tested empirically in the following years by scholars, with controversial results (Brouwer and Kleinknecht, 1999; Geroski and Walters, 1995; Kleinknecht and Verspagen, 1990; Pianta, 2001; Scherer, 1982).

The response from the SPRU school soon arrived, mainly with two contributions, by Dosi (1997) and Freeman (1994). Freeman's (1994) argument revolves around the distinction between radical and incremental innovation, and the pattern of diffusion of innovation. He contends that in early stages of radical innovation science and technology are prominent, while demand can take a part once the technological trajectory has been established. This is where the diffusion mechanisms step in, as diffusion entails both supply and demand. Thus, Freeman concludes that the majority of demand-led innovation consisted of relatively minor innovation along established trajectories, while the counter-Schmookler type of innovation was typical of the early stage of innovation in many industries. This argument is based on the insights provided by the chain linked model by Kline and Rosenberg (1986), which emphasizes the presence of continuous feedback loops between innovation, diffusion, and further generation of new solutions (for a review of this debate, see Ruttan, 1997).

The latter point regards what the neo-Schumpeterian strand of literature has to say about labour markets and therefore policy recommendation. This research has been extremely helpful in broadening our understanding about technical change, innovation, and the behaviour of the firm. Accordingly, a vast array of policy recommendations have been elaborated, mainly confined to science, technology, and innovation policy (Archibugi and Iammarino, 1999; Archibugi *et al.*, 1999; Borras, 2003; Fagerberg *et al.*, 2009; Hall, 2007; Lundvall, 1999; Lundvall and Borras, 2005; Pavitt, 1987; Scherer, 2000). However, it has little to say about the more 'traditional' economic policies – such as, for instance, labour market policies. We believe the key challenge for this research is that of exploring the linkages between its understanding of economic change and the traditional field of economic policy involving the role of institutions, the functioning of labour markets, fiscal arrangements, unemployment, underdevelopment and so on. So far, some notable attempts have been made, like those related to growth (for review, see Verspagen, 2005), international trade (Archibugi and Michie, 1997; Fagerberg, 1988; Filippetti *et al.*, 2011; Laursen, 2000; Meliciani, 2001) and employment (Bogliacino and Pianta, 2010a; Pianta, 2004). However, clear theoretical developments as well as systematic empirical research in these directions are still lacking.

In this book we try to address some of the problems raised above. Specifically, the role of finance, along with the importance of demand, is taken into account at the country level in Chapter 5, and at the level of the firm in Chapter 9, while Chapter 6 addresses the role of labour market institutions in affecting a firm's decision to invest in innovation during a recession. In what follows, we set the scene to explore the role of National Systems of Innovation and labour market institutions.

Institutions, economic change and innovation

Institutions have become key in a substantial part of the mainstream literature dealing with growth and economic development. As such, they have become the fundamental ingredient of the 'augmented' Washington Consensus (Easterly, 2002; Rodrik, 2007). True, the fundamental importance that institutions play in shaping the economics and social environment in which the economic activity takes place has been emphasized since the work of Veblen (2008 (1899)), followed by the Davis and North studies (Davis and North, 1971; North, 1990, 2005) and those of Joel Mokyr (2002), among others. This research has placed institutions at the centre of understanding the functioning and evolution of the economic system, as they shape its incentive structure.

Institutions are broadly defined as 'the rules of the game' of the socio-economic context. They provide both opportunities and constraints for agents' choices and behaviours. The main idea is that completely abstraction from the specific context in which the economic activity and economic change take place leaves aside an important part of the story. Some elements that could play a key role in *explaining* the patterns of economic change and economic behaviour are omitted. For instance, an Arrow–Debreu world would not be considered a useful tool for addressing the problem this literature is concerned with – that is, the pattern of economic change, the working of technical change, and the heterogeneity in the behaviour of economic agents. Within this context, firms' choices (i.e.

firms' reaction to a major recession) are shaped by institutional factors. It is therefore reasonable to assume that the behaviour of the firm is particularly shaped by the institutional arrangements during a major economic downturn. This is the central concern of Part II of this volume.

In the domain of innovation studies, the seminal work by Freeman (1987) has been developed further by the National Systems of Innovation (NSI) literature by Lundvall (1992) and Nelson (1993), who have considered the role played by institutions in the dynamic of innovation. In the same line, Coriat and Dosi (2000) have proposed the 'institutional embeddedness dimensions of economic change', while Coriat and Weinstein (2002) have put forward a framework to investigate the roles of organizations and institutions in the development of innovation. All these studies, among others, give a great deal of prominence to the role of institutions in shaping innovation activity, mainly at the country level (and at the sectoral level, as in Malerba, 2004). One of the key issues in this merging of institutional and innovation streams of literature is, what institutions (and differences among them) are relevant in explaining different innovation patterns and dissimilar behaviours across economic systems? In the following, we consider two streams of literature that have addressed this issue: that associated to the NSI (Lundvall, 1992; Lundvall *et al.*, 2002; Nelson, 1993) and the so-called Varieties of Capitalism (VoC) research (Hall and Soskice, 2001; Hanckè, 2009).

So far, the relationship between the VoC literature and that of the NSI has been largely unexplored. However, there are important overlaps and similarities. First, in both cases the firm is explored as *embedded* in its environment, which is shaped by institutions. Further, the analysis is centered on the relations that the firm has to establish outside its boundaries to solve its problems concerning labour, knowledge and innovation. The latter point has, in recent years, been particularly emphasized by the Open Innovation paradigm (Chesbrough, 2003; Chesbrough *et al.*, 2008). Second, both of them stress the importance of the linkages: the VoC research emphasizes the role of *complementarities* in institutional dimensions, while NSI insists upon the *systemic* nature of the innovation activity. Third, in both cases there is no such a thing as a necessary convergence of economic systems towards a single or optimal configuration. As Freeman (1995) puts it, 'national variation in circumstances may often lead to different paths of development and to increasing diversity rather than standardization and convergence' (p. 15). Finally, in both these theoretical frameworks, and very much in the spirit of institutional theory, history matters. Thus, the current institutional arrangements and characteristics of NSI of countries can be understood as the result of a path-dependent process, and the outcome of historical processes in which the development of firms, organizations and industries interacted with national policies, institutional development, culture and informal rules over time (Fagerberg *et al.*, 2009; Hall and Soskice, 2001; North, 2005).

In this book, both the VoC and NSI concepts are employed to test empirically their influence on the behaviour of the firm in terms of innovation investment in response to the current economic crisis. This is pretty much in the spirit of both innovation studies and institutional theories, such as those addressed here. In fact, as explained in Chapter 2, innovation activity is characterized by having a structural, long-term and path-dependent nature. Thus it is very likely that innovation activities co-evolve with institutional change and economic growth along specific patterns. The fact that these patterns can be country-specific is exactly at the core of the NSI claim.

If innovation, technical change and institutions consistently co-evolve over the long term, what happens in the short term in conjunction with a deep global recession? Do different NSI structure and labour market institutions matter? Do they shape the innovation behaviour of the firm in a systematic fashion across countries? If so, in which direction? In other words, do specific configurations of NSI and labour market institutions provide a comparative institutional advantage in times of crisis? As a matter of fact, it is possible that all firms react in a similar way in the face of a major recession. It is thus possible that in such a peculiar macroeconomic environment, structural characteristics of the country are less relevant in opposition to short-term macroeconomic dynamics. The first general question at stake is therefore whether structure matters vis-à-vis demand during a big recession. We turn to this point in Chapters 5 and 6.

The National System of Innovation

The concept of NSI was introduced in the mid-1980s, drawing largely from the field of evolutionary economics. It points to the endogenous nature of innovation activities as embedded in a specific national context, in opposition to the exogenous nature of innovation in neoclassical studies. It was defined as 'the network of institutions in the public and private sectors whose activities and interactions initiate, import, modify and diffuse new technologies' (Freeman, 1987). As such, NSI include firms, universities, public bodies and non-profit organizations that support the generation and diffusion of science, technology and innovation within national borders.[1]

The NSI concept resides on one fact and two well-established beliefs: (1) countries exhibit systematic differences in terms of economic performance; and (2) the latter largely depends on different technological and innovation capabilities on the one side, and development of institutions on the other side (North, 1990, 2001; Fagerberg, 1994; Landes, 1998; Mokyr, 2002); (3) innovation and technology policies are an effective tool for fostering innovation performance of countries. The persistent difference in terms of innovative capabilities across countries is one of the factors that explain their different economic performance, as stressed by the NSI literature (Castellacci, 2008; Fagerberg and Srholec, 2008; Freeman, 1995; Lundvall, 1992; Nelson, 1993). The way in which firms carry out innovation activities and set their learning processes is affected by a number of specific national factors (Archibugi and Michie, 1997; Lorenz and Lundvall, 2006), including the nature of the scientific and technological institutions, the education and training system, the financial system, and industrial specialization.

This is also associated with the fact that innovative activities are cumulative and persistent at the micro level (Cefis and Orsenigo, 2001; Geroski *et al.*, 1997; Nelson and Winter, 1982; Patel and Pavitt, 1997). Previous literature has already shown how the sectoral dimensions of patterns of innovation are country-specific, as well as firms' persistency in innovating (Cefis and Orsenigo, 2001).

In their conceptualization of NSI, Lundvall and colleagues (Lundvall, 1992; Lundvall *et al.*, 2002) go beyond the 'technonationalism' that had inspired Nelson's conceptualization of a NSI (Nelson, 1993) in order to recognize that the ability of countries to foster innovation is dependent upon social capabilities, and is not solely based on science and technology. Within this broadened context, a national system of innovation is constituted by the institutions and economic structure affecting the rate and direction of technological change in the society (Edquist and Lundvall, 1993, p. 267). At the core of the latter definition of a NSI resides the microeconomic theory of innovation derived from the neo-Schumpeterian strand of literature, the assumptions of bounded rationality of agents, the role of tacit knowledge, as well as the role played by institutions upon economic activities. Regarding the former, the main message taken on board in NSI is the systemic nature of innovation activity. Firms carry out innovation through extensive interactions with several actors outside their boundaries, such as universities, research centres, users and suppliers. Crucially, this activity occurs within a specific (national) institutional context.

Figure 3.1 summarizes the elements of the NSI (Archibugi and Michie, 1997). Both education and training, and science and technology capability, reflect the major role played by human capital and knowledge generation in modern economies. The industrial structure, in terms of technological specialization, has also been demonstrated to heavily condition the nature of the innovative activity (Archibugi and Pianta, 1992). Moreover, science and technology (S&T) strengths and weakness are very country-specific. Some countries specialize in leading-edge technologies, while others have strengths in areas that are likely to

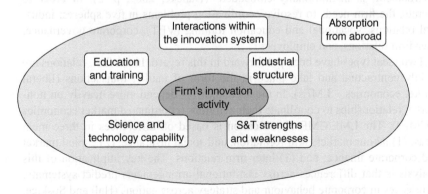

Figure 3.1 National Systems of Innovation (source: authors' elaboration).

provide only diminishing returns in the future. The resulting S&T specialization may influence the future patterns of innovation of a nation, and its competitiveness. The degree of the interactions within the NSI is also a key element. In some countries, such as Germany and Japan, or the Italian districts, the firm is more likely to coordinate its economic activity by interacting strongly with the rest of the NSI elements. Here, the similarities with the VoC research are relevant. Finally, the capacity to absorb foreign technology and adapt it to the national economic system is central for fostering technical change and economic growth.

The varieties of capitalism: labour market institutions, skills, education and corporate governance

Over the past decade, the so-called Varieties of Capitalism (VoC) research has investigated the importance of the institutional structure across advanced countries (Hall and Soskice, 2001). This stream of studies is nested within a well-established tradition of studies that emphasize the role of institutions in shaping the behaviour of economic agents, the evolution of organizations, and the pattern of economic development (Landes, 1998; Mokyr, 2002; Nelson, 2001; North, 1990, 2005). In brief, this research claims that: (1) countries systematically differ in terms of institutional structures, and there is no necessary condition for countries to converge; and (2) this considerably shapes the way firms carry out their activity.

Institution structure includes the organization of the labour market, industrial relationships, corporate governance, skills of the labour force, provisions pertaining to employment and unemployment protection. The unit of analysis of this research is the firm. The latter, along with its necessity to coordinate several activities within a specific institutional context, is substantially affected by the real configuration of the institutional structure of its country. However, in contrast to standard economic theory, the VoC research 'treats the firm as a relational network: the firm, operating in its markets and other aspects of the relevant environment, is institutionally embedded' (Hanckè, 2009, p. 2). In order to operate, the firm needs to resolve coordination problems in five spheres: industrial relations, vocational and education training (VET), corporate governance, inter-firm relations, and employees.

Two ideal types have been put forward in this regard. In the first, relations are mainly contractual and take place in the form of market transactions (liberal market economies – LMEs). In the second, firms depend more heavily on non-market relationships to coordinate their activities (coordinated market economies – CMEs). The LME/CME classification is based on differences in three main areas: (1) labour market, skill formation, and social insurance; (2) capital market and corporate finance; and (3) inter-firm relations. The key implication of this analysis is that differences across institutional arrangements predict systematic differences in corporate behaviour and strategy across nations (Hall and Soskice, 2001).

Here, the idea is that such a wide spectrum of institutional arrangements leads to different structures of incentives for the economic agent – namely the firm – resulting in different functioning of the economic systems. For instance, regarding innovation, Hall and Soskice (2001) maintain that LMEs are more likely to carry out radical innovation activities, while in turn CMEs are more likely to be involved in incremental forms of innovation (for an assessment, see Akkermans *et al.*, 2009; Hanckè, 2009).[2] Further than innovation activities, the functioning of economic systems across the varieties of capitalism differs in many respects. Hall and Soskice (2001) analyse the differences between the Unites States and Germany. They show that company needs regarding corporate governance, education and training, and industrial and inter-firm relations are addressed and solved in very different ways. Japan is a case in point. The Japanese economic system has been defined as 'relationalism' (Keller and Samuels, 2003), as its functioning is organized along three main ties: (1) the government–business tie, (2) the business–business tie, and (3) the management–labour tie. These strong relationships profoundly shaped the pattern of economic development and technical change in Japan in the second half of the twentieth century.

The VoC literature initially drew on the clear-cut distinction between LMEs and CMEs. These were depicted as two ideal types of modern advanced market systems, often related to the US on the one side, and Germany on the other (Hall and Soskice, 2001). Over recent years both the VoC and comparative labour market literature have gone beyond this stylized distinction, in order to investigate different sub-types of capitalistic systems reflected by different provisions in the labour market as well as in the capital market. Thus, different institutional arrangements have been identified, along three main dimensions: (1) unemployment security, (2) employment protection, and (3) vocational and educational training (VET).

A crucial point emphasized in this research is that regarding *institutional complementarities*. The idea is that labour market institutions and labour relations, skills and education, and corporate finance, tend to reinforce each other. Thus, CMEs are characterized by the prominence of non-market relations, collaborations, and long-term commitment, while in LMEs one can observe the prevalence of arms-length relations between the economic agents.

The complementarities of institutional arrangements in economic system are well explained in Estevez-Abe *et al.* (2001), where the authors show that different types of social protection are complementary to different skill equilibria. Their argument is that workers (and firms) are more encouraged to invest in specific skills in the presence of an implicit agreement for long-term employment and real wage stability. Thus, social protection becomes important as much as it assures this form of agreement. The main message, then, is that the shape of the social protection has a bearing on national competitive advantage in terms of skills and education of the workers. Specific institutional arrangements that provide higher incentives and expected returns for specific skills explain the different levels of specific skills investment of workers and companies across

countries. Thus, wage protection through collective bargaining systems reinforces the effects of both employment protection and unemployment protection,
as it reduces the risk that the wage-level for specific skills might drop in the
future. As a result, one is expected to observe wage-bargaining systems in highly
coordinated economies with a higher level of specific skills, and non-coordinated
systems where it is low.

This is evident in Figure 3.2, in which Estevez-Abe *et al.* (2001) have plotted
countries along an index of employment protection on the horizontal axis, and
unemployment protection on the vertical axis. One can note that LMEs are clustered in the lower left-hand corner, with low levels of both employment and
unemployment protection. One can also observe a lot of variation between
CMEs, even if overall job security is higher in all CMEs than in any LMEs. The
range of unemployment protection is extremely high, and goes from very low
figures for Italy and Japan to very high figures for Denmark, Switzerland and
The Netherlands. There is also a clear pattern as far as the levels of skills are
concerned, with LMEs showing lower figures in opposition to CMEs (see Tables
3.1 and 3.2 for a summary).

A crucial implication for this book's argument is that this observed persistency in capitalist differences provides a different structure of incentives for

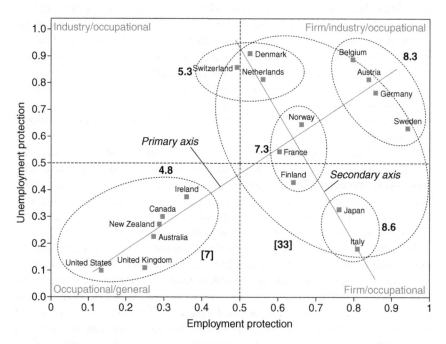

Figure 3.2 Social protection and skills profiles (source: Estevez-Abe *et al.*, 2001; reproduced with permission).

Note
Bold numbers are mean tenure rates for the cluster of countries circled; bracketed numbers are the
percentage of an age cohort going through vocational training.

Table 3.1 Institutional arrangements in LMEs and CMEs

Assets	Labour market	Skills and education	Corporate governance
Liberal market economies			
Switchable (i.e. assets whose value can be realized if diverted to other purpose)	Low employment protection and low unemployment security	Low vocational training and high general skills and education	Short-term, venture capital
Coordinated market economies			
Co-specific (i.e. assets that cannot readily be turned to another purpose)	Different mix of employment protection, unemployment security, and active policies for labour market	Overall, high vocational and education training	Long-term 'patient' capital

Source: Author's elaboration from Estevez-Abe *et al.* (2001).

Table 3.2 Institutional arrangements *within* CMEs

Models	Labour market institutions	Skills
Flexicurity (e.g. Denmark)	Low employment protection coupled with high unemployment security, pro-active labour market policies, social security systems providing adequate income support during employment transitions	Industry-specific, lifelong learning strategies
Continental (e.g. Germany)	High employment protection and high unemployment protection	Industry-specific and firm specific
Club-med (e.g. Italy and Japan)	High employment protection coupled with low security for unemployment	Firm-specific

Source: Author's elaboration from Estevez-Abe *et al.* (2001).

agents, which in turn generate different behaviours in terms of economic adjustment. This can be even more prominent in the case of a recession, as

> in the face of an exogenous shock threatening return to existing activities, holders of mobile assets will be tempted to 'exit' those activities to seek higher returns elsewhere, while holders of specific assets have higher incentives to exercise 'voice' in defence of existing activities.
>
> (Hall and Gingerich, 2004).

Conclusions

To sum up, starting from the role that institutions play in economic theory, we have described the NSI and VoC main arguments. As explained, there are significant similarities between these two fields of research that put the institution at the centre of the understanding of the functioning and evolution of economic systems. They can be summarized as follows:

- institutional arrangements vary across countries, and are the result of historical processes in which technological change and industrial evolution interact with formal and informal rules, culture, and policies;
- countries do not necessarily convergence towards an 'optimal' system of organization of the economic system;
- the firm is at the centre of the stage, and it is conceptualized in terms of its relationship with the economic system. These relationships are key to solving its coordination problems, in the goods market, labour market, and capital market;
- they both emphasize the paramount role of the institutional environment in which the firm is 'embedded' in affecting the behaviour of the firm.

The last point calls for an exploration of the role that institutional arrangements, in the form of both NSI structure and labour market institutions, played during the current economic downturn in affecting the innovative behaviour of the firm. We turn to this in the next part of the book.

PART II

The uneven impact of the crisis across countries: some explanation

4   Is the crisis hampering innovation convergence in Europe?

Introduction

The European Union (EU) is grounded on three main pillars: cohesion, integration and convergence. It will be important for analysis and policy advice to investigate what the impact of the 2008 global financial crisis will be on each of these pillars (Hodson and Quaglia, 2009). While a few recent studies have addressed the impact of the financial crisis in terms of income, productivity and employment convergence, less attention has been devoted to the impact on innovation performance.[1] Convergence in innovation is a crucial component of a successful European integration, since on the one hand innovation provides a key asset to enhance economic competitiveness and on the other hand it facilitates cohesion in the social and political sphere. We assume, in fact, that the lack of convergence in innovative activities will also jeopardize EU cohesion policies, since it will make the least developed countries more dependent on the knowledge generated elsewhere or, even worse, will not allow them to benefit at the same level from the available knowledge.

The existence of major technological gaps *within* Europe has traditionally been recognized as constraining the building of a European System of Innovation (Lorenz and Lundvall, 2006; Pavitt and Patel, 1988). Enlargement has led to a more heterogeneous EU in terms of innovation capabilities and technological development. Moreover, New Member Countries are more vulnerable not only in terms of scientific and technological infrastructure, but also in terms of financial institutions, and are therefore likely to be hit more severely by adverse economic effects. The reduction of national disparities in scientific and technological competences is therefore a key priority in allowing the EU to close the gap with the US and Japan (Archibugi and Coco, 2005a). This chapter's aim is to investigate the dynamics of countries' technological convergence and innovation performance in the light of two major events: the EU enlargement, and the impact of the global financial crisis.

European policy makers have widely recognized the importance of science, technology and innovation for the continent's economic growth and well-being. The 'Lisbon strategy' puts the 'Knowledge Economy' at the centre of its economic policy and asks Member States to make a major effort to invest more in

R&D and other innovation-related activities. But the European Union is composed of countries that vary considerably in terms of technological expertise. While some of them, such as Sweden and Finland, are world innovation leaders, others are lagging behind. Moreover, the 2004 and 2007 enlargements have substantially increased not just the number of Member States, but also the range of countries' technological expertise and stages of development. Even more than before, EU policy needs to take explicitly into account the existing variety in technological competence, innovation performance and industrial structure. In contrast to the United States and Japan, a proper European System of Innovation is still far from being in place. Rather, the EU still appears to be an agglomeration of autonomous and highly diverse national innovation systems (Lorenz and Lundvall, 2006).

A large body of literature has already demonstrated the fundamental role played by innovation and technological capabilities in fostering long-term growth performance (Castellacci, 2008; Fagerberg, 1994). In order to catch up, emerging countries need to develop an endogenous capability allowing them to absorb the knowledge and technology developed elsewhere (Cohen and Levinthal, 1989; Griffith *et al.*, 2004). As far as the European case is concerned, differences in economic growth across European regions have already been explained by looking at the differences in generating and adapting technologies developed abroad (Cantwell and Iammarino, 2003; Cappelen *et al.*, 1999; Fagerberg and Verspagen, 1996). This has led policy makers to rely on EU innovation policy as a fundamental instrument in reaching convergence, including key variables such as productivity and income (Borras, 2003; Lundvall and Borras, 2005; Von Tunzelmann and Nassehi, 2004). The free circulation of commodities, capital and people should in fact also facilitate the transmission of know-how, equipment and infrastructure from the most to the least advanced parts of the EU.

International economic integration may have opposite effects on the distribution of innovative activities. In the optimistic view, economic, social and political integration helps to disseminate best-practice technologies and to diffuse expertise. Through trade, scientific exchanges, technological collaborations and direct foreign investment, backward countries have windows open which allow them to exploit the technological opportunities offered by the most developed countries (Perez and Soete, 1988). In the pessimistic view, on the contrary, the strongest areas will attract the most knowledge-intensive economic activities, providing job opportunities to the best talents. Eventually, backward areas will find themselves confined in an economic specialization in the low technology industries and with decreasing returns, while the most developed areas will further reinforce their leadership (Rodriguez-Pose, 1999).

In the real world, both mechanisms are at work, since innovative activities are not homogeneous entities. As shown by a large theoretical and empirical literature, innovation is nurtured by a variety of different sources, including R&D, design, engineering, equipment and machinery, and infrastructure (Pavitt, 1984; von Hippel, 1998). The effect of economic integration is not necessarily the same on all these activities. While economic integration may help in disseminating innovative infrastructure, such as ICT and other general-purpose technologies, integration may have an opposite effect on core activities associated to the generation of new knowledge and innovation, which may agglomerate in the most advanced areas.

This chapter discusses the dynamics of innovation performance across EU Member States and the effect of the crisis. We address empirically the following crucial questions:

1   *Has convergence in innovation been achieved in recent years?* This will follow previous research carried out for the EU15 (Archibugi and Coco, 2005b) and that can now be expanded to include the New Member States (NMS).
2   *To what extent is the current economic downturn impairing the convergence process across the European Union in terms of innovation performance and technological capabilities of countries?*

The next section presents the dataset that is employed throughout the book.

The data: the Innobarometer Survey and the European innovation scoreboard

The empirical part of this book is mostly grounded on the Innobarometer Survey 2009, which is designed and collected by the European Commission (2009b). In each of the twenty-seven EU Member States, plus Norway and Switzerland, 200 enterprises from most manufacturing and private service industries with twenty or more employees were sampled.[2] A total of 5238 telephone interviews were completed during the period 1–9 April 2009. The sample was a random sample, stratified by country, enterprise size (five size bands) and industry (two-digit industry codes).[3]

Since 2001, the Innobarometer has been conducted on a yearly basis. Each year the survey highlights a different issue/theme, which is picked up on in additional and specific questionnaire items over and above a core set of variables. The focus of the current (2009) survey was on innovation-related expenditures and the effects of the economic downturn on such expenditures. It is this section of the questionnaire from which our key variables are developed.

The dependent variables

Our dependent variables measure change in innovation-related investment as it is reported by the firms themselves and with reference to different time periods (before, during and following on from the crisis). Innovation-related investment is captured in a wide sense, incorporating expenditures not only on in-house R&D but also on technology, embodied in the purchase of machinery, equipment and software, licensed-in technology (patents or other know-how), training of staff in support of innovation, and expenditures on design of products, process and services. This broad definition (in line with the definition adopted in the Community Innovation Surveys) has advantages over a narrow definition, such as investment in R&D. R&D expenditures will not be able to capture short-term responses to the financial crisis on the grounds that R&D projects are typically commitments made for several years. Moreover, R&D is also concentrated in a few firms and sectors. In contrast, the wider definition of innovation-related investments used in this chapter, which includes other innovation-related expenditures over and above R&D, is better suited to capturing short-term adjustments due to changes in the economic environment. Firms are quicker in cutting training for innovation, design budgets or purchases of software than they are in adjusting R&D projects.

The dependent variables are based on firms' responses to the following three questions.

1   before the crisis: '*Compared to 2006 has the total amount spent by your firm on all innovation activities in 2008 increased, decreased or stayed approximately the same?*'
2   during the crisis: '*In the last six months[4] has your company taken one of the following actions as a direct result of the economic downturn; increased total amount of innovation expenditures, decreased [...] or maintained [...]?*' and
3   following on from the beginning of the crisis: '*Compared to 2008, do you expect your company to increase, decrease or maintain the total amount of its innovation expenditure in 2009?*'

The observations feeding into the empirical analysis are all from those firms that were innovation-active, and thus firms that stated that they increased, decreased or maintained their innovation investment in the three periods respectively.

The weakness of our dependent variable – change in innovation-related investment – is that the scales are categorical rather than continuous (e.g. three choices as opposed to the total amount spent on innovation), but the strength is that they provide a unique possibility to distinguish between three different time periods around the crisis.

Table 4.1 provides the descriptive statistics for the three dependent variables, including the number (frequency) and percentage of enterprises that increased, maintained and decreased innovation investment under (1) time proxy for 'before the crisis' – we also refer to this as T1, (2) proxy for 'during the crisis' that we also refer to as T2, and (3) proxy for 'following on from the crisis', referred to as T3.

Table 4.1 reveals two patterns. First, 38 per cent of enterprises reported that they increased innovation-related investment in 2008 compared with their investment in 2006 (see Table 4.1 '%' column under T1); but in T2 only 9 per cent and in T3 13 per cent of enterprises reported increased investment. Thus, there is a strong drop in the number of firms that increased innovation-related investment

Table 4.1 Investment in innovation-related activities before, during and following on from the crisis

Dependent variable: change in innovation-related investment	Before the crisis (T1)		During the crisis (T2)		Following on from the beginning of the crisis (T3)	
	Frequency	%	Frequency	%	Frequency	%
Increase	1985	38	453	9	659	13
Decrease	472	9	1231	24	1560	30
Maintain	2207	42	2961	57	2452	47
Innovation active firms	4664	89	4645	90	4671	90
No innovation activities	328	6	457	9	343	7
Missing observations	242	5	132	3	220	4
Number of observations	5234	100	5234	100	5234	100

Notes
T1 refers to the change in innovation-related investment in the calendar year 2008 compared to 2006; T2 refers to the change in innovation-related investment in the six-month period October 2008 to March 2009; T3 refers to the expected change in innovation-related investment in 2009 compared with 2008.

during the crisis and following on from the crisis. This pattern is mirrored in a shift from few firms to many firms reporting decreased investment over the three time periods. In T1 only 9 per cent of firms decreased their innovation-related expenditures, but in the midst of the financial crisis – in T2 – 24 per cent decreased investment and 30 per cent planned to decrease investment in 2009 compared to investment levels in 2008. Second, a large share of firms (about half of all firms) reported that they maintained innovation-related investment irrespective of the crisis. Thus, there are broadly two main patterns here. The first is related to a change in the innovation investment behaviour of a part of the firms in response to the crisis. The second pertains to those firms which reported maintaining their innovation investment at the same level, thus suggesting the presence of persistency in the innovation behaviour. These two patterns will be at the centre of the empirical analysis throughout the entire volume.

Data on innovation at the country level are taken from the *European Innovation Scoreboard* (EIS) (European Commission, 2009a). The EIS is a Report of the European Commission – Directorate of General Enterprises and Industry.[6] It aims at measuring and comparing the innovation performance at the country level using a synthetic composite indicator. For our analysis we will use the current EIS composite indicator methodology, which is based on twenty-nine indicators addressing several dimensions of a country's system of innovation (see Table A4.1 in the Appendix to this chapter for a detailed list of the indicators). The composite indicator, the *Summary Innovation Index* (SII), has been calculated with the same methodology over the period 2004–2008. This allows us to address the convergence of innovation performance of countries over a period of five years using both the SII as a whole, and its seven dimensions (see Table A4.2 in the Appendix).

Cohesion, enlargement and economic convergence in the European Union

In this chapter, we concentrate on a specific dimension of economic convergence, namely *convergence in innovation capabilities*. In this section we first introduce the notion of convergence; we then examine research dealing with convergence in the EU and present the most important empirical results. Most of the studies discussed below deal with convergence in income and productivity, although there is a general consensus that technological capabilities and innovation are crucial determinants of economic growth. Both new growth (Grossman and Helpman, 1991; Romer, 1986) and neo-Schumpeterian theories (Fagerberg and Godinho, 2005) would in fact agree in emphasizing the role of technology and innovation in explaining different growth rates across countries.

The economics of growth literature has always questioned whether there is some kind of mechanism at work leading to convergence across countries in terms of level of income per capita. Boldrin *et al.* (2001) have distinguished four main hypotheses about convergence proposed by the literature, from a strong convergence hypothesis *à la* Solow (1956) to a non-convergence one caused by the presence of strong increasing returns, as proposed by the new growth literature (Grossman and Helpman 1991; Romer 1986) and reinforced by the new geography literature that emphasizes the role of agglomeration economies (Krugman, 1991).

The convergence versus divergence argument has been central to the European integration debate since the very beginning. This is the result of the importance of the socio-political dimension of the EU process of integration – cohesion – which profoundly differentiated EU integration from other regional organizations such as NAFTA or MERCOSUR. During the 1970s, the Community regional policy, inspired by the hypotheses of Gunnar Myrdal (1957), tried to counterbalance the agglomeration of capital and human resources towards the more developed regions at the expense of the peripheral ones. Both the Structural Funds and, later, the Cohesion Fund were grounded on the non-convergence hypothesis, and therefore aimed to compensate regions that were lagging behind due to the asymmetric effects of integration (Boldrin *et al.*, 2001; Leonardi, 1995).

A great deal of empirical research has investigated the convergence versus divergence hypothesis across European countries at both national and regional levels. In a comprehensive study, Leonardi (1995) analyses per capita income convergence relating to the period 1970–1995, finding convergence at both regional (NUTS II) and national levels. Using data for sixty-four European regions in the 1980s, Fagerberg *et al.* (1997) show that innovation and the diffusion of technology are important factors behind European growth. Most of the regions fail to take advantage of more advanced technologies developed elsewhere due to a lack of R&D absorptive capabilities, and therefore they show lower growth rates with respect to rich regions. Boldrin *et al.* (2001) find neither significant income convergence nor divergence across EU15 regions during the

1980s and the first half of 1990s, while labour productivity shows a moderate tendency to convergence. Martin (2001) provides additional analysis of patterns of regional productivity trends and employment growth over the period 1975–1998. Whilst labour productivity shows very weak convergence across the EU regions, there is a sharp divergence in regional employment.

Taking into account the effects of innovation in the EU countries from 1969 to 1998, Jungmittag (2004) shows that technology diffusion is a driving force for growth and labour productivity convergence of catching-up countries. He concludes by claiming that EU policy should encourage catching-up countries in 'setting up efficient national innovation systems and, at the same time, participate in a gradually emerging European innovation system' (p. 272). Using three alternative methodologies to measure convergence, Neven and Gouymte (2008) investigated the pattern of convergence in output per head across regions in the European Community for the period 1975–1990. They found strong differences across sub-periods and across subsets of regions. Southern European regions seem to have caught up in the early 1980s, but not in the second part of the 1980s, while the regions in the north of Europe tended to stagnate or diverge in the first part of the 1980s but converged strongly thereafter. In recent years, increasing attention has been devoted to innovation and convergence at the subnational regional level.[7] There is, in fact, a rising concern that increasing cross-country interactions are intensifying regional disparities within countries due to intense spillover effects, proximity effects and agglomeration economies.[8]

More recent studies have addressed convergence in technology across Europe.[9] Zizmond and Novak (2007) found significant technology convergence between fifteen old EU Member States and the eight New Member States. Krammer (2009) explores the main driver of innovation in sixteen Eastern European transition countries. He emphasizes the role played by universities and the national knowledge base, complemented by both public and private R&D expenditure, as well as the important part played by inflows of foreign direct investment and trade. Johnson *et al.* (2010) describe the technological development of thirteen countries in Europe, claiming that there is substantial potential growth in the technological development of Eastern European nations, and that there are high expectations that they will catch up over the coming fifteen years.

Finally, Filippetti and Peyrache (2011) show, in a study covering forty-two countries, how EU New Member States are part of a global trend of technological capabilities convergence over recent decades. This is also reflected in a recent paper (Filippetti and Peyrache, 2010) investigating the dynamic of labour productivity in Europe, including both the NMS and three of the Candidate Countries (namely Croatia, Iceland and Turkey). Figure 4.1 provides some impressionist evidence that an overall process of convergence in labour productivity has been occurring for the considered twenty-nine European countries relative to the period 1993–2007. That is, lagging-behind countries seem to be catching up the more advanced EU Member States in terms of labour productivity. They find that, for Europe as an average, the relative contributions to labour productivity growth of capital deepening and total factor productivity (TFP)

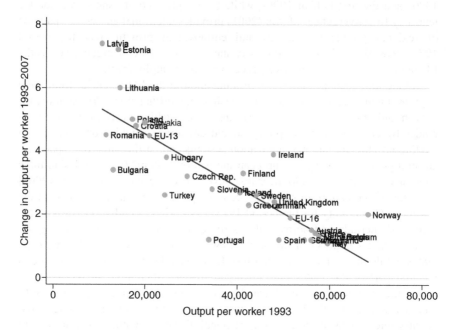

Figure 4.1 Convergence in output per worker over the period 1993–2007, twenty-nine European countries (source: Filippetti and Peyrache, 2010, reproduced with permission).

respectively account for around 53 per cent and 47 per cent. By further decomposing TFP they find that change in technological capabilities explains 71 per cent of change in TFP, thus accounting for 33 per cent of labour productivity growth.

Summing up, a huge number of empirical studies have addressed the convergence issue in terms of per capita income, productivity, employment and, more recently, technological capabilities.[10] The difficulties in coming to definitive conclusions arise from the fact that the geometry of the EU is a variable one due to the continuous process of integration and enlargement. Most of the studies reviewed do not take into account the recent enlargement process, and therefore do not include the EU New Member States. However, these studies show a general confirmation that domestic technological capabilities – in terms of R&D activities, infrastructure and human resources – are key factors in enhancing catch-up processes, which our empirical exercise will build upon. Our contribution will in fact try to shed new light on innovation performance convergence across the EU27 countries, taking into account the process of enlargement, but also looking at how the current economic downturn is impacting, and will continue to impact, on the convergence in progress.

The good news: the convergence in innovation performance across the EU

As already mentioned, economic convergence represents one of the main pillars of the EU project and enlargement. Since the very beginning of European integration, a good deal of effort and resources has been put forward by policy makers to achieve this goal. In this section, we assess to what extent convergence across EU Member States[11] has occurred in terms of innovation performance.

Methodology

To address convergence, we use the SII and its seven dimensions as a measure of innovation performance at a country level (see Table A4.1 in the Appendix). Composite indicators of innovation and technological capabilities have demonstrated that they are quite stable over time (Archibugi *et al.*, 2009), which is not surprising, considering they capture an economic structural dimension. The emergence of a convergence over a medium-term period of five years would already be a significant achievement. Moreover, the SII also allows exploration of convergence in the seven innovation dimensions of the SII indicator, disentangling the areas in which convergence is actually occurring, and shedding some light on its components' dynamics.

In order to make our results robust, we have applied two different methodologies already used to address convergence in the growth literature (Barro and Sala-i-Martin, 2005). Both rely on the simple concept that, in case of convergence, lagging-behind economies tend to grow faster than the best performer. The first model is usually referred to as the 'beta-convergence model', and takes into account only the first and last years – in our case, 2004 and 2008 respectively. We use the following equation for the beta-convergence model:

$$\ln\left[\frac{y_{T,i} - y_{0,i}}{y_{0,i}}\right] = \alpha + \beta \ln y_{0,i} + \varepsilon_i \qquad (1)$$

where the dependent variable represents the entire period variation rate (2004–2008), α is a constant, $y_{0,i}$ is the initial value (at time 0) relative to country i, and ε is the error term. We run eight different regressions for this model; one relative to the SII index, and the others relative to the seven sub-indexes which feed into the SII (see Table A4.1 in the Appendix). Thus, in the first case y represents the SII Index, while in the other cases it represents the sub-indexes, such as *Human resources, Finance & Support*, and so on. This allows us to check the presence of beta-convergence relative to the global innovation performance, as measured by the SII Index, and relative to the seven innovation dimensions in the considered period. If the parameter β is significantly negative, one can conclude in favour of unconditional beta-convergence.

The second model is instead based on the entire longitudinal data set, usually referred to as *panel data*. Panel data have become increasingly used thanks to two characteristics. First, they allow controlling for individual heterogeneity, which is a relevant characteristic when dealing with countries. Second, they are more informative with respect to time series or pure cross-sectional data. For our analysis, we use the *fixed effects* specification. The following equation is used for the fixed-effects model:

$$\ln\left[\frac{y_{t,i} - y_{t-1,i}}{y_{t-1,i}}\right] = \alpha_i + \beta \ln y_{t-1,i} + \varepsilon_{t,i} \tag{2}$$

where the dependent variable is the log of the SII annual variation rate relative to the country i, the regressor is represented by the log of the SII value for country i at time $t-1$, and α_i is interpreted as a parameter to be estimated, as in the fixed-effect model specification. This model refers only to the SII, and is not run for the seven dimensions.

Results

Figure 4.2, where we plot the SII performance in 2004 against the 2004–2008 SII variation rate, shows the achievement of convergence in technological capabilities and innovation performance across European countries. Countries with a low SII figure in 2004, including Bulgaria, Romania, Latvia and Slovakia, have

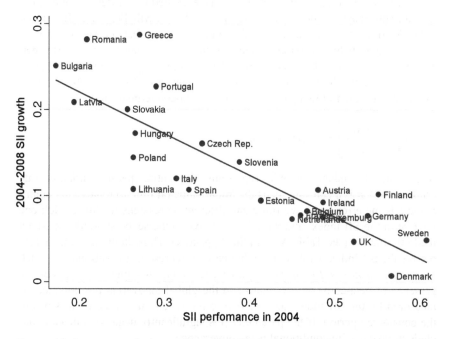

Figure 4.2 Convergence in innovation performance across the EU27 countries over the five years 2004–2008 (source: authors' elaboration on European Commission (2008, 2009a) – SII: Summary Innovation Indicator).

been performing relatively better over the past five years in comparison with the countries that were better performing in 2004 – i.e. Denmark, Sweden and the United Kingdom.

Table 4.2 summarizes the 'robust' estimates of the two models showing the coefficients related to the SII indicators. As a whole, the results of both the models confirm the hypothesis of convergence among European countries. Both coefficients are negative, as expected, and significant. In Table 4.3 we report the results of the beta-convergence model relative to the seven EIS dimensions. Also in this case, coefficients have negative and significant signs with the only exception being the 'Innovators' dimension.[12] Our results also show that 'Finance & Support', which includes Public R&D, venture capital, private credit and broadband, and 'Throughputs', which includes patents, trademarks, design registrations and the technology balance of payments, are the two dimensions in which convergence occurs at a faster rate.

As we have already mentioned, composite indicators like the SII are likely to show a stable dynamic performance over time due to the structural nature of the phenomena they deal with. The fact that both models account for convergence over a period of five years signals the presence of a significant process of cohesion across Europe in innovative activities. An analysis of the coefficients for the seven SII sub-indices related to the innovation dimensions of the SII also shows that convergence has been faster in less structural variables such as venture capital and broadband access. On the other hand, structural dimensions such as 'Firm investment', 'Human Resources' and 'Economic Effects' consistently show a slower convergence over the considered period.

In Figure 4.3, we report the dynamic of the SII and the seven innovation dimensions for New Member States (NMS) compared to the EU27 simple average over the period 2004–2008. Romania, Bulgaria and Latvia show a faster growth of the SII composite indicator. As a whole, the NMS show a similar growth composition to the EU27 average, with some notable exceptions. Specifically, Bulgaria and Hungary seem to be relatively weak on 'Human Resources', while Poland shows a strong dynamic regarding 'Firm Investment' relatively to its other dimensions. With regard to the 'Firm Investment' dimension, all the NMS perform better than the EU27 average.

Table 4.2 Results of the Model 1 (beta-convergence) and Model 2 (fixed effects), relative to the SII performance

	Beta-regression estimates	*Fixed-effects estimates*
Independent variable	SII variation rate (2004–2008)	Yearly SII variation rate (2004–2008)
β	−0.36***	−1.76***
Observations	32	96
F-test		0.04

Note
Robust standard errors: *** $P<0.01$, ** $P<0.05$, * $P<0.1$.

Table 4.3 Results of the Model 1 (beta-convergence) relative to the seven innovation dimensions* of the SII

Independent variable	Human resources	Finance and support	Firm investment	Linkages and entrepreneurship	Throughputs	Innovators	Economic effects
β	−0.90***	−1.46***	−0.34**	−0.35**	−1.51***	−0.02	−0.59***
Observations	32	32	32	32	32	32	32

Notes
Robust standard errors: *** $P<0.01$, ** $P<0.05$, * $P<0.1$.
* The seven dimensions are derived from the EIS (Table A4.1 in the Appendix)

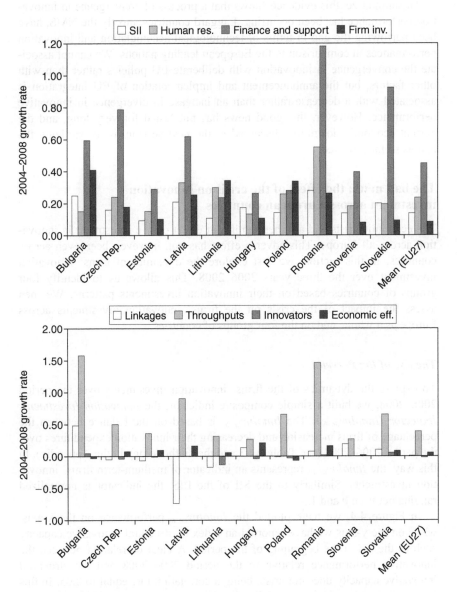

Figure 4.3 Growth rates for the SII and the seven innovative dimensions of the SII* for the New Member States and EU27 mean, 2004–2008.

Note
* The seven dimensions are derived from the EIS (Table A4.1 in the Appendix).

To summarize, this evidence shows that a process of convergence in innovation performance has been occurring. Laggard countries, mostly the NMS, have been narrowing the gap in terms of technological accumulation and innovation performances in comparison to the European leading nations. We cannot associate the convergence in innovation with deliberate EU policies rather than with other factors, but the announcement and implementation of EU integration is associated with a decrease rather than an increase in divergence in innovative performance. However, this good news has not lasted for very long, and the current economic downturn, discussed in the next session, is jeopardizing the results so far achieved.

The bad news: the effect of the crisis on innovation investment across European countries

The economic crisis had a rather significant effect on the investment in innovation across all Europe. This adverse effect has not, however, been even across countries. In this section, we first explore the dynamics of firms' innovation investment over the three years 2006–2008. This allows us to identify four groups of countries based on their innovation investments patterns. We then assess the impact of the crisis on the firms' innovation investments across Europe as a whole, and on the four groups of countries.

The rise of the Parvenu

To explore the dynamics of the firms' innovation investments over the period 2006–2008, we built a simple composite indicator, the *Innovation Investments Indicator (InnoInv$_{06-08}$)*. The *InnoInv$_{06-08}$* is based on the balance between the percentage of firms increasing and decreasing their innovation expenditures over the period 2006–2008 (see Table A4.3 and the methodology in the Appendix). In this way, the *InnoInv$_{06-08}$* represents an indicator of medium-term firms' innovation investments. Similarly to the SII of the EIS, the indicator is normalized ranging between 0 and 1.

In Figure 4.4, we have plotted the *InnoInv$_{06-08}$* performance on the x-axis, while on the y-axis we have reported an index of structural innovative capacity such as the SII at the beginning of the period. A clear correlation between the innovative performance relative to the period 2006–2008 and the structural innovative capacity does not arise, being a correlation rate equal to 0.05. In this way we are able to define the following four quadrants and relative groups of countries:

1   The *Parvenu*: although they do not exhibit high strength in their national innovation systems, they have been increasing their investments more than the average relative to the considered period. This group includes several NMS, including Poland, Slovakia, Lithuania, Bulgaria, Romania and Slovenia, which come from the ex-Socialist block.

2 The *Aristocracy*: this group consists of those countries that show both a structural consolidated leadership of their innovation performance, and at the same time are continuing to increase their investments in innovation. These countries are Sweden, Austria, Germany, Finland and Belgium. This brilliant performance is associated not only with hereditary privileges, but also with continuous efforts in learning and innovation.

3 The *Declining Nobility*: these countries, even though they have a strong national innovation system, have been increasing their innovation expenditures relatively less over the 2006–2008 period. They include Denmark, Ireland, the United Kingdom, Luxembourg, France and The Netherlands. A new member country, Estonia, also belongs to this group.

4 The *Third State*: this group of countries is characterized by both a low innovation performance at the national level and a low performance in firms' innovation spending. Interestingly, this group includes not only NMS such as Hungary, Latvia and the Czech Republic, but also the Southern European countries (Italy, Spain and Portugal).

The data presented in this section confirm the results reported in the previous section and based on the EIS. Until the financial crisis, Europe as a whole was expanding its investment in innovation, and firms in at least some of the laggard countries were expanding their innovative investment more than the EU average.

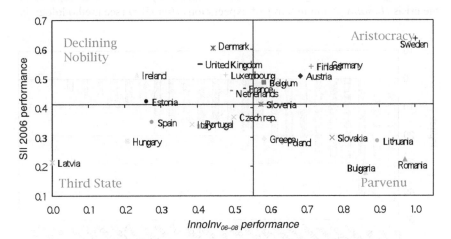

Figure 4.4 Medium-term firms' innovation performance (*InnoInv₀₆₋₀₈*) and national innovation system strength 2006 SII (source: authors' elaboration on *Innobarometer* data, and on *EIS* data (see Tables A4.2 and A4.3 in the Appendix)).

Note
Axes cross at average values.

The impact of the crisis across European countries

The huge impact of the economic downturn on firms' innovation spending is evident by looking at the data at the country level, as reported in Figure 4.5. The figures report the difference between the share of firms increasing and those firms decreasing their innovation investments in response to the crisis. In general, apart from Austria, Finland and Sweden, in all other countries the share of firms reducing innovation investments exceeds that increasing them in response to the crisis. Crucially, among the countries with the strongest negative impact, most belong to the *Parvenu* group. It is worth observing that we find Greece within this group of countries. Among those relatively less affected by the recession, we find advanced and dynamic economies such as Austria, Finland and Sweden. Let us look at this evidence in greater detail.

How bad is the bad news? The impact of the crisis within the four groups of countries

Our hypothesis is not only that the crisis is affecting countries to a different extent, but also that it is somehow reversing the convergence in innovation performance achieved in the past. In order to test this hypothesis, we put together all three questions of the Innobarometer (see Tables 4.1 and A4.3). Also, for the second and third questions we used the balance between the percentage of firms increasing and decreasing their innovation respectively in 2009 as a response to the crisis *(InnoInv$_{09}$)* and in terms of expectations *(InnoFor)* (see methodology in

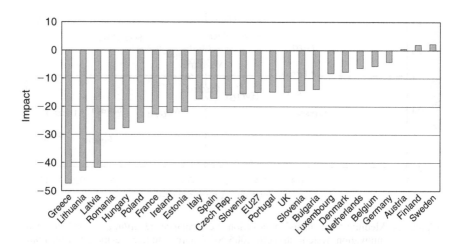

Figure 4.5 The impact of the current recession on firms' innovation investments* (source: authors' elaboration on *Innobarometer* data (see Tables A4.3 and A4.4 in the Appendix)).

Note
* Calculated as the difference between the share of firms increasing and firms decreasing their innovation investments.

the Appendix). This will allow testing of whether the reduction of innovation investment is occurring in the short term only, or if it will instead have consequences in the medium term as well.

In Figure 4.6, we summarize the results for the three indicators. As expected, the *Parvenu* is the group of countries with the greatest increase in innovation investment over the period 2006–2008. However, the *Parvenu* is also the group most negatively affected by the crisis, followed by the *Third State*. The other two groups, the *Aristocracy* and the *Declining Nobility*, are also those with the highest innovative rate, as shown by the SII. In a nutshell, *as a direct result of the crisis*, the innovation leaders are doing relatively better that the catching-up and lagging-behind countries. This is exactly the opposite of the convergence process highlighted above.

However, when we turn to look at the prospects as shown by *InnoFor*, the picture seems to change again. First, the groups *Aristocracy*, *Declining Nobility* and *Third State* seem to be persisting in reducing further their innovation expenditures: the number of firms reducing innovation investment is even larger then in the previous case *(InnoInv$_{09}$)*. And the only group that is showing a moderate counter-cyclical behaviour is the *Parvenu*. That is, in this case the number of firms that foresee reducing their expenditures in innovative activities is lower than in the previous situation. Although the *Parvenu* figure remains the highest among the four groups, it is quite close to those of the *Declining Nobility* and *Third State*.

To sum up, if we also take into account firms' expectations on innovation investment, the impact of the recession is even more profound than emerged in the previous section. The *persistence* of the crisis is emphasized by the fact that there is a marked tendency of the firms in the *Aristocracy*, the *Declining Nobility* and the *Third State* countries to keep on decreasing innovation investment.

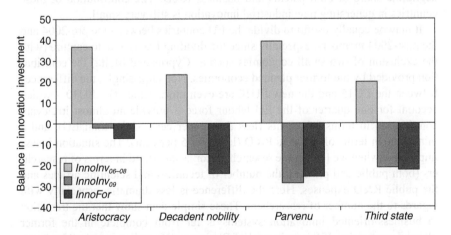

Figure 4.6 Balance between firms' innovation investment before (*InnoInv$_{06-08}$*), during (InnoInv$_{09}$) and after the crisis (InnoFor) (source: authors' elaboration on the three questions of the *Innobarometer* (see Tables A4.3–A4.4 in the appendix)).

This is true in particular for the Western countries that belong to the first two groups, but it holds to a lesser extent for the *Third State* as well. On the contrary, the *Parvenu* show a moderate signal of prompt recovery.

The polarization of innovation capabilities across the EU countries

So far, our analysis has been based on the innovation intensity of European countries. This method of presenting the data is certainly relevant in guiding policy-making, since the bulk of it is still carried out at the national level, but it may hide the reality that some countries are larger than others. In Table 4.4 we report some of the most relevant variables that address the state-of-the-art of the innovation capabilities relative to the four groups of identified countries in the EU in comparison to the United States. A broader distinction between the EU15 and the ten countries of Central and Eastern Europe that joined the EU in 2004 and 2007 (what we call EU10) is also put forward.[13]

The differences across the four groups are striking. The *Aristocracy*, which accounts for nearly one quarter of the total EU labour force and population, concentrates more than half of the triadic patent and around 45 per cent of business R&D: this group of countries, dominated by Germany and shaped by Sweden, Finland, Austria and Belgium, appears as the engine of the European industrial innovation. The *Declining Nobility* is the largest group of countries in terms of labour force and population, and plays an even greater role in terms of public knowledge: it has the largest share of public R&D and scientific articles. Not surprisingly, this group is dominated by the United Kingdom and France, both countries with large governmental activities in science and technology. The *Parvenu*, accounting for less than 18 per cent of the EU27 labour force, shows a negligible share of both patents and business R&D. The contribution of these countries in generating new industrial innovation is still very small.

It may be equally useful to divide the EU countries between the pre-2004 and the post-2004 members, especially since the dividing line is able to capture (with the exclusion of two small economies such as Cyprus and Malta) the contribution provided by the former planned economies. Not surprisingly, the differences between the EU15 and the new EU10 are even more acute. The EU10 – which account for one quarter of the EU labour force – provide an almost irrelevant contribution in terms of patents (less than 1 per cent of the total EU), and a minor one in terms of business R&D (less than 5 per cent). The situation is less impressive when we look at the research sector as measured in terms of researchers (both public and private), the number of technical and scientific articles and the public R&D expenses. Here the difference is less dramatic, especially with regards to the number of researchers. These simple data show that the transition to business-oriented innovation systems is far from complete in the former planned economies. If the main goal of EU innovation policy is to build a European System of Innovation, it seems obvious that the core priority is to better integrate such an important part of the continent.

Table 4.4 Innovation variables for group of countries ordered by labour force and population, 2007

	Total researchers	Triadic patents	BERD	PUBR&D	Articles	Population	Labour force
Declining Nobility	35.78	37.40	38.47	38.02	40.33	30.85	31.36
Third State	21.15	7.22	14.97	22.62	22.69	27.47	26.55
Aristocracy	32.65	54.89	44.62	33.04	30.05	23.48	24.62
Parvenu	10.26	0.46	1.85	6.17	6.84	18.14	17.39
EU15	86.73	99.18	95.32	91.76	91.45	78.84	79.53
EU10	13.27	0.82	4.68	8.24	8.55	21.16	20.47
European Union	100.00	100.00	100.00	100.00	100.00	100.00	100.00
United States	112.28	107.57	159.52	94.17	83.41	61.35	66.61

Source: Authors' elaboration on OECD Main Science and Technology Indicators 2009, and World Bank World Development Indicator, 2009.

Notes

BERD is business R&D; PUBR&D is public R&D; articles are scientific and technical articles in international journals recorded by the Institute of Scientific Information.

EU15: Member countries up to 2004.

EU10: Eastern and Central European member countries that joined the Union in 2004 and 2007: Bulgaria, Czech Republic, Estonia, Hungary, Latvia, Lithuania, Poland, Romania, Slovak Republic, Slovenia.

We have also drawn, in Table 4.4, a comparison between the EU27 and the United States.[14] The USA has 66 per cent of the European labour force,[15] but it is far ahead, compared to the EU, in business sector innovation expenditure and number of researchers. In quantitative terms, the EU still has to make substantial changes before becoming the largest knowledge economy of the world. In terms of internal disparities, it is certainly true that across the United States there are differences as large as those in Europe (for example, compare Silicon Valley with the Midwest).

However, there are at least three main reasons for believing that these differences play a greater role across the EU: (1) within the US national system of innovation there exist consolidated mechanisms of *transmission of knowledge and technology* which have been built over the last century; (2) the US system of innovation shares the same institutional setting, such as the same education system, STI policies, industrial policies and immigration policies, and the same rules of the game in general (Rodriguez-Pose, 1999); and (3) human resources represent a fundamental mechanism of diffusion of knowledge, especially of tacit knowledge (Polanyi, 1966). The high mobility of human resources within the US, also encouraged by a homogeneous labour market, is a fundamental driver of the diffusion of knowledge generated in specific areas across the country (Zimmermann, 1995, 2005).[16]

Is the economic downturn impairing the convergence in innovation performance in Europe?

A decade has passed since the 2000 Lisbon summit, in which the European Council declared its intention of making the European research area the 'world's most competitive and dynamic knowledge-based economy' in the world. As a result of the process of enlargement, we have shown that the EU has become not only larger but also more heterogeneous and polarized in terms of knowledge generation, innovation performance, and development of technological capabilities. In the South and in the East, there are substantial European areas that are still lagging behind in knowledge and competence-building, but the current gap in innovation performance can also be an opportunity for the NMS to catch-up with the more advanced countries. In just a few years, these countries have managed to narrow, albeit to a limited extent, their divergence from the leading nations. This still leaves these countries far behind the scientifically and technologically more developed European countries, but we show that there is at least a trend towards reduction of the divergence. The emerging countries, however, are those most vulnerable to external shocks; these are also the countries that have most reduced their innovative investment as a direct consequence of the economic crisis. This casts some doubt on the structural nature of the observed convergence process in innovation capabilities.

Our results reinforce the idea that specific innovation policies should be considered as important as structural policies in the overall cohesion strategy of the EU. To fully exploit the benefits of these policies, three specific factors of the EU context should be considered: (1) the high polarization in terms of the creation of knowledge, (2) the potential offered by a system of public R&D and human resources that has not yet been transformed into a consistent business innovation strategy, and (3) the weakness of the newcomers in sustaining their innovative projects when there are external shocks, such as the recent financial crisis.

In the light of our findings, can we argue that the economic downturn is hampering the convergence in innovation in Europe? Answering this question is complicated by the fact that many other interrelated elements play a role, such as fiscal imbalances, capital flows, and the credit and currency markets among others. However, we can certainly conclude from our results that the negative effects of the crisis are remarkable, and that this, at least from the innovation investment viewpoint, is not likely to improve in the immediate future. Insofar as the NMS are the worst hit by the recession, this is also affecting the process of convergence in innovation performance. The possibility that some countries will take a long time to recover is not good news for the EU as a whole. This could seriously hinder the reduction of regional disparities, which is a key factor for the EU to compete with the US and Japan today, and in the very near future also with emerging economies such as China, India and others. Strengthening the innovative potential of laggard countries may become a crucial priority to allow the EU to grow and to compete in the global economy.

This chapter has introduced in a descriptive fashion the effects of the economic crisis on innovation investment of the firm at a country level. Important differences arise across countries. The next two chapters aim to investigate the root of these differences along two lines of enquiry: (1) the specificities of the National Systems of Innovation and demand; and (2) the differences in the labour market institutions and skills of the labour force.

Appendix

Methodology: the three indicators

1   The $InnoInv_{06-08}$ Indicator is based on the following *Innobarometer 2009* question: '*Compared to 2006, has the amount spent by your firm on all innovation activities in 2008 increased, decreased, or stayed approximately the same (adjust for inflation)?*'

$$InnoInv_{06-08country-i} = (X_{country-i} - X_{country-min})/(X_{country-max} - X_{country-min})$$

where $X_{country-i} = (\%$ firms increasing $-\%$ firms decreasing$)$ – see Table A4.1.

2   The $InnoInv_{09}$ Indicator is based on the following *Innobarometer 2009* question: '*In the last six months has your company taken one of the following actions [increased, decreased or maintain the innovation spending] as a direct result of the economic downturn?*'

$$InnoInv_{09country-i} = (X_{country-i} - X_{country-min})/(X_{country-max} - X_{country-min})$$

where $X_{country-i} = (\%$ firms increasing $- \%$ firms decreasing$)$ – see Table A4.2.

Table A4.1 Indicators for the InnoStruct of the European Innovation Scoreboard 2008

Dimension	Indicators
Human resources	S&E and SSH graduates per 1000 population aged 20–29 (first stage of tertiary education)
	S&E and SSH doctorate graduates per 1000 population aged 25–34 (second stage of tertiary education)
	Population with tertiary education per 100 population aged 25–64
	Participation in life-long learning per 100 population aged 25–64
	Youth education attainment level
Finance and support	Public R&D expenditure (% of GDP)
	Venture capital (% of GDP)
	Private credit (relative to GDP)
	Broadband access by firms (% of firms)
Firm investments	Business R&D expenditures (% of GDP)
	IT expenditures (% of GDP)
	Non-R&D innovation expenditures (% of turnover)
Linkages and entrepreneurship	SMEs innovating in-house (% of SMEs)
	Innovative SMEs collaborating with others (% of SMEs)
	Firm renewal (SME entries plus exits) (% of SMEs)
	Public–private co-publications per million population
Throughputs	EPO patents per million population
	Community trademarks per million population
	Community designs per million population
	Technology Balance of Payments flows (% of GDP)
Innovators	SMEs introducing product or process innovations (% of SMEs)
	SMEs introducing marketing or organizational innovations (% of SMEs)
	Share of innovators where innovation has significantly reduced labour costs (% of firms)
	Share of innovators where innovation has significantly reduced the use of materials and energy (% of firms)
Economic effects	Employment in medium-high and high-tech manufacturing (% of workforce)
	Employment in knowledge-intensive services (% of workforce)
	Medium and high-tech manufacturing exports (% of total exports)
	Knowledge-intensive services exports (% of total services exports)
	New-to-market sales (% of turnover)
	New-to-form sales (% of turnover)

Source: *European Innovation Scoreboard 2008* (Merit 2009).

3   The *InnoFor* Indicator is based on following *Innobarometer 2009* question: '*Compared to 2008, do you expect your company to increase, decrease or maintain the total amount of its innovation expenditures in 2009?*'

$$InnoFor_{country-i} = (X_{country-i} - X_{country-min})/(X_{country-max} - X_{country-min})$$

where $X_{country-i} = $ (% firms increasing – % firms decreasing) – see Table A4.3.

Table A4.2 SII values of the European Innovation Scoreboard, 2004–2008

Countries	2004	2005	2006	2007	2008
Belgium	0.47	0.48	0.49	0.50	0.51
Bulgaria	0.17	0.17	0.18	0.21	0.22
Czech Republic	0.34	0.35	0.37	0.39	0.40
Denmark	0.57	0.57	0.61	0.60	0.57
Germany	0.54	0.54	0.55	0.57	0.58
Estonia	0.41	0.41	0.42	0.44	0.45
Ireland	0.49	0.50	0.51	0.53	0.53
Greece	0.27	0.28	0.30	0.33	0.36
Spain	0.33	0.34	0.35	0.36	0.37
France	0.46	0.46	0.47	0.50	0.50
Italy	0.31	0.32	0.34	0.36	0.35
Cyprus	0.37	0.36	0.38	0.43	0.47
Latvia	0.19	0.20	0.22	0.24	0.24
Lithuania	0.26	0.27	0.29	0.29	0.29
Luxembourg	0.49	0.49	0.51	0.50	0.52
Hungary	0.27	0.27	0.29	0.31	0.32
Malta	0.27	0.28	0.29	0.32	0.33
Netherlands	0.45	0.45	0.46	0.47	0.48
Austria	0.48	0.49	0.51	0.52	0.53
Poland	0.26	0.27	0.28	0.29	0.31
Portugal	0.29	0.32	0.34	0.34	0.36
Romania	0.21	0.21	0.22	0.25	0.28
Slovenia	0.39	0.39	0.41	0.43	0.45
Slovackia	0.26	0.27	0.30	0.30	0.31
Finland	0.55	0.55	0.54	0.59	0.61
Sweden	0.61	0.61	0.64	0.63	0.64
United Kingdom	0.52	0.53	0.55	0.56	0.55
Croatia	0.28	0.29	0.28	0.29	0.29
Turkey	0.19	0.20	0.20	0.21	0.21
Iceland	0.38	0.39	0.42	0.45	0.47
Norway	0.36	0.37	0.37	0.38	0.38
Switzerland	0.61	0.62	0.63	0.66	0.68

Source: *European Innovation Scoreboard 2008* (European Commission, 2009a).

Table A4.3 Results from the three questions from the *Innobarometer* 2009*

Country	Question no. 1 (2006–2008)				Question no. 2 (2009)				Question no. 3 (forecast)			
	Increased %	Decreased %	Stayed the same %	Total	Increased %	Decreased %	Stayed the same %	Total	Increased %	Decreased %	Stayed the same %	Total
Austria	40.8	5.8	53.4	100	11.2	10.7	78.1	100	15.25	17.88	66.88	100
Belgium	40.1	9.4	50.5	100	12.0	17.6	70.5	100	16.23	20.56	63.21	100
Bulgaria	52.6	10.1	37.3	100	11.9	25.7	62.3	100	20.09	30.06	49.85	100
Czech Republic	40.3	13.1	46.6	100	13.8	29.6	56.5	100	16.86	35.98	47.15	100
Denmark	35.2	10.4	54.4	100	17.2	24.9	57.9	100	13.42	34.63	51.95	100
Estonia	32.0	14.9	53.1	100	7.9	29.6	62.5	100	6.61	43.11	50.28	100
Finland	42.7	6.4	50.9	100	16.7	14.8	68.5	100	19.58	20.94	59.48	100
France	35.3	7.0	57.7	100	7.0	29.7	63.2	100	8.61	37.81	53.58	100
Germany	43.2	5.2	51.5	100	10.3	14.4	75.3	100	10.1	20.94	68.96	100
Greece	45.8	15.0	39.2	100	2.0	49.3	48.7	100	11.61	45.06	43.33	100
Hungary	36.0	21.3	42.7	100	4.6	32.2	63.2	100	17.59	37.85	44.56	100
Ireland	30.8	14.9	54.3	100	9.9	32.1	58.0	100	12.43	42.32	45.25	100
Italy	35.8	13.4	50.8	100	8.9	26.1	65.0	100	9.84	35.46	54.7	100
Latvia	27.3	21.2	51.5	100	9.2	51.0	39.8	100	11.23	53.41	35.36	100
Lithuania	54.9	11.0	34.2	100	6.3	49.1	44.6	100	14.5	61.3	24.2	100
Luxembourg	31.9	5.6	62.5	100	8.6	16.9	74.5	100	11.9	31.81	56.28	100
Netherlands	35.6	8.7	55.7	100	10.4	16.8	72.8	100	9.16	27.8	63.05	100
Norway	35.8	6.9	57.3	100	12.9	27.2	59.8	100	16.74	27.2	56.06	100
Poland	46.1	13.3	40.6	100	8.2	33.8	58.0	100	17.84	31.07	51.09	100
Portugal	37.2	14.0	48.8	100	13.4	28.2	58.4	100	18.7	26.67	54.62	100
Romania	56.4	9.2	34.4	100	10.7	38.8	50.5	100	18.24	39.65	42.12	100
Slovakia	48.6	9.9	41.5	100	16.5	30.7	52.7	100	15.1	41.79	43.11	100
Slovenia	39.5	9.1	51.3	100	5.1	20.6	74.2	100	9.06	31.98	58.96	100
Spain	28.8	11.2	60.0	100	10.1	27.2	62.7	100	11.55	40.89	47.55	100
Sweden	54.2	5.8	40.0	100	14.8	12.6	72.6	100	21.99	25.4	52.61	100
Switzerland	47.8	8.9	43.4	100	17.5	9.0	73.5	100	13.7	18.2	68.1	100
UK	32.9	9.6	57.5	100	8.5	23.2	68.4	100	14.21	25.53	60.27	100

Source: *European Innovation Scoreboard 2008* (European Commission, 2009a).

Note

* With respect to the *Innobarometer* 2009, the results have been re-scaled to make them comparable across countries.

5 National Systems of Innovation, Structure and Demand

Introduction

The descriptive analysis carried out in the previous chapter has shown that the effects of the crisis have been relevant as well as different across the European countries. This chapter aims to investigate the root of these differences. Concerning the relationship between innovation and business cycles, two extreme hypotheses can be outlined: according to the first, innovation is *cyclical* and therefore firms tend to reduce their innovation efforts during the downswing of the economy; according to the second, innovation is instead *counter-cyclical*, leading to claims that recessions are a fertile environment for firms to innovate.

The macroeconomic dynamic is the result of firms' behaviours: while some firms will exhibit persistency in investing in innovation during recessions, others will not. Persistency of innovative activities can be contingent on several factors. Some can depend on firm-specific characteristics, such as strategies, management's attitude, stage of development and so on. Others can impinge on the cumulative and path-dependent nature of innovation, technological change and scientific research. Particular trends of cash flows and profits can also play a role. Finally, industry-specific dynamics of the demand, profit opportunities and technological opportunities can also play a part.

However, as discussed in Chapter 3, a good deal of theoretical, empirical and historical research has demonstrated that the national institutional setting has a major impact upon how the economic agents behave and how firms perform (Freeman, 1995; Hall and Soskice, 2001; Nelson, 2001; North, 2005). National institutions shape not only the structural conditions of countries, but also *their ability to respond to changes*. We assume that this is even more prominent in the event of a major economic downturn. The National System of Innovation (NSI) approach – an institutional conception *par excellence* – has framed innovative activities and the way firms do things within the institutional national context (Freeman, 1995; Lundvall, 1992; Nelson, 1993). This chapter aims to investigate the role that structural characteristics of NSI, along with demand, play in explaining persistency in the innovation behaviour of the firm during a major recession.

A significant drop in demand represents the usual landscape throughout severe recessions. While scholars largely accept the fact that a major fall in demand would bring about a reduction in innovation activity, other fundamental issues are at stake here. *How important are structural characteristics of the countries vis-à-vis the dynamic of the demand?* Further, *which are the structural dimensions that are more relevant? How do structural dimensions and demand interact at the country level?* These questions are central for a broader under-standing of the role played by national institutions and policies – as encom-passed along the NSI dimensions – as a source of persistency of innovation over the business cycle. The NSI literature has already widely shown the prominence of some country-specific factors in shaping the patterns of innovation of firms, as discussed in Chapter 3. The current chapter builds on this research by shed-ding some light on the role of country-specific characteristics as determinants of firms' innovation behaviour, in cases of adverse events such as a major financial crisis. This would provide some relevant theoretical insights, as well as policy recommendations for recovery and long-term growth.

National Systems of Innovation and the persistence of innovation during recessions: structure, investment and demand

National Systems of Innovation and the persistence of innovation

In Chapter 3 we discussed the NSI research. Building on this literature, here we explore whether some structural features of the NSI also affect firms' innovation behaviour in cases of economic downturn. Investigating the role played by some specific characteristics of NSI in relation to exogenous shocks is something new and worth exploring, and also raises some key issues. Do countries which have been accumulating larger 'stocks' of knowledge embodied in human resources, learning institutions and companies show a greater persistency in their innovat-ive activities? Which kind of industrial structure and technological specialization is more sensitive to a macroeconomic shock in terms of innovation? In what follows, we develop on the conceptualization of NSI in order to derive the central argument to this chapter's analysis.

In their conceptualization of NSI, Lundvall and colleagues (Lundvall, 1992; Lundvall *et al.*, 2002) go beyond the '*technonationalism*' that inspired Nelson's conceptualization of NSI (Nelson, 1993), in order to recognize that the ability of countries to foster innovation is dependent upon social capabilities, which are not solely based on science and technology. Within this broadened context, the National System of Innovation is constituted by the institutions and economic structure affecting the rate and direction of technological change in the society (Edquist and Lundvall, 1993). At the core of the latter definition of NSI resides the microeconomic theory of innovation derived from the neo-Schumpeterian strand of literature, the assumptions of bounded rationality of agents, the role of tacit knowledge, as well as the role played by institutions in economic activities. Regarding the former, the main message taken on board in the NSI is the sys-temic nature of innovation activity. Firms carry out innovation through extensive interactions with several actors outside their boundaries, such as universities, research centres, users and suppliers. Crucially, this activity occurs within a specific (national) institutional context.

Chapter 3 maintained that a large body of research has shown the substantial role played by institutions in influencing the behaviour of firms (Hall and Soskice, 2001) and their organizational structures (Coriat and Dosi, 2000; Coriat and Weinstein, 2002), as well as the patterns of economic change (North, 1990, 2005). Here, it is enough to say that institutions, broadly defined as the rules of the game, represent both a *constraint* and a *source opportunity* for agents within economic systems. The way firms innovate, search and learn over time is, then, significantly affected by a large array of institutions, including the way the labour market works, industrial patterns of specialization, industrial relationships, the education system and financial structure. In this chapter, we refer to the current NSI characteristics of countries as *structure*. The current structure of countries can be understood as the result of a path-dependent process. NSI configurations of countries are the outcome of historical processes in which the development of firms, organizations and industries interacted with national policies and institutional development over time (Fagerberg *et al.*, 2009).

In order to put forward our central argument, we take stock of three major insights drawing from the discussion carried out so far. (1) NSI characteristics heavily affect firms patterns of innovation and learning. (2) These characteristics are the result of path-dependent processes in which firms' organizational structures and industrial specialization co-evolved along institutional change and national policies. This leads to different, and sometimes divergent, paths of learning and development of the states that ultimately brings about (3) considerable cross-country *differences* in their structures. This brings us to the main concern of the chapter: that is, to investigate the role of systematic differences in the structures of countries, along with demand, in explaining persistency in the innovation behaviour of the firm during a major recession.

The considered dimensions of National Innovation Systems

A number of factors play a role in shaping the national environment and affect firms' innovation behaviours during an economic downturn. Schumpeter has already emphasized the relationship between finance and innovation (Santarelli, 1995; Schumpeter, 1911 (1934); see discussion in Chapter 2). A robust financial system might play a role in macroeconomic shocks if it can provide firms with resources to be invested in innovative activities. Inasmuch as firms are inclined to rely on internal funds to finance their innovation activities (O'Sullivan, 2005), financial constraint is very likely to play a major role during recessions. Different levels of education and training systems of the labour force, together with different configurations of the labour market and welfare state, can generate different patterns of recovery, since workers can be easily transferred from mature towards growing sectors of the economy (OECD, 2009a, 2009b). Finally, a different industrial specialization – for example, in high-tech manufacturing or the knowledge-intensive service sector – could lead to a different impact of the depression on firms' innovation investment, depending on the magnitude of the drop in the domestic and external demand across the sectors.

In the empirical analysis carried out in the second part of this chapter, four main components of the NSI structure are taken into account: (1) the quality of the 'stock' of the human resources of a country, in terms of levels of education and participation in life-long learning activities; (2) the stock of accumulated knowledge, including R&D and non-R&D expenditures, patents and ICT expenditures; (3) the 'financial depth' of the economic system in terms of the share of venture capital investment and credit towards the private sector from deposit-taking financial institutions; and (4) the specialization of NSI in terms of the relative importance of the high-tech manufacturing sector and the knowledge-intensive service sector.

Investment and innovation over the business cycle

Both Keynes and Schumpeter agreed that decisions to invest play a crucial role in economic fluctuations. But while Keynes and his followers are mostly concerned with investment as the most dynamic and volatile component of aggregate demand, Schumpeter and his followers argue that the nature of investment is equally important in shaping economic trends. Focusing on investment in innovations, the Schumpeterian tradition indicates that attempts to introduce new products and processes in the market are the qualifying condition for economic growth. Freeman *et al.* (1982) further elaborated on Schumpeter's intuition by claiming that, in adverse economic environments, investments are likely to be reduced because of a low profit margin and a general 'pessimistic mood', while in periods of economic expansion there are opportunities for new technology systems to emerge. In this chapter, we focus on how a remarkable macroeconomic shock such as the current economic downturn has shaped firms' *innovation investment* in comparison to the previous period.

Demand and innovation

Jakob Schmookler (1966) has already emphasized the role of demand as an innovation driver, pointing out a strong relationship between investment in capital good user industries and patent applications in the same industries. Other scholars have empirically revisited and re-examined Schmookler's hypothesis (Brouwer and Kleinknecht, 1999; Kleinknecht and Verspagen, 1990; Scherer, 1982), producing some evidence which lends support to the demand-pull determinants of innovation at the firm level.

Demand-pull arguments have been suggested both in favour and against the cyclical hypothesis. On the one hand, it has been argued that established firms might delay the introduction of innovations as this requires a diversion of resources from ongoing activities, and they prefer to exploit the value of their existing rents (Mensch, 1979). Given that the value of existing rents decreases in a recession, firms might be encouraged to introduce new products and processes. On the other hand, two arguments based on the role of demand suggest that innovations are more likely to be introduced during business-cycle upswings. The first claims that rising demand during a boom provides more favourable conditions to absorb new products than a recession. The second argument suggests that because firms have only a limited period of time to appropriate the returns from their innovations, they are more likely to introduce new products and processes in an expanding market regardless of when they produce them (for a review on this issue, see Geroski and Walters, 1995). Geroski and Walters (1995) also show the presence of a long-run association between the level of demand and innovative activity, and they find that demand appears to Granger to cause innovation. In a recent empirical study at the firm level, Bogliacino and Pianta (2009) conclude that demand-side factors have a significant influence on the growth of profits and on the innovation-related turnover (see also Piva and Vivarelli, 2007).

Given the prominent role played by demand in the current economic downturn (OECD, 2009b), the question addressed here is, *to what extent is the macroeconomic environment, in terms of the drop in the demand, playing a role in firms' decisions about innovation investments?* Two sources of demand are taken into account in the analysis: domestic demand and export.

The impact of the global economic turmoil and the uneven effects on European countries[1]

In the previous chapter it became clear that the crisis is having uneven effects across Europe, and the NMS are the countries most affected by the crisis in terms of innovation investment. In Figure 5.1, we have plotted the *InnoStruct* performance on the y-axis, while on the x-axis we have reported the $InnoInv_{09}$ indicator (as in the Appendix to Chapter 4). Overall, Figure 5.1, in opposition to Figure 4.4 of Chapter 4, suggests that the relationship between the NSI strength and the firms' innovation behaviour in response to the crisis is much deeper than prior to the crisis. As a consequence of the crisis, the distance between the *Aristocracy* and other countries is increasing.

To recap, two major points arise:

1   *The uneven effects of the crisis.* The impact of the current global economic downturn on firms' investment in innovative activities has not been of the same magnitude across all European countries. On the contrary, the most severely struck have been those NMS which were catching up over the years 2006–2008.

2   *Structure matters.* Considering the effects of the economic downturn on the firms' innovation behaviour, countries endowed with stronger national innovation systems are also those less affected, in relative terms, by the recession. This clearly emerges in opposition to the 2006–2008 period, in which we do not observe a significant relationship between trends in firms' innovation investments and the strength of the NSI.

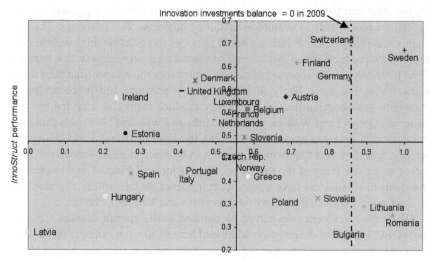

Figure 5.1 Short-term firms' innovation performance (*InnoInv₀₉*), and national innovation system strength (*InnoStruct*) (source: author's elaboration on question no.
2 of the *Innobarometer* data, and on *EIS* data (see Appendix in Chapter 4)).

Note
Axes cross at average values.

Why have countries been affected differently by the crisis? And which characteristics of the NSI which are playing a role in making some countries relatively
less affected by the crisis? How are these characteristics relevant vis-à-vis the
role of demand? The next section attempts to answer these questions.

The uneven effects of the crisis on innovation investment across countries: some explanations

We will now attempt to provide some explanations for the uneven effects of the
crisis across countries. Two categories of explanations are addressed: (1) some
structural characteristics of the NSI, and (2) the drop in domestic demand and
exports.

The variables

In order to carry out the analysis, a new variable has been developed merging the
first two questions from the Innobarometer as presented in Chapter 4. The new
dependent variable – INVchange – reflects a change in the behaviour of the firm
related to its innovation investment as a response to the crisis vis-à-vis the period
before the crisis (Table 5.1). Three different behaviours are then identified by jux-
taposing firms' innovative behaviours before and in response to the recession:

Table 5.1 Change in the behaviour of the firm related to its innovation investment as a response to the crisis vis-à-vis the period before the crisis

Variable	*Value assumed by the variable*	*Behaviour of the firm*
Change in innovation behaviour (INVchange) = [–(INVEST2 – INVEST1)]	= 1	Cyclical (e.g. firms which were increasing and pass to maintaining or decreasing in response to the crisis)
	= 0	Neutral (e.g. firms which were increasing and keep on increasing)
	= –1	Counter-cyclical (e.g. firms which were decreasing and pass to increasing or maintaining)

Note
INVEST1 and INVEST2 relate respectively to the three-year period before the crisis and to the crisis. They are categorical variables which assume the following values: = 1 if firm increases investment, = 0 if firms maintain investment at the same level, and = –1 if decreases investment.

cyclical, neutral and counter-cyclical. Two reasons lead us to construct this new variable. First, it allows us to summarize the different behaviours of the firms in the two different periods in one single variable, with a relevant gain in the simplicity and robustness of the analysis, as well as in the interpretation of the results. Second, it allows us to look at the changes in firms' innovative behaviour in response to the crisis. For example, firms which were decreasing investment in the previous period and continue to decrease them during the crisis are not considered as changing their behaviour. This allows us to identify the effect of the crisis in changing the attitude of the firms: cyclical vs counter-cyclical behaviours.

In Figure 5.2, the INVchange variable is plotted. What emerges clearly is the prominence of the cyclical behaviour of the firms. Nearly 50 per cent of the firms in the sample exhibit cyclical behaviour, and 40 per cent of firms are instead neutral. Finally, only 6 per cent of the firms in the sample seem inclined to exploit the current situation by investing more in innovation, while in the previous period they were either maintaining or decreasing innovation expenditures. From the operational standpoint, in what follows we try to point out those country-specific features that have a role in offsetting the cyclical behaviour of the firms, and therefore have a positive influence on persistency of innovation investment. The following different characteristics of the NSI have been derived from the EIS: (1) the stock of knowledge; (2) the quality of the human resources; (3) the depth of the financial and credit system; and (4) the specialization of the country (see Table 5.2; see also Table A5.1, in the Appendix to this chapter, for the construction of the composite variables 'knowledge' and 'human resources').

In order to capture the role played by the short-term macroeconomic environment, we build two different variables. The first – domestic demand drop – reflects the drop in the domestic demand of the country, and is calculated as the percentage variation between the third term 2009 and the first term 2008.

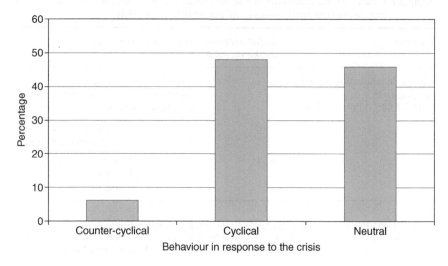

Figure 5.2 Firms' innovation investment behaviour in response to the crisis (source: author's elaboration on *Innobarometer* data (as for Figure 5.1)).

The second – export drop – reflects the drop in the exports of the country, and is calculated in the same way over the same period of time. In this way we seek to gauge the drop of the demand during the crisis, distinguishing among domestic and external demand. In Figure 5.3, we report these variables for the countries considered. While the drop in exports has been remarkable for nearly every country, there is a good deal of variance in the drop in domestic demand. New Member States and, to a lesser extent, Sweden, Ireland and the UK are facing the larger drops in domestic demand.

The results

Table 5.3 presents the 'robust' estimates of an ordered logit model in which the dependent variable is INVchange (positive values of the independent variable reflect *cyclical* behaviours of the firm, thus a negative coefficient signals those country-effects which offset cyclical behaviour). Three sets of independent variables are included (correlation rates are reported in Table A5.2). The first reflects the magnitude of the drops in domestic demand and exports. The second group includes the variables accounting for the characteristics of the NIS. The third group includes the interaction effects between demand effects and NIS effects. Finally, as already stated in the Introduction, both firm-specific and industry-specific factors can play a role in affecting innovation behaviour of the firm during recessions. Accordingly, a set of variables controlling for the individual characteristics of the firms is included. Specifically, we introduce three binary variables at the firm level – i.e. size, innovation intensity and internationalization – in order to control for firm idiosyncratic effects, together with industry dummies.

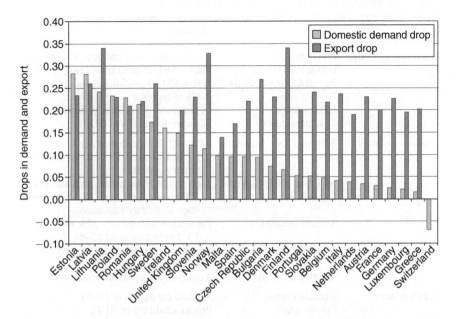

Figure 5.3 The drops in the domestic demand and export, 1st term 2008–3rd term 2009 (source: author's elaboration on Eurostat data 'Euro-indicators').

In the first model, only the demand effects are included, together with the control variables. Both domestic demand and exports are statistically significant and positive. In the first place, this seems to suggest that the drop in demand plays a substantial role in explaining the cyclical behaviour of the firms. When, in the second model, the NSI effects are added, both private credit and technological manufacturing specialization are negative and significant. That is, these are the country characteristics of the NSI which tend to offset the cyclical behaviour of firms. In this model, demand effects no longer show up as significant.

The third model is a multiplicative interaction model. These models are common in the quantitative political science literature in which it is frequently implied that the relationship between political inputs and outcomes varies depending on the institutional context. It has been acknowledged that the intuition behind the relevance of context, or 'context conditionality', is captured quite well by multiplicative interaction models (Aiken and West, 1991; Friedrich, 1982). In interaction models, the interaction variables are added to the independent variables – the constitutive variables, which thus take the following form:

$$Y = \beta_0 + \beta_1 X + \beta_2 Z + \beta_3 XZ + \varepsilon \tag{1}$$

In these models, Z is usually a binary variable in order to make the results easier to interpret. It should be kept in mind that β_1 must not be interpreted as the average effect of a change in X on Y, as it can be in a linear-additive regression

Table 5.2 Characteristics of the NSI included in the analysis

NIS characteristics	Variable	Indicator
Stock of knowledge	Business R&D	Business R&D expenditures (% of GDP)
	Public R&D	Public R&D expenditures (% of GDP)
	Non-R&D expenditure	Non-R&D innovation expenditures (% of turnover)
	EPO patents	EPO patents per million population
	IT expenditures	IT expenditures (% of GDP)
Human resources	S&E and SSH graduates	S&E and SSH graduates per 1000 population aged 20–29 (first stage of tertiary education)
	S&E and SSH doctorate graduates	S&E and SSH doctorate graduates per 1000 population aged 25–34 (second stage of tertiary education)
	Tertiary education	Population with tertiary education per 100 population aged 25–64
	Life-long learning	Participation in life-long learning per 100 population aged 25–64
	Youth education	Youth education attainment Level
Credit system	Venture capital	Venture capital (% of GDP)
	Private credit	Private credit (% of GDP)
Industrial specialization	Employment in medium-high & high-tech manufacturing	Employment in medium-high & high-tech manufacturing (% of work-force)
	Employment in knowledge-intensive services	Employment in knowledge intensive services (% of workforce)

Source: European Commission (2009a).

model. Rather, β_1 captures the effect of a one-unit change in X on Y when condition Z is absent. When condition Z is present ($Z = 1$), equation (1) becomes:

$$Y = (\beta_0 + \beta_2) + (\beta_1 + \beta_3)X + \varepsilon \tag{2}$$

Hence, the effects of the constitutive variable X can be calculated as $(\beta_1 + \beta_3)$. Our model includes two sets of constitutive variables; the NIS variables and the demand ones. In this way we are able to explore the interaction effects of the two different dimensions of a country which, as a matter of fact, interact in reality. Both the drop in demand and the drop in exports have been transformed into binary variables, taking a value equal to 1 when the drop in domestic demand (or exports) is higher than the average and 0 if lower.[2]

The results of the third model are shown in Table 5.3. If we consider the overall effects of the NIS variables (by adding all the related coefficients, see Eq. 2), the variables offsetting the cyclical behaviour of firms are human resources, private credit and high-tech manufacturing sectors, similarly to the previous model (apart from the human resources coefficient). The only coeffi-

Table 5.3 Ordered logit model, robust estimates (dependent variable: INVchange)

	Model no. 1	*Model no. 2*	*Model no. 3*
Demand effects			
Domestic demand drop	1.26***	0.52	0.72
Export drop	1.72***	–0.60	–0.43
National Innovation System effects			
Knowledge		0.07	1.82
Human resources		–0.13	4.77**
Venture capital		–0.02	–0.15
Private credit		–0.41***	–0.54***
High-tech manufacturing specialization		–0.73***	–3.33***
Knowledge-intensive service specialization		0.29	–2.25**
Interaction effects			
Demand*knowledge			0.19
Demand*human resources			–4.81**
Demand*high-tech specialization			1.35
Demand*KIS service specialization			2.45**
Export*knowledge			–1.57
Export*human resources			–4.75**
Export*high-tech specialization			2.72***
Export*KIS service specialization			3.46**
Firm-level control variables			
Medium and large firms	0.24***	0.22***	0.22***
Highly innovative firms	0.78***	0.79***	0.82***
Internationalized firms	0.06	0.13	0.13
Industry dummies	included	included	included
Observations	3072	3072	3072

Notes
Robust standard errors in parentheses (country clustered errors provide the same results)
*** $P<0.01$, ** $P<0.05$, * $P<0.1$
Reference control variables: small firms; low innovative firms.

cient predicting the overall cyclical behaviour of the firm is the specialization in knowledge-intensive service. By looking at the interaction effects, one can observe the remarkable role played by the presence of qualified human resources in contrasting the cyclical behaviour of the firms in countries characterized by a large drop in both domestic demand and exports. On the contrary, in those countries the specialization in knowledge-intensive service sectors predicts cyclical behaviour. As far as the manufacturing sector is concerned, specialization in high technology is associated to cyclical behaviour of firms in the case of a large drop in exports.

Discussion and policy implications

Is innovation cyclical or persistent?

One of the most significant results of our analysis is that about 65 per cent of the firms declare that they have kept their innovation investment unchanged in spite of the crisis. This somehow confirms the importance of technological accumulation (stressed, among others, by Grandstrand *et al.*, 1997; Nelson and Winter, 1982; Patel and Pavitt, 1997), and lends substantial support to the persistency of innovative activities over time (Cefis and Orsenigo, 2001; Geroski *et al.*, 1997). But accumulation and persistency do not explain all firms' behaviour: we also observe a good deal of cyclical innovative behaviour across firms. Significantly, firms which exhibit cyclical behaviour are the major innovators. In fact, firms which are more likely to reduce investment in response to the crisis are characterized by: (1) larger innovation intensity (in terms of share of turnover invested in innovation), and (2) larger size (see Table 5.3). We can speculate that firms are maintaining innovation activities related to ongoing projects, which are often characterized by some degree of rigidity and consistent sunk costs, but appear less willing to start new innovation projects.

The uneven effects of the crisis and the role of National Systems of Innovation

It has clearly emerged that the crisis has not been of the same magnitude across all European countries. On the contrary, we have shown that the most negatively affected by the downturn are those EU New Member States which were catching up over the 2006–2008 period. Countries endowed with stronger NSI are, on the contrary, less affected and are better able to respond, at least in relative terms, to the recession. And this should be contrasted with the previous period of moderate economic expansion (2006–2008), when firms were expanding their investment in innovation in most countries, and regardless of the strength of their NSI.

We have attempted to explain this evidence on the grounds of the structural characteristics of the NSI and the role played by domestic demand and exports. The structural characteristics of the NSI seem to play a more relevant role than demand. Hence, the hypothesis that characteristics of the NSI can affect the way firms react to an external shock such as the actual global turmoil is confirmed by the results. Specifically, the presence of qualified human resources plays a crucial role in cushioning the effects of a downswing in innovation in frontrunner countries. This seems to be less the case in catching-up countries; this result reflects mostly the ex-Socialist nations, the largest group of catching-up countries considered here. Apparently, the high level of human resources in the previously planned economies have not yet been fully incorporated into the new competitive economy and therefore do not have the 'braking' effect in terms of reduction of investment in innovation. When the interaction with demand is also included, the availability of human resources becomes the most important factor in contrasting a reduction of firms' innovation expenditures. Firms are very reluctant to fire qualified workers even when facing a drop in their demand.[3]

Our results show that the decision to invest in innovation relative to the knowledge-intensive sector is particularly sensitive to the domestic demand. This can be explained by the fact that this sector includes both the financial inter-mediation industry and the real-estate industry, which have been severely hit by the crisis. That decisions to invest in innovation are particularly sensitive to exports in both the high-tech manufacturing and knowledge-intensive sectors comes as no surprise: firms' internationalization and their innovative activities go hand in hand (Filippetti *et al.*, 2011; Frenz and Ietto-Gillies, 2009).

The 'depth' of the financial system, in terms of the dimension of private credit, seems to play an important role in counteracting the effect of the crisis on firms' innovation expenditures. In general, this finding reinforces the importance of the financial sector for innovation, not only as an engine in times of growth, but also as a buffer during a downswing. This is particularly important for the EU New Member Countries which have not developed a sufficiently robust domestic financial market. The substantial withdrawal of foreign capital that occurred quickly as the crisis erupted, coupled with an insufficient supply of domestic credit, is very likely to have played a substantial role in the reduction of innovation investment of firms.

Which policies in times of crisis?

On the grounds of our results, what will the economic crisis bring in terms of innovative capabilities across Europe? And what can we learn to inspire policy analysis? There is evidence that the crisis is hitting countries with a less developed NSI, namely the New Member States. This will lead to an increase in their technological gap, which, especially for ex-Socialist economies, is still huge. It will not be easy to recycle the skills and the human resources available into a competitive economy. There is the risk that the effects of the downturn will turn out to be structural, and, as a result of the crisis, at least some of the New Member States will be no longer be able to sustain the catching-up process they started before the recession.

It remains to be seen how these countries will be able to react, since compe-tences, skills and knowledge are not ephemeral phenomena, but are rather embedded in organizations' routines, firms' capabilities, workers' skills and capital goods (Evangelista, 1999; Lall, 1992; Massini *et al.*, 2002). Will the structural components of competence and skills prevail over the adverse short-term economic environment? And how will the new economic environment be transformed by the crisis? There is no guarantee that, after the turmoil, the *loci* of the competitive advantage will remain the same. New sectors can emerge as a result of new technological opportunities, as well as of substantial public pol-icies that governments are enacting to hamper the effects of the crisis. A case in point is the 'green industry', which is believed to represent a fundamental source of innovation and growth for the coming future (OECD, 2009a).

Periods of technological breakthroughs can represent a crucial 'window of opportunity' for lagging-behind countries to catch up (Perez and Soete, 1988). However, catching-up processes based on the adoption of technology require a reliable base of internal knowledge, human resources and infrastructures. Winners and losers are not easily identifiable when the game is still ongoing, but the winners are more likely to be those countries which are equipped with both strong innovative infrastructures and domestic knowledge base. On the other hand, the capacity of the catching-up countries to recover their previous catching-up patterns cannot be taken for granted. This will, crucially, depend on their capacity to maintain their acquired knowledge, skills, competences and human resources in their business sector and *within their borders*.

The empirical analysis has shown the crucial role played by qualified human resources in reducing the effects of the crisis. In some countries, the crisis is already leading to the emigration of skilled workers, budget cuts to the R&D public spending and to the educational system, as well as the weakening of the credit system and infrastructures. If these factors are not properly counteracted by public and business policies, there is the risk that NSI will be substantially weakened and that the potential for growth in the coming years will be undermined. The large public expenditures programmes put forward by most of the States in response to the crisis do represent crucial means to sustain current innovation capabilities. The choice of sectors and the design of public procurement policies can provide new opportunities, and it is very likely that those who manage to capture them will be the winners, and those who do not will become the losers.

As argued by the technological accumulation hypothesis, technological discontinuities do not necessarily imply new and different competences and skills (Pavitt, 1988). Continuing investment in knowledge, human resources and structures is the best way to cope with (uncertain) scientific and technological evolution. New sectors and technological opportunities will emerge after the crisis, and a process of re-specialization is expected to be crucial for recovery (Perez, 2009). Those countries that maintain their innovation capabilities will be more likely to be ready to exploit the recovery and expansion of the market in the new emerging sectors. This will be key for creating new job opportunities along with the phase of recovery. A recent study by the OECD (2009b) reports paradigmatic examples of counter-cyclical policies carried out during recent periods of recession in Finland and Korea. In line with our argument, they claim that policies aimed at supporting business and public R&D (the latter was *increased* during the recession by these governments), as well as policies directed at stimulating job opportunities for skilled labour, were very important in putting these economies on a stronger and more knowledge-intensive growth path (OECD, 2009b).

Conclusions

This chapter represents an attempt to explore empirically the effects of the current economic crisis on innovation across European countries, and to propose some explanations for it. A substantial number of firms have managed to maintain their investment for innovation, but the number of firms able to expand it has dramatically dropped, and the number of firms that have decreased it has also substantially risen. This trend is not distributed uniformly across the European economic space. The most affected have been the European catching-up countries, namely the New Member Countries of Central and Eastern Europe.

A possible explanation for these patterns that has not been taken into consideration here is the role played by multinational corporations (MNCs) and by international division of labour. Several manufacturing and service firms in the New Member Countries are suppliers to core companies placed in advanced countries. Hence, it is likely that these firms are those suffering larger cuts when compared with the strategically more important nodes placed in other countries. This trend is confirmed by the results from the 2008 EU Survey on R&D Investment Business Trends (European Commission, 2010a), where one can read that, in the economic downturn, outside MNCs' subsidiaries may face the strongest cuts in R&D. The crisis has, so far, stopped a tiring process in which these countries were also trying to increase their efforts as a consequence of joining the EU market.

We have seen that the countries that have been relatively less affected are those with stronger NSI. Switzerland, Sweden, Finland, Germany and Austria will emerge from this crisis with a relatively stronger innovative capacity, while the United Kingdom and France, and, to a larger extent, the Southern European countries are likely to lose additional relative positions. Within a perspective of increasing integration, this calls for a stronger and more cooperative innovation policy at European level, not only in good times but especially in bad times.

Severe recessions are prominently characterized by a major fall in demand. While scholars agree that negative demand shocks affect investment, the ultimate effect on innovation investment can differ across countries. This emerges from the descriptive analysis, and this is what we seek to explain, relying on the NSI literature. This literature claims that economic and institutional structure differs between countries, and this would be a major factor in determining the direction of learning and innovation. We have shown that this also plays a role in affecting patterns of innovation of firms during major recessions. In particular, competences and quality of human resources, the specialization in the high-technology sector, along with the development of the credit system, seem to be the structural factors that are able to mitigate the effects of the economic downturn on innovation investments of firms across Europe. The fact that some structural characteristics of NSI explain persistency of innovation in response to major exogenous shocks is an important finding. It sheds some light on the behaviour of firms during crises, and represents a step forward in terms of understanding the mechanisms underlying the relationship between macro and micro determinants of innovation which lie at the heart of the NSI theory.

Appendix

Table A5.1 The construction of the variables 'Human resources' and 'Knowledge' from the EIS

Country	Innostruct	(1) S&E graduates	(2) S&E doctoral	(3) Tertiary education	(4) Life-long learning	(5) Youth education	(6) Human resources	(7) Business R&D	(8) Public R&D	(9) Non-R&D expenditure	(10) Patent	(11) IT expenditure	(12) Knowledge
Austria	0.53	21.60	1.72	17.60	12.80	84.10	0.42	1.81	0.75	0.73	183.10	2.80	0.63
Belgium	0.51	33.10	0.94	32.10	7.20	82.60	0.46	1.30	0.57	0.79	129.10	2.80	0.46
Bulgaria	0.22	31.50	0.36	22.40	1.30	83.30	0.31	0.15	0.33	0.88	1.40	2.00	0.17
Czech Rep.	0.40	25.80	0.86	13.70	5.70	91.80	0.33	0.98	0.55	0.51	7.30	3.20	0.39
Denmark	0.57	46.80	0.93	32.20	29.20	70.80	0.59	1.65	0.88	3.36	174.60	3.20	0.58
Estonia	0.45	38.20	0.57	33.30	7.00	80.90	0.45	0.54	0.58		5.60	2.90	0.47
Finland	0.61	38.30	2.17	36.40	23.40	86.50	0.72	2.51	0.94	0.33	267.60	3.20	0.82
France	0.50	62.00	1.13	26.80	7.40	82.40	0.55	1.31	0.74	1.07	119.20	3.10	0.48
Germany	0.58	25.90	1.56	24.30	7.80	72.50	0.38	1.77	0.76	0.74	275.00	2.90	0.63
Greece	0.36	25.30	0.58	22.00	2.10	82.10	0.30	0.15	0.41	0.72	6.50	2.90	0.63
Hungary	0.32	30.20	0.42	18.00	3.60	84.00	0.30	0.49	0.46	0.96	7.80	2.50	0.27
Ireland	0.53	62.10	1.11	32.20	7.60	86.70	0.61	0.88	0.44	1.10	64.10	1.50	0.29
Italy	0.35	32.10	0.89	13.60	6.20	76.30	0.29	0.55	0.52		76.10	1.70	0.32
Latvia	0.24	56.40	0.24	22.60	7.10	80.20	0.42	0.21	0.42		5.70	2.30	0.21
Lithuania	0.29	60.30	0.61	28.90	5.30	89.00	0.54	0.23	0.58		1.30	1.80	0.20
Luxembourg	0.52			26.50	7.00	70.90	0.39	1.36	0.27	0.64	194.90		0.40
Netherlands	0.48	36.00	0.87	30.80	16.60	76.20	0.49	1.03	0.67	0.90	173.30	3.30	0.48
Norway	0.38	29.40	0.94	34.40	18.00	93.30	0.58	0.81	0.77	0.29	95.50	2.40	0.37
Poland	0.31	52.90	0.86	18.70	5.10	91.60	0.47	0.18	38.00	0.17	3.00	2.60	0.26
Portugal	0.36	30.60	2.75	13.70	4.40	53.40	0.31	0.61	0.46	1.03	7.40	1.80	0.25
Romania	0.28	40.90	0.48	12.00	1.30	77.40	0.26	0.22	0.31	0.95	0.70	2.10	0.20
Slovakia	0.31	24.40	0.89	14.40	3.90	91.30	0.32	0.18	0.27	1.08	5.80	2.50	0.28
Slovenia	0.45	41.00	0.96	22.20	14.80	91.50	0.51	0.94	0.60	1.51	32.20	2.20	0.38
Spain	0.37	27.30	0.67	29.00	10.40	61.10	0.32	0.66	0.55	1.12	29.30	1.40	0.22
Sweden	0.64	29.70	2.25	31.30	32.00	87.20	0.72	2.64	0.99	0.49	184.80	3.80	0.74
Switzerland	0.68	48.50	2.33	31.30	22.50	78.10	0.69	2.14	0.69	0.66	411.10	3.70	0.72
UK	0.55	52.00	1.61	31.90	26.60	78.10	0.68	1.08	0.64	0.92	91.40	3.50	0.55

Source: *European Innovation Scoreboard 2008* (European Commission, 2009a).

Note

The variable 'Human resources' is derived aggregating the variables in the first five columns, while the variable 'Knowledge' is derived aggregating the other five variables from the seventh to the eleventh columns (see Table A4 for the description of the variables). Both the variables have been normalized between 0 and 1 (see methodological appendix for the normalization procedure).

Table A5.2 The correlation rates between the independent variables

	Demand drop	Export drop	Knowledge	Human resources	Venture capital	Private credit	High-tech man.	Kis service
Demand drop	1.00							
Export drop	0.09	1.00						
Knowledge	-0.29	0.21	1.00					
Human resources	0.07	0.12	0.69	1.00				
Venture capital	0.06	0.07	0.55	0.66	1.00			
Private credit	-0.31	-0.58	0.28	0.38	0.53	1.00		
High-tech man.	-0.28	0.02	0.33	-0.07	-0.32	-0.29	1.00	
Kis service	-0.44	-0.19	0.69	0.60	0.67	0.67	0.05	1.00

6   Varieties of capitalism and the impact of the crisis[1]

Introduction

The ongoing crisis is likely to be a key factor in drafting the new European strategy. The European Commission (EC) acknowledges that 'European labour markets will be changed profoundly by the crisis'. Over the past decade, the 'flexicurity' model – that is, flexibility in the labour markets with appropriate levels of security – has been endorsed by European Union (EU) as a way of solving the Union's employment problem (Kok, 2003). However, as a new Commission faces up to Europe's worst recession for many decades, doubts have emerged as to how committed member states are towards flexicurity and making it work across the EU (European Commission, 2009c). In addition, criticisms have been raised regarding the recent EU labour harmonization policy – as, for instance, by the European Trade Union Confederation (ETUC). These days, the reform of the EU labour market is still a centrally debated issue.

The European Commission's Lisbon Agenda aims to improve both flexibility and security in the labour markets in order to reconcile economic growth with more and better jobs, as well as greater social cohesion. The pursuit of a balance between flexibility and security addresses simultaneously (1) the flexibility of labour markets, work organization and labour relations, and (2) security, including employment and social security for weaker groups in and out of the labour market. In a recent study of the Joint Research Centre – Institute for the Protection and Security of the Citizen (Manca *et al.*, 2010) exploring flexicurity in Europe, the authors concluded the following:

> results of country scores and ranking highlight substantial heterogeneity across EU Member States in terms of how close they are to fulfilling flexicurity 'requirements'. Geographical clusters [...] such as Nordic, Continental, Anglo-Saxon, Mediterranean and New Member States are to some extent confirmed.
>
> (p. 61)

Thus, the policy argument in the current debate on labour market reform in EU revolves around the 'best' labour market model to be employed in Europe to foster sustainable growth and social welfare. Should the EU tend to harmonize the labour market according to the flexicurity model? To put it another way, does the flexicurity model systematically work better than the other models across countries?

This chapter addresses one fundamental dimension of the working of different labour market institution model; that is, the innovation performance. Specifically, we examine innovation performance across labour market institutions in the realm of the current financial crisis. We compare the persistence of firm-level investments in innovation in twenty-one European countries from the early days of the financial crisis up to mid-2009. Our interest is in how differences in labour market institutions and in the provision of human capital affect a firm's innovation investment during a severe financial crisis-cum-recession.

We might, broadly, expect investment in innovation to decline in such a setting, due both to diminished financial resources and to increased uncertainty. On the other hand, the disruptive effects of crisis may bring opportunities, or simply a perceived imperative to adapt in order to survive. Innovative activities are characterized by *resilience* to a considerable extent, not only during less turbulent times (Cefis and Orsenigo, 2001; Gerosky et al., 1997) but even during severe recessions (Gerosky and Walters, 1995). Deep and long recessions are often characterized by major shifts in technological paradigms, deep technical discontinuities and industry change (Antonelli, 2002; Dosi, 1982; Perez, 2010); Field (2003) finds that the period 1929–1941 was, in the case of the United States, 'the most technologically progressive decade of the century'.

This chapter concerns innovation investments at the company level, and the way in which those investments may be affected by a country's labour market institutions and skill base. A firm's choices regarding investment in innovation during a crisis may be shaped by such considerations as (1) the availability in the market of skilled labour capable of undertaking the innovative activity; (2) the desire to retain skilled employees already with the firm; and (3) the cost of dismissing skilled (or any) employees.

The relationship between national institutions, and the level and character of innovation, has emerged as an object of study at the intersection of innovation studies and comparative political economy (see also the discussion in Chapter 3). On the innovation side, following Freeman (1987), is work that comes under the rubric of 'National Systems of Innovation' – Lundvall (1992), and Nelson (1993). In the same line, Coriat and Dosi (2000) propose the 'institutional embeddedness dimensions of economic change' while Coriat and Weinstein (2002) have put forward a framework to investigate the roles of organizations and institutions in the development of innovation. On the comparative political economy side, the interest in systems of innovation grows out of the study of national differences in systems of production, and associated differences in labour- and capital-market institutions (Hall and Soskice, 2001).

With reference to skill, the innovation literature has tended to focus on advanced science and engineering knowledge, while the comparative political economy literature has shown more interest in shop-floor skills. Of particular interest to us in the latter category is the relationship, outlined by Estevez-Abe *et al.* (2001), between investment in industry- or firm-specific skills through vocational education and training (VET), and the level and type of 'social protection' in the labour market; broadly, participation in VET is very low in countries which have neither a strong safety net for the unemployed ('unemployment protection') nor strong job security provisions ('employment protection'). The low-VET countries are the Liberal Market Economies (LMEs), which happen to be the English-speaking industrial countries. Among those rich industrial countries which do have high levels of VET, Estevez-Abe *et al.* identify four clusters of interest: one which we can call the 'flexicurity' countries, best exemplified by Denmark, with high unemployment protection and low (as non-LMEs go) employment protection; a second in which social protection is provided primarily through security of employment, with very weak unemployment protection (Italy, Japan); a third in which both employment and unemployment protection are very high (e.g. Germany); and a fourth with moderate (for non-LMEs) levels of both (e.g. France).

Europe has maintained a wide variety of different labour market, education and training institutions despite the integration of its markets (Manca *et al.*, 2010). It has also maintained (Lorenz and Lundvall, 2006), and even increased (Archibugi and Coco, 2005) its heterogeneity in terms of innovation performance and technological development. Differences of innovation and technological capabilities make an important contribution to differences in growth rates (Fagerberg, 1994; Filippetti and Peyrache, 2010) and are thus a factor in the convergence – or lack of it – between European economies (Fagerberg *et al.*, 2007; Filippetti and Peyrache, 2011).

Our interest here is in whether labour market institutions and human capital provision map into differences in firm-level innovation investment during a particular difficult period. Controlling for firm-level characteristics (including prior investment in innovation) and country-level changes in aggregate demand, we seek to identify country-specific effects on private investment in innovation during the crisis. We then analyse the relationship between the country-specific effects and a small number of institutional characteristics: an index of employment security; enrolment in vocational education and training (VET) programmes; and the short-term income replacement rate for unemployment benefits (our measure of unemployment security).

In the empirical analysis, we employ data at the micro (firm) and macro (country) levels. For the former, we use the last Innobarometer Survey carried out by the European Commission (European Commission, 2009b). For the country-level analysis, our data are from the OECD, Eurostat, and the World Bank's *World Development Indicators*.

The chapter is organized as follows. The next section outlines the theoretical background of the analysis, while the following section presents the data. We then analyse the current institutional setting across European countries, before presenting and discussing the empirical results. The final section concludes.

How might labour market institutions affect firms' innovation decisions during a financial crisis?

Employment- and unemployment protection may have direct effects on firms' innovation decisions. The skills of the workforce may also affect these decisions; the stock of skills is in turn affected by the employment- and unemployment-protection provisions previously in place, and in important respects the system of skill provision and the systems of employment- and unemployment protection may be mutually determined. At the risk of simplifying this web of causation, let us trace a few ways in which these labour market institutions may affect the innovation choices of firms during a financial crisis.

In liberal economic doctrine, employment protection is almost certain to retard innovation by discouraging reallocation of labour and/or by removing incentives for innovative effort. Indeed, there is almost no upside to employment protection in liberal economic doctrine, and as part of their response to the crisis the IMF and the OECD have prevailed on Spain to reduce statutory employment protection, with the aim of boosting job creation (see Rodrik, 2010, for a critique of this policy). Yet it is plausible that employment protection can encourage innovation, if the reduced threat of job loss encourages employees' cooperation in productivity improvement, or if the lock-in motivates employers to innovate in order to find productive uses for otherwise surplus labour.

During a crisis, the effects (positive or negative) of employment protection should be especially strong: sharp changes in demand will require greater reallocation of labour; the reduced financial capabilities of firms tighten constraints on their ability to reallocate labour internally, but financial market conditions (elevated liquidity preference of private investors; curtailed bank lending) also constrain the ability of the labour market to reallocate labour between firms; the elevated threat of job loss may increase effort or, if job loss appears imminent, may shift workers' attention elsewhere.

Many of the possible effects of employment protection do not – for better or worse – hold for unemployment protection, as the latter does not lock firms into employment relationships. It does, however, lower a worker's cost of job loss, and might for this reason reduce incentives for work effort generally; it could inhibit innovation through that channel or, on the contrary, encourage it by reducing employee resistance to productivity-enhancing innovation.

A more highly skilled workforce should be better able to contribute to innovation, thereby increasing the return on investment in innovation by employers. As noted above, innovation literature tends to focus on the skills of those involved in formal, science-based innovation: for instance, the European Commission's *European Innovation Scoreboard* (2010b) tracks a number of variables dealing with patents, R&D expenditures, university–industry linkages, tertiary education, and science and engineering PhDs, but completely ignores VET and any other indicator of production-level skills. In a broader view of innovation, however, we need to consider production-level skills. There is good reason to believe that both the level of the supply of such skills, and the mode of their provision, are affected by the strength of employment- and unemployment protection.

Both employment- and unemployment protection reduce the risk to individual workers inherent in investing time or money in acquiring skills which are specific to a firm, industry or technology. This is the explanation given by Estevez-Abe *et al.* (2001) for the fact that, in their sample of countries, those with low levels of *both* employment- and unemployment protection also had very low levels of participation in VET. However, while both employment- and unemployment protection seem efficacious in encouraging VET participation, the way in which VET is provided differs considerably, and we should not take for granted that the different VET systems would necessarily provide skills which feed through to innovation in the same way.

In countries with high strong employment security and weak unemployment security (e.g. Italy and Japan in the Estevez-Abe sample) VET provision tends either to occur within large firms, or to be sponsored by local associations of smaller ones: in either case, responsibility for VET provision falls on employers. In countries where unemployment security is strong and employment security is relatively weak (e.g. Denmark, The Netherlands), public bodies take the lead in VET provision; in recent years, this institutional package of institutions has come to be labelled 'flexicurity' (Manca *et al.*, 2010). The countries with 'dual' apprenticeship systems (Germany, Austria, Belgium) are, not surprisingly, ones in which both employment- and unemployment security are strong. Crouch *et al.* (1999) provide a good overview of differences in VET provision in selected industrial countries. Employers' choices about investment in skills also differ among these institutional configurations. In particular, the lock-in of employment protection may motivate firms to select more skilled workers when hiring, and also to seek ways to protect the firm's investment in skills; with respect to the latter, the various forms of inter-firm cooperation, from industry participation in public apprenticeship programmes to anti-poaching conventions, are well documented (Culpepper, 2001).

The interplay between employment- and unemployment security and the type of skill can play a key role during a major recession. In fact, firms might be more reluctant to fire skilled workers when skills are firm-specific, especially in those cases in which most of the investment in training has been carried out by the firm itself. In this case, the firm can decide to maintain labour surplus within the firm during a period of low demand associated with a recession. Here, the public policy of employment security can play a decisive role. Something along this line is occurring in Italy, where the government has extended financial benefits to those firms which keep their workers employed. We may envisage a very different situation in the case of a general-skilled labour force. In this case, the firm might be less reluctant to dismiss workers for two main reasons: first, because it is more confident of finding workers with the same competences in the future; and second, because it has not invested in workers' training. In this view, the 'lock-in' effect of the worker within the firm associated to the type of skill, and investment associated to it, can be as strong as that associated with forms of employment protection.

Data sources

Firm-level variables

As in previous chapters, the following two questions are taken as dependent variables (see Table 4.1, first and second columns):

1. *'Compared to 2006, has the total amount spent on innovation in 2008, increased, decreased, or stayed the same?'*
2. *'In the last six months has your company taken one of the following actions: increased total innovation expenditures, decreased [...] or maintained [...]?'*

Although 'innovation expenditures' is not a category that many people would have clearly in mind most of the time, and is one of which we might ordinarily expect people to have widely varying interpretations, the fact that these questions come immediately after a series of more specific questions about the company's innovation activities gives us some confidence that respondents would have had a reasonable common understanding of the term.

The definition of innovation implicit in this series of questions is in line with the definition adopted in the Community Innovation Surveys and similar surveys elsewhere in the world. While there are obvious drawbacks to using a set of subjective self-assessments to measure innovation activity, this approach has the considerable advantage of getting a broad measure of innovation: certain aspects of innovation activity, such as formal R&D and patent applications, can be more precisely and objectively measured, but they capture a narrow and unrepresentative slice of overall innovation activity, and are heavily concentrated in a few industries and in larger firms. Moreover, with respect to the question addressed in this chapter, R&D/patent measures alone are problematic because firms typically commit to such projects for extended periods, and the response over six months is likely to be slight; in contrast, items such as training or design budgets, or new equipment purchases, can be – and often are – cut quickly.

The survey also collected data on changes in the firm's turnover from 2006–2008, number of employees and industry classification, among others (see Table A6.1 in the Appendix to this chapter). In our analysis, we use binary variables for decreased turnover (turn_fall) and firms with more than 250 domestic employees (LARGE). Pair-wise correlations of firm-level variables are reported in Table 6.1.

To get a rough picture of how these results differ by country, we treated the responses as scales running from –1 (decreased spending) to 1 (increased), took the mean by country, and plotted them (Figure 6.1).

Country level variables

Several variables have been considered at the level of the country, divided into three main groups: macroeconomic aggregate, labour market institutions and skills, and education. As for the first, the change in GDP has been considered, namely change in GDP in the first term of 2008 with respect to the first term of

Table 6.1 Correlation matrix for firm-level variables

	Innovation 2008–2009	Innovation 2006–2008	LARGE	turn_fall
Innovation 2008–2009	1			
Innovation 2006–2008	0.245*	1		
LARGE	−0.013	0.077*	1	
Turn_fall	−0.123*	−0.215*	−0.787*	1

Note
* Pairwise correlation significant at 0.01.

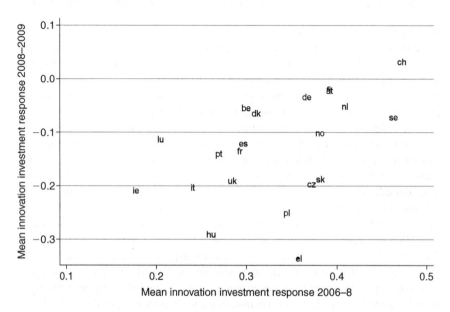

Figure 6.1 Innovation investment prior to and during the crisis.

Note
See Table 6.2 for country abbreviations.

2007, and change in GDP in the first term of 2009 with respect to the first term of 2008. Regarding labour market institutions three main variables are taken into account: (1) replacement rate as defined by the OECD as 'net income replacement rates for unemployment benefits (Percentage of earnings)'; (2) the OECD Employment Protection Index representing a synthetic indicator of the strictness of regulation on dismissals and the use of temporary contracts[2]; and (3) vocational and education training defined by the World Bank – World Development Indicator – as 'Technical/vocational enrolment in ISCED 3 as percentage of total enrolment in ISCED 3'. The third group of variables includes science and engineering doctorates per population (Eurostat), science and engineering degrees per population (Eurostat), and the share of the labour force with tertiary education (World Bank – World Development Indicators) (see Table 6.2 for an overview of the variables).

Table 6.2 Country-level variables

Country	Replacement	Employment protection index	VET	S&E doctorate	S&E graduates	Tertiary education	GDP0801	GDP0901
Switzerland (ch)	0.97	0.16	0.77	0.82	0.66	0.78	3.0	-2.2
Austria (at)	0.72	0.47	1.00	0.56	0.00	0.18	3.4	-5.2
Finland (fi)	0.90	0.48	0.58	0.75	0.41	1.00	2.6	-7.5
Denmark (dk)	0.99	0.30	0.56	0.22	0.62	0.82	-0.2	-3.4
Germany (de)	0.74	0.55	0.63	0.49	0.11	0.47	2.1	-6.4
Belgium (be)	0.74	0.57	0.60	0.22	0.28	0.81	2.1	-4.1
Netherland (nl)	0.97	0.48	0.82	0.19	0.36	0.75	3.6	-4.5
Luxembourg (lu)	1.00	1.00	0.69		–	0.57	3.4	-6.0
Norway (no)	0.87	0.78	0.59	0.22	0.19	0.91	0.5	1.2
France (fr)	0.72	0.92	0.38	0.30	1.00	0.58	1.7	-3.3
Spain (es)	0.58	0.89	0.38	0.11	0.14	0.68	1.9	-3.9
Sweden (se)	0.82	0.45	0.67	0.79	0.20	0.78	0.9	-6.7
Portugal (pt)	0.68	0.96	0.18	1.00	0.22	0.00	0.9	-4.4
Poland (pl)	0.59	0.46	0.43	0.19	0.77	0.22	6.5	0.9
Slovakia (sk)	0.45	0.28	0.90	0.20	0.07	0.04	9.7	-5.7
Italy (it)	0.15	0.46	0.68	0.20	0.26	0.00	0.3	-6.4
United Kingdom (uk)	0.64	0.00	0.68	0.51	0.75	0.80	2.0	-4.9
Czeck Republic (cz)	0.75	0.48	0.94	0.19	0.10	0.00	2.7	-4.4
Ireland (ie)	0.84	0.14	0.17	0.30	1.00	0.82	-1.4	-9.3
Hungary (hu)	0.72	0.36	0.06	0.00	0.21	0.19	1.9	-6.7
Greece (el)	0.00	0.79	0.16	0.07	0.09	0.37	3.4	0.3

Note
Except for the GDP variables, these have been standardized with a maximum of 1 and minimum of 0.

Empirical analysis

The strategy for analysing the data is to estimate an ordered logit model on the firm-level data and macroeconomic variables, with country-level random effects. We then rank the country-level effects and compare them in tables with the tertile ranks of the country-level variables. In principle, the random effects estimated in the first stage could be modelled as functions of the country-level variables – that is, an alternate strategy would have been to estimate a two-level model. We do not do this because, with only twenty-one countries, the statistical properties of the second-stage estimates are not good. Moreover, there are plausible and important hypotheses which could only be tested using both levels and *interactions* of country-level variables: we can get nice-looking results with up to three country-level institutional variables, but when we add further variables or interactions the results become unstable – unsurprisingly, given the number of independent observations. This difficulty is commonly encountered in doing statistical analysis of comparative international data, and it presents a choice between making heroic statistical assumptions (including the omission of variables of interest) or resorting to a low-tech tabular or visual presentation. We opt for the latter.

The regression model is:

$$\text{Innovation2009}_{i,k} = b1*\text{Innovation2008}_{i,k} + b2*\text{Large}_{i,k} + b3*\text{turn\_fall}_{i,k} +$$
$$b4*\text{INMKT}_{i,k} + b5*\text{GDP0801}_k + b6*\text{GDP0901}_k + \text{industry controls} + e_k + u_{i,k}$$

where e_k is the country random effect. This is estimated in Stata using the GLLAMM package (Rabe-Hesketh and Skrondal, 2004).

Results of this estimation are reported in Table 6.3. The innovation trajectory in 2006–2008 is a strong predictor of the innovation trajectory in the six months prior to the survey. Reduced turnover during 2006–2008 dampens innovation investment in 2009, and innovation in 2009 is similarly dampened by low (or negative) GDP growth in 2008 and 2009. Similarly, the fact that the firm is internationalized (INMKT) and firm size (LARGE) have little effect.

The country effects from this regression, with their standard errors, are shown in Figure 6.2. The countries in which firms showed the strongest innovation performance during the crisis are all in north-western continental Europe, and are among what Hall and Soskice (2001) would classify as 'coordinated market economies': Switzerland tops the ranking, followed by Austria, Finland, Denmark, Germany, Belgium and The Netherlands. There are, of course, significant differences among these countries' economic institutions, but those seem small compared with the differences among the countries in the lower tail: starting at the bottom, we have Greece, Hungary, Ireland, Czech Republic, the UK, Italy and Slovakia. One might think that what the countries performing worst have in common is a particularly bad experience with the financial crisis, but we have controlled for change in GDP.

Table 6.4 shows the country effects alongside each country's ranking for unemployment replacement (REPLACE), VET enrolment (VET) and employ-

Table 6.3 Regression output

Dependent variable: inno2009	
inno2008	0.768***
	–0.063
LARGE	–0.157
	–0.084
INTMKT	–0.042
	–0.082
GDP0901	–0.027
	–0.029
GDP0801	–0.027
	–0.033
turn_fall	–0.422***
	–0.102
industry dummies	included
_cut11	
Constant	–1.160***
	–0.247
_cut12	
Constant	2.412***
	–0.251
coun1	
Constant	0.285***
	–0.062
R-squared	
N	3237

Notes
* *P*<0.05, ** *P*<0.01, *** *P*<0.001.

ment protection (EMPLOY). We have grouped these variables so that one-third of the countries with the lowest rankings for, for example, REPLACE get a 1 in that column, those in the middle third get a 2, and those in the top third get a 3.

Two things are striking about this table. One is that all of the countries in the top one-third of the table – that is, those with relatively persistent firm-level innovation during the financial crisis – are in the top two-thirds in terms of both the earnings replacement rate *and* VET enrolment. In the bottom half of the table, many countries rank highly in either earnings replacement *or* VET enrolment, but only one (Czech Republic) is strong in both of them; all other countries in the bottom half of the table are in the bottom one-third of either earnings replacement *or* VET – or, in a few cases, both. A good earnings replacement safety net together with a strong system of VET are, of course, key elements of 'flexicurity'.

The second striking thing about the table, however, is that while it shows clearly that the unemployment security and training elements of flexicurity are, in combination, associated with greater resilience of investment in innovation by firms, it is not clear at all about labour market flexibility. The 'flexi' end of flexicurity is, of course, limited employment security. But what we see in Table 6.4

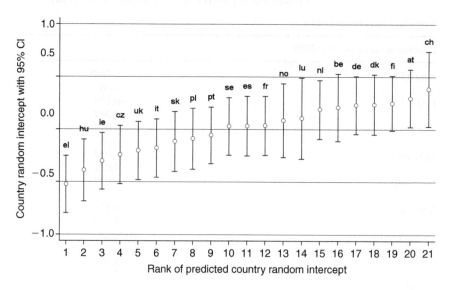

Figure 6.2 Country effects.

Note
See Table 6.2 for country abbreviations.

Table 6.4 Country innovation effects and labour market institutions

Country	Country effect	Replacement rate	Vocation and education training	Employment protection
ch	0.385	3	3	1
at	0.297	2	3	2
fi	0.251	3	2	2
dk	0.237	3	2	1
de	0.232	2	2	2
be	0.210	2	2	3
nl	0.191	3	3	2
lu	0.106	3	3	3
no	0.086	3	2	3
fr	0.037	2	1	3
es	0.032	1	1	3
se	0.029	2	2	1
pt	−0.055	1	1	3
pl	−0.088	1	2	2
sk	−0.115	1	3	1
it	−0.177	1	3	2
uk	−0.202	1	1	1
cz	−0.242	2	3	2
ie	−0.302	3	1	1
hu	−0.389	2	1	1
el	−0.523	1	1	3

Note
See Table 6.2 for country abbreviations.

is an extremely weak association between employment security and the persistence of investment in innovation: the countries with the strongest employment security are grouped together in the middle of the pack, while countries at the top and bottom are both decidedly mixed in their levels of employment security. For the present question, at least, the level of employment security (or its inverse, numerical flexibility for employers) does not appear to be very important. These impressions are reinforced by Figures A6.1–A6.3 in the Appendix, which plot the country effect against the replacement rate, VET enrolment and employment protection variables, respectively.

In Table 6.5, we present a similar breakdown for the three higher-education variables. These are of interest both as additional measures of skill in a country's workforce, and as indicators of the country's science base. These are also, of course, the sort of education variables more commonly associated with innovation in the academic literature on the subject. The patterns here are not so clear-cut. Science and engineering degrees (the middle column) bear no apparent relation to the country effect, but most of the countries that rank high in the persistence of innovation also rank high in science and engineering doctorates, and in tertiary education generally.

Table 6.5 Country innovation effects and tertiary education

Country	Country effect	S&E doctorate	S&E graduates	Tertiary education
ch	0.39	3	3	2
at	0.30	3	1	1
fi	0.25	3	2	3
dk	0.24	2	3	3
de	0.23	2	1	2
be	0.21	2	2	3
nl	0.19	1	2	2
lu	0.11	–	–	2
no	0.09	2	1	3
fr	0.04	2	3	2
es	0.03	1	1	2
se	0.03	3	2	2
pt	–0.05	3	2	1
pl	–0.09	1	3	1
sk	–0.11	1	1	1
it	–0.18	1	2	1
uk	–0.2	3	3	3
cz	–0.24	1	1	1
ie	–0.30	2	3	3
hu	–0.39	1	2	1
el	–0.52	1	1	2

Note
See Table 6.2 for countries abbreviations.

Concluding remarks

Firm-level investment in innovation in Europe during the onset of the financial crisis in 2008–2009 was strongest in countries with high earnings replacement rates, high participation in vocational education and training, and high numbers of people completing doctoral degrees in science and engineering subjects. We see no relationship, good or bad, with employment protection or with lower-level science and engineering degrees. These results must be treated with caution, due to both the short timeframe covered by the data (six months into the crisis), and the small number of independent units for country level data.

They are, nonetheless, striking in three respects. One is the clear association between the persistence of innovation and the replacement rate/VET combination, in keeping with the flexicurity model. The second is the apparent *unimportance* of employment security: a great deal of political and academic energy is spent both attacking and defending it, but, at least within the very limited scope of the present question, the stakes seem small. The third is the place of science and engineering doctorates, which suggests (together with the replacement/VET result) a synergy between production skills and the research system.

Appendix

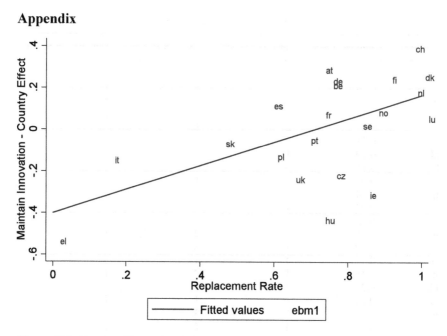

Figure A6.1 Country effect and replacement rate.

Note

See Table 6.2 for country abbreviations.

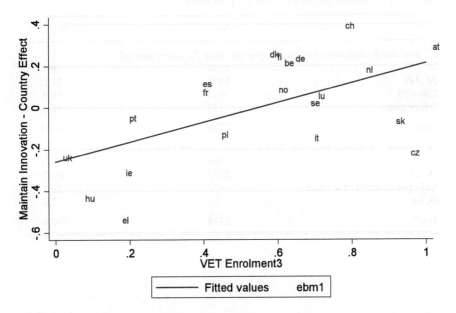

Figure A6.2 Country effect and VET enrolment.

Note
See Table 6.2 for country abbreviations.

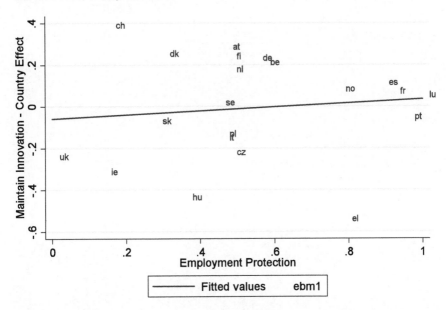

Figure A6.3 Country effect and employment protection.

Note
See Table 6.2 for countrys abbreviations.

Table A6.1 Domestic employment and turnover trend

	No.	*%*
d2. how many employees does your company have [in your country]?		
20–49	1330	39.4
50–249	1075	31.8
250–499	634	18.8
500 or more	337	10.0
Total	3376	100.0
d4. comparing your turnover of 2008 to that of 2006, did the annual turnover		
decrease	561	16.6
increase	2032	60.2
stay approximately the same	692	20.5
dk/na	91	2.7
Total	3376	100.0

PART III

The innovative behaviour of the firm in times of crisis

7 The shift of the innovation environment: from creative accumulation to creative destruction[1]

Introduction

As shown in the first part of the book, the financial crisis has severely reduced the short-term willingness of companies to invest in innovation. While, on the whole, firms' investment in innovation declined during the economic downturn, a small but significant minority of firms are 'swimming against the stream' and have increased their expenditures in innovation. This chapter explores the characteristics of these firms, and compares them with those that increased investment into innovation prior to the crisis.

Who are these firms that have decided to respond to the crisis by innovating more rather than less? There are two possible scenarios:

1   These firms are the most dynamic ones; those that cannot survive without changing their products and services. The competitive advantage of these firms resides in the generation and upgrading of new knowledge, and they innovate continuously irrespective of the business cycle.
2   Alternatively, these firms are new entrants that were not necessarily involved in innovation before the crisis. These firms might be smaller in size or entirely new enterprises that exploit the crisis to compete for market shares of incumbent firms.

Point (1) assumes that innovation and technical change is rooted in cumulative learning processes, leading to path-dependent patterns that are woven into organizational routines and that favour innovation by established firms (Dosi *et al.*, 2002; Nelson and Winter, 1982). Point (2) is based on the assumption that economic turbulence makes it possible for new and small firms to emerge in a competitive market through innovation (Henderson and Clark, 1990; Perez, 2002; Simonetti, 1996; Tushman and Anderson, 1986).

As with most insights in the field of innovation, points (1) and (2) are also derived by the theorizing of Joseph A. Schumpeter. As discussed in Chapter 2, Schumpeter and his followers suggested that economic cycles are the consequence of innovation, but also that innovative activities and the nature itself of innovative organizations are re-shaped by economic crises. In particular, we interpret the canonical debate between the two models elaborated by the young and the old Schumpeter in the following way: during an upswing in the business cycle, innovation is carried out in a cumulative fashion. Firms carry out innovation along established technological trajectories, and develop into incumbents that carry out innovation as a routine and to prevent the entrance of newcomers (Bell and Pavitt, 1993; Schumpeter, 1942). Following Malerba and Orsenigo (1995), we call this process *creative accumulation*. Economic turmoil, on the contrary, generates a shake-out in established industries and technological fields; new firms in new sectors play a relatively bigger role than the incumbent firms in inducing innovations. New firms are eager to exploit new technological opportunities as a way to challenge incumbent corporations: as the young Schumpeter suggested, 'it is not the owner of the stage-coaches who builds railways' (Schumpeter, 1911 (1934)). Following Schumpeter, we call this process *creative destruction.*[2]

The evolutionary perspective claims that changes at the aggregate level emerge from the dynamics at the micro level (Dosi, 1997; Nelson and Winter, 1982), and it is the micro level that this chapter explores. Phenomena observed at the aggregate level, such as economic cycles, are the result of dynamic interactions among agents at the micro level characterized by a high degree of heterogeneity, in terms of both behaviour and characteristics. For the purpose of this chapter, the two ideas of creative accumulation and destruction (linked to points (1) and (2) above) are ideal types of two possible aggregate outcomes that emerge from the micro behaviour, and are operationalized at the level of the firm.

This chapter seeks to test the interplay between the forces of creative destruction and accumulation in innovation before, during and after the financial crisis that started in the autumn of 2008. The chapter is structured as follows. It first discusses the state of the art against which the chapter is set. The following section develops the conceptual framework by providing a sketch of the two ideal typical models of creative accumulation and creative destruction. We then introduce the variables and methodology, before presenting the results that are discussed in the last section.

Innovation generated through technological accumulation and economic creative destruction

The concepts of technological accumulation and creative destruction are at the very core of Schumpeter and Schumpeterian economics. The young Schumpeter looked at innovation as an event that could revolutionize economic life by bringing to the fore new entrepreneurs, new companies and new industries. The mature Schumpeter, on the contrary, observed and described the activities of large oligopolistic corporations, able to perform R&D and innovation as a routine by building on their previous competences.

On the ground of these insights, the Schumpeterian tradition has further investigated the relative importance of the two processes (Breschi *et al.*, 2000; Malerba and Orsenigo, 1995; Nelson and Winter, 1982; Patel and Pavitt, 1994).

Creative destruction is described as a result of a regime characterized by low cumulativeness and high technological opportunities, leading to an environment with greater dynamism in terms of technological ease of entry and exit, as well as a major role played by entrepreneurs and fierce competition. Creative accumulation is associated with a technological regime that is characterized by high cumulativeness and low technological opportunities, bringing about more stable environments in which the bulk of innovation is carried out by large and established firms incrementally, leading to a market structure with high entry barriers and oligopolistic competition.

There are arguments supporting the relevance of cumulativeness and of reinforcing patterns of technological development and innovation, and arguments lending support to a 'destruction/discontinuous hypothesis'. Concerning the former, several studies suggest that learning processes that underlie innovation activities are both local and cumulative, resulting in path-dependency (Antonelli, 1997). In addition, empirical evidence indicates that there is a degree of persistence in innovation and among innovators (Cefis and Orsenigo, 2001; Geroski *et al.*, 1997).

Regarding the latter, it has often been stressed that there are periods of turbulence associated with a change in the leading sectors and/or the emergence of new sectors, which brings about a decline of technological and profit opportunities in established industries (Perez, 2002, 2009). This, in turn, might lead to a change in the knowledge and technological base for innovation activity, and could substantially affect the hierarchy of innovators. Other research has stressed the fact that firm-specific organizational routines and capabilities can bring about inertia and hamper the capacity of established firms to keep up with major discontinuities (Henderson and Clark, 1990; Leonard-Barton, 1992; Levinthal and March, 1993).

This should also be related to the 'continuity' thesis advocated by Chandler (1977) and his followers on the grounds of the fact that the population of incumbent, large firms has remained stable over recent decades. This thesis has been challenged by Simonetti (1996), Louca and Mendonca (1999) and Freeman and Louca (2001), who claim that a stream of new firms has joined incumbent firms during periods of radical discontinuities. This can also be contingent to the specific knowledge base and technical skills attached to different industries. For example, while Klepper and Simons (2000) show that firms established in making radios were successful in developing colour TVs, Holbrook *et al.* (2000) illustrate that this pattern is not mirrored in the evolution of the semiconductor industry.

In this chapter the emphasis is not on specific industries or technologies, but rather on how an external shock, represented by the financial crisis, is affecting companies' innovative strategies. As a result, we expect to find an array of different innovation drivers both before and in response to the crisis. These are examined in view of the changes at the macro level, as we aim to understand whether the crisis has led to some variation/discontinuity at the aggregate level as a result of a different composition among innovating firms.

An attempt to identify the core characteristics of creative destruction and technological accumulation

To guide the analysis, we elaborate on the ideal typical models of creative destruction and creative accumulation as two possible aggregate outcomes of micro behaviours. Creative destruction describes a dynamic environment in which new firms emerge as the most significant innovators as a result of a major discontinuity such as an economic downturn. Creative accumulation is underpinned by a more stable pattern of innovation which emphasizes cumulativeness and persistency of innovative activities in response to the crisis. Here, we make an attempt to identify these two patterns in relation to firm behaviour rather than to the evolution of technological regimes. In this sense, our approach is complementary to the research pioneered by Malerba and Orsenigo (1995) to identify Schumpeterian patterns of innovation with reference to various technological fields.

A sketch of the differences between the models of creative destruction and creative accumulation is given in Table 7.1, where four categories are singled out: (1) characteristics of the innovating firm; (2) types of knowledge source dominant in the innovation process; (3) types of innovation; and (4) characteristics of the market.

In the empirical part of the chapter some of these factors, those more directly associated to our data, will be used to test if the two ideal typical models can be related to the patterns of innovation investment of firms.

Characteristics of the innovating firms

The creative accumulation model assumes that incumbent firms systematically explore technological opportunities. For them, to innovate is routine, and it is one of the core things that the top management supervises. They have to upgrade their products periodically, often because they operate in concentrated oligopolistic industries. A stream of incremental innovation guarantees not only that costs and prices are kept competitive, but also that products are differentiated and improved compared to those of the competition. This provides the opportunity to accumulate knowledge, and often not just in the areas of their core products (Grandstrand *et al.*, 1997). When new technological opportunities are identified, these companies may also be quick in entering into new fields and industries, thanks to their wide accumulated knowledge. However, when firms diversify, they tend to do so along some kind of technological relatedness, defined as *coherence* (Piscitello, 2004; Teece *et al.*, 1994). Pavitt makes this point clear: 'Given the increasingly specialized and professional nature of the knowledge on which they are based, manufacturing firms are path-dependent. [...] it is difficult if not impossible to convert a traditional textile firm into one making semiconductors' (Pavitt, 2005, p. 95).

By contrast, the creative destruction model emphasizes the role played by individual inventors and entrepreneurs. This model reflects a more uncertain

Table 7.1 Innovative firms' characteristics under the creative accumulation and creative destruction models

Categories	Creative accumulation	Creative destruction
Characteristics of the innovating firms	Innovations are driven by large, incumbent firms that seek new solutions through formal research, exploiting their pre-existing capability.	Small firms, new entrants are the key drivers in the innovation process. They use innovation and economic turbulence to acquire market share from incumbent firms or to open new markets.
Types of knowledge source	High relevance of past innovations and accumulated knowledge. Importance of formal R&D, in-house but also jointly performed or externally acquired.	Higher relevance of collaborative arrangements leaning towards the applied knowledge base (other firms). Exploration of new markets and technological opportunities.
Types of innovation	The innovation process is dominated by a large number of incremental innovations. Organizational routines dominate the generation of innovations.	The emphasis is on path-breaking innovations often able to create new industries. New organizational forms contribute to generate innovations.
Characteristics of the market	Barriers to entry are high due to relative importance of appropriation and cumulativeness of knowledge and high costs of innovation. Dominance of oligopolistic markets. Technological advancement based on path dependent and cumulative technological trajectories.	Low barriers to entry into the new industries. A high rate of entry and exit leads to low levels of concentration and high competition. Discontinuous technologies are available that generate growing markets and new opportunities.

Source: Authors' elaboration.

landscape of early stages of new technologies. By anticipating or even creating technological opportunities, these far-sighted individuals manage to generate new firms and often new industries that substantially change the economic landscape. These individuals can be independent – for example, setting up or owning their own business – but they can also be dependent and employed by (sometimes large) organization.

These individuals do not find the most conducive environment in existing organizations, since learned and accumulated routine activities, organizational settings, and decision processes somehow discourage an entrepreneurial stance. Moreover, the larger the company, the greater might be a resistance to change by the company as a whole. Thus, patterns linked to creative destruction are associated, at the firm level, with innovation driven by smaller size, and new entry into markets alongside established firms, as entrepreneurial activities might be greater due to lower inertia, greater flexibility and responsiveness to changes in demand conditions and technological discontinuities. This type of innovative behaviour could be found in spin-offs from established companies, in universities or simply in new businesses.

Types of knowledge source

In creative accumulation, routine-based research is more important as a key source in the innovation process than sudden insights. This favours the large firm that (1) has the capacity and the resources to set up and maintain internal R&D laboratories, (2) can use interactions with others, and (3) has well-established internal functions (including design, production and marketing). High-tech companies are also able to plug into the knowledge base of other companies, public institutions and countries. They are in the position to reduce the risks and costs associated with exploring new technological opportunities through strategic technological agreements, they have qualified personnel able to interact periodically with universities and public research centres, and they can also establish intra-firm but international research networks through subsidiaries in other countries. All these factors allow them to build on their existing competences.

Creative destruction, on the contrary, will be based on internal sources that on some occasions, and for limited periods of time, represent the bulk of the firm's economic activity, as has happened for companies in emerging fields such as biotechnology and software. This will also be combined with the concentric exploration of new opportunities, with specific ventures with companies operating in other industries, or with generating symbiotic contacts with university departments (see Breschi *et al.*, 2000). In the case of small or newly established firms, the development of new products, services or processes is likely to favour external collaborations and strategic alliances over and above than is the case for large corporations. Such set-ups help to overcome possible resource, finance and capability constraints within new and comparatively small firms.

Types of innovation

Creative destruction is linked to patterns of path-breaking innovations and radically new solutions that are incompatible with traditional solutions. Several scholars have argued that in this case innovations are more likely to be introduced by new firms, as existing firms can face problems in terms of a lack of adequate new skills and competences (Henderson and Clark, 1990; Leonard-Barton 1992; Tushman and Anderson, 1986), organizational adaptation (Levinthal and March, 1993) and difficulties in changing context (Christensen, 1997; Christensen and Rosenbloom, 1995).

Creative accumulation is linked with frequent, but more incremental, innovation patterns. Accumulation or cumulativeness suggests that firms' innovation activities are driven by past innovation activities. Current technologies build on past experience of production and innovation specific to the firm. Malerba and

Orsenigo (1995) and Breschi *et al.* (2000) suggest that cumulativeness of techno-logical change is high when: (1) the firm is established and can build on a history of innovation success, and (2) there is a tradition of research carried out inside the firm.

Pavitt and his colleagues suggested that incumbents might have the resilience to survive and to adapt to major changes (Grandstrand *et al.*, 1997; Patel and Pavitt, 1994). Methé *et al.* (1996) present empirical evidence showing that estab-lished firms are often sources of major innovations, for example in telecommu-nications and medical instruments. In a similar vein, Iansiti and Levien (2004) suggest that, despite the many predictions about incumbents' failures, technolo-gical transitions in the computer industry were survived by the overwhelming majority of firms.

Characteristics of the market

In a Schumpeterian model, firms compete to become oligopolistic in their market. This allows them to gain extra profit through the appropriation of the return of their innovations. In a dynamic context, the oligopolistic structure is seen as a necessary evil to foster dynamic efficiency led by the continuous intro-duction of innovations (Galbraith, 1952; Scherer, 1992; Schumpeter, 1942; Sylos Labini, 1962). Creative destruction has been associated with a market structure characterized by high dynamism and competition, as well as a high rate of change in the hierarchy of innovators. On the contrary, creative accumulation patterns are linked to oligopolistic market structure, with high entry barriers and a high degree of stability of innovators.

Nelson and Winter (1982) suggest that the market structure in a specific industry, the degree of concentration and rate of entry, are influenced by the degree to which technological opportunities arise and the ease with which inno-vations can be protected from imitation (i.e. the appropriability conditions). High technological opportunity together with low appropriability causes lower con-centration in an industry, and vice versa. These arguments are picked up and empirically tested by Breschi *et al.* (2000) and Malerba and Orsenigo (1995, 1997) in their work on technological regimes and their role in the evolution of industrial structures, hierarchy of innovators and innovation activities.

Technological opportunities are often associated with the productivity of R&D. The higher the technological opportunities, the higher the expected return of a unit of R&D expenditure (under a given level of appropriability).[3] Within this perspective, high levels of new technological opportunities favour creative destruction because the presence of technological opportunities increases the expected return of insight and idea generation of entrepreneurs and new firms. On the other hand, industries characterized by low technological opportunities are less attractive for new entrants and potential innovators. Consequently, low technological opportunities are associated with the creative accumulation model.

Variables and methodology

The dependent variables

As in previous chapters, our dependent variables are based on firms' responses to the following three questions from the Innobarometer Survey (European Commission, 2009b):

a   before the crisis: '*Compared to 2006 has the total amount spent by your firm on all innovation activities in 2008 increased, decreased or stayed approximately the same?*',

b   during the crisis: '*In the last six months[4] has your company taken one of the following actions as a direct result of the economic downturn; increased total amount of innovation expenditures, decreased [...] or maintained [...]?*', and

c   following on from the beginning of the crisis: '*Compared to 2008, do you expect your company to increase, decrease or maintain the total amount of its innovation expenditure in 2009?*'

The observations feeding into the empirical analysis are all those firms that were innovation-active, and thus firms that stated they increased, decreased or maintained their innovation investment in the three periods respectively. The weakness of our dependent variable – change in innovation-related investment – is that the scales are categorical rather than continuous (e.g. three choices as opposed to the total amount spent on innovation), but the strength is that they provide a unique possibility to distinguish between three different time periods around the crisis.

Table 7.2 provides the descriptive statistics for the three dependent variables, including the number (frequency) and percentage of enterprises that increased, maintained and decreased innovation investment under (1) time proxy for 'before the crisis' – we also refer to this as T1, (2) proxy for 'during the crisis' that we also refer to as T2, and (3) proxy for 'following on from the crisis', referred to as T3.

Table 7.2 reveals two patterns. First, 38 per cent of enterprises reported that they increased innovation-related investment in 2008 compared with their investment in 2006 (see Table 7.2 '%' column under T1); but, in T2 only 9 per cent and in T3 13 per cent of enterprises reported increased investment. Thus, there is a strong drop in the number of firms that increased innovation-related investment during the crisis and following on from the crisis. This pattern is mirrored in a shift from few firms to many firms reporting decreased investment over the three time periods. In T1 only 9 per cent of firms decreased their innovation-related expenditures, but in the midst of the financial crisis – in T2 – 24 per cent decreased investment and 30 per cent planned to decrease investment in 2009 compared to investment levels in 2008. This might at the aggregate level point towards destruction. Second, a large share of firms (about half of all firms)

Table 7.2 Investment in innovation-related activities before, during and following on from the crisis

Dependent variable: change in innovation-related investment	Before the crisis (T1)		During the crisis (T2)		Following on from the beginning of the crisis (T3)	
	Frequency	%	Frequency	%	Frequency	%
Increase	1985	38	453	9	659	13
Decrease	472	9	1231	24	1560	30
Maintain	2207	42	2961	57	2452	47
Innovation active firms	4664	89	4645	90	4671	90
No innovation activities	328	6	457	9	343	7
Missing observations	242	5	132	3	220	4
Number of observations	5234	100	5234	100	5234	100

Source: Authors' elaboration on the *Innobarometer*, European Commission (2009a).

Notes
T1 refers to the change in innovation-related investment in the calendar year 2008 compared to 2006; T2 refers to the change in innovation-related investment in the six-month period October 2008 to March 2009; T3 refers to the expected change in innovation-related investment in 2009 compared with 2008.

reported that they maintained innovation-related investment irrespective of the crisis, leaning towards an accumulation hypothesis.

In Table 7.3 we report the cross-tabulations and Chi-squared statistics between the dependent variables, producing three cross-tabulations: before the crisis (T1) with during the crisis (T2); before the crisis (T1) with following on from the crisis (T3); and during the crisis (T2) with following on from the crisis (T3). We present the cross-tabulations to gain insight into the level of continuity/ discontinuity in innovation investment decisions. For example, are the firms that increased investment during the crisis also among the firms that increased investment before the crisis?

In the cross-tabulations, we report frequencies and column percentages below the frequencies. In the first column total of the top cross-table we report that 438 firms increased investment during the crisis (T2), and in the first cell of the first cross-tabulation we report that, of these 438 firms, 332 also increased investment before the crisis (T1). This is the same as stating that 76 per cent of firms that increased investment during the crisis are firms that already increased investment before the crisis. These 76 per cent of (or 332) firms indicate some consistency of investment patterns, and may already point towards – despite the crisis – a confirmation of the importance of technological accumulation.

However, of the 438 firms that increased investment during the crisis (and 620 that increased investment following on from the crisis; see the middle cross-tabulations), 24 per cent (and 42 per cent) decreased or maintained investment before the crisis. And it is among these firms that we can see a shift in firm characteristics and market conditions associated with increased innovation investment before, during and following on from the crisis.

Table 7.3 Innovation investment before, during and following on from the crisis: cross-tabulations of the dependent variables

			During the crisis (T2)			Total
			Increase	Decrease	Maintain	
Before the crisis (T1)	Increase	*Frequencies*	332	445	1124	1901
		Column percentages	76	38	40	43
	Decrease	*Frequencies*	18	255	167	440
		Column percentages	4	22	6	10
	Maintain	*Frequencies*	88	469	1538	2095
		Column percentages	20	40	54	47
	Total	*Frequencies*	438	1169	2829	4436
		Column percentages	100	100	100	100

Notes
Chi^2(4)=463; $P<0.01$.

			Following on from the crisis (T3)			Total
			Increase	Decrease	Maintain	
Before the crisis (T1)	Increase	*Frequencies*	358	631	907	1896
		Column percentages	58	43	39	43
	Decrease	*Frequencies*	62	225	158	445
		Column percentages	10	15	7	10
	Maintain	*Frequencies*	200	625	1270	2095
		Column percentages	32	42	54	47
	Total	*Frequencies*	620	1481	2335	4436
		Column percentages	100	100	100	100

Notes
Chi^2(4)=168; $P<0.01$.

			Following on from the crisis (T3)			Total
			Increase	Decrease	Maintain	
Before the crisis (T1)	Increase	*Frequencies*	192	73	159	424
		Column percentages	32	5	7	10
	Decrease	*Frequencies*	61	812	256	1129
		Column percentages	10	57	11	26
	Maintain	*Frequencies*	350	544	1832	2726
		Column percentages	58	38	82	64
	Total	*Frequencies*	603	1429	2247	4279
		Column percentages	100	100	100	100

Notes
Chi^2(4)=1400; $P<0.01$.

From the information presented in Table 7.3 we also know that there is greater stability in the investment choices of firms between the two periods during (T2) and following on from (T3) the crisis, also resulting in the higher measure of association (Chi^2(4) = 1400; $P < 0.01$), compared with before the crisis (T1 and T2, T1 and T3).

To fully address our research question of who the firms are that increased investment (top row of Table 7.2) in the midst of the crisis – (1) the most dynamic ones that compete largely on continuous upgrading or (2) new players that could be newly established firms or firms less relevant in aggregate innovation – we used a set of measures capturing firm and market characteristics to which we now turn, and that we use to predict innovation-related investment across T1, T2 and T3 in the results section of the chapter.

The independent variables

Table 7.4 contains an overview of the independent variables arranged by the categories already introduced in Table 7.1: (1) characteristics of the innovating firms; (2) types of knowledge source; (3) types of innovation; and (4) market characteristics.

The first column in Table 7.4 gives the variable names of the independent variables, and the second column the variable description. All our independent variables are dummy variables, coded 1 if a characteristic is met and zero otherwise. We rely on dummies because of a lack of more detailed information. In the first category, entitled 'characteristics of the firm', the first variable is called 'newly established', and this variable is coded 1 if a firm was established after 1 January 2001 and 0 if it was established earlier. This variable is used as a proxy to identify new entrants. The second set of variables is made of three dummies that we use to proxy firm size. Small firms (20–49 employees) are used as the base comparison group in the regressions. The final variable proxies the innovation intensity of firms or the stock/level of investment in innovation-related activities with reference to the calendar year 2008. High innovation intensity is measured as a share of turnover – at least 5 per cent is spent on innovation-related activities.[5] Low innovation intensity (i.e. below 5 per cent of turnover) is the base group.

Under the heading 'types of knowledge source' are six variables; first, a variable that captures if the enterprise is engaged in in-house R&D, second, if it is engaged in extramural R&D. The remaining four variables relate to linkages or joint knowledge sources; specifically, collaboration on innovation with other businesses, collaboration on innovation with educational and other research institutions, collaboration with partners located abroad, and investment in companies located abroad. All variables are coded 1 for yes answers and zero for no answers.

Under 'types of innovation' or innovators we include four variables that are proxies for the strategic orientation of the firms with respect to their innovations: whether or not firms compete (1) based on their innovations, (2) based on

Table 7.4 Characteristics of the innovating firms, types of knowledge source, types of
innovation, and characteristics of the market: overview of the independent
variables

Characteristics of the innovating firms

Newly established	The enterprise was established after 1 January 2001
Small enterprise	There are four dummies that we use to measure the size of the enterprise; small enterprises here have 20–49 employees
Medium enterprise	The variable selects all enterprises with 50–249 employees
Large enterprises	The variables selects all enterprises with more than 250 employees
Low-innovation intensity	The enterprise invests less than 5% of turnover in innovation-related activities in 2008
High-innovation intensity	The enterprise invests at least 5% of turnover in innovation-related activities

Types of knowledge source

In-house R&D	The enterprise has had expenditures on in-house R&D since 2006
Bought-in R&D	The enterprise has had expenditures on R&D performed for the company by other enterprises or by research organizations since 2006
Link with other firms	The enterprise has developed strategic relationships in support of innovation with customers, suppliers or other companies since 2006
Link with the knowledge base	The enterprise has developed strategic relationships in support of innovation with research institutes and educational institutions since 2006
International collaboration	The enterprise has started or increased cooperation with local partners in other countries in support of innovation since 2006
Investment in companies abroad	The enterprise has invested in companies located in other countries in support of innovation since 2006

Types of innovation

Enterprise competes on innovations	The enterprise sees the main competitive advantage in new products, services and processes
Enterprise competes on improvements	The enterprise sees the main competitive advantage in the modification of existing products, services and processes
Enterprise competes on new business models	The enterprise sees the main competitive advantage in the developments of new business models or ways to market products and services
Enterprise competes on cost	The enterprise sees the main competitive advantage in reducing costs of existing products

Characteristics of the market

IPRs	The enterprise has applied for a patent or registered a design since 2006
Technological opportunities	New technologies have emerged in the enterprise's market since 2006
Market opportunities	New opportunities to enter into new markets or expand sales in existing markets have emerged since 2006
International market	The enterprise operates in international markets

---

improvements to existing products, (3) based on a new business model, or (4) based on cost savings. Competing on innovation might lean more closely to activities at the frontier, and might be seen as more closely related to path-breaking developments vis-à-vis the remaining categories. While improvements lean towards incremental innovations, new business models might be indicative of a new service. Competing on cost might favour the upgrading of processes. There is, of course, much blurring and overlap across such categories when attempting to translate competitive orientation into 'types of innovation'.

Under the final heading, 'characteristics of the market', are four variables. The first one captures the use of IPRs – specifically, whether or not the firm applied for a patent or registered a design. The next two variables are used to capture the technological opportunities and market opportunities as assessed by the responding firms: 1 indicates that the firm perceived that there were oppor-tunities (technological or market) and zero suggests a lack of opportunities. The final variable takes values of 1 if the enterprise operates in international markets, and zero otherwise. Table 7.5 provides an overview of the descriptive statistic for all independent variables.

Table 7.5 Descriptive statistics of the independent variables

Independent variables	Number of observations	Mean	Standard deviation
Characteristics of the innovating firms			
Newly established	4664	0.08	0.28
Small enterprise (base group)	4664	0.40	0.49
Medium enterprise	4664	0.32	0.47
Large enterprise	4664	0.28	0.45
Low innovation intensity (base group)	4298	0.68	0.47
High innovation intensity	4298	0.32	0.47
Types of knowledge source			
In-house R&D	4635	0.48	0.50
Bought-in R&D	4631	0.32	0.47
Link with other firms	4627	0.67	0.47
Links with the knowledge base	4628	0.38	0.49
International collaboration	4602	0.29	0.45
Investment in companies abroad	4620	0.11	0.31
Types of innovation			
Enterprise competes on innovations	4558	0.24	0.43
Enterprise competes on improvements	4558	0.23	0.42
Enterprise competes on business models	4558	0.16	0.37
Enterprise competes on cost (base group)	4558	0.34	0.47
Characteristics of the market			
IPRs	4613	0.15	0.36
Technological opportunities	4594	0.40	0.49
Market opportunities	4596	0.58	0.49
International market	4588	0.50	0.50

Source: Authors' elaboration on the Innobarometer, European Commission (2009a).

Most of the dependent variables are observed for 4664 firms (out of 5234 observations in the initial database) in T1 (and 4645 and 4671 in T2 and T3 respectively), and Table 7.5 presents descriptive statistics for the independent variables based on these 4664 observations. With respect to some of the independent variables, there are missing observations where respondents stated that they did not know the answer. Specifically, 4298 respondents provided a valid response with respect to their innovation intensity and so on. Because of missing values (and missing values not occurring systematically by appearing within the same observations) we have a final dataset of 3959 observations in T1 (3886 T2 and 3890 T3) that is used in the regressions. This dataset is the largest possible dataset that contains observations for all dependent and independent variables.

In Table 7.5, the column entitled 'mean' gives the mean value for our variables. Because these are all dummy variables, this column is the share of enterprises that engage in a specific activity – for example, 0.08 or 8 per cent of firms were newly established, 40 per cent were small, and 50 per cent of firms reported that they operated in international markets.

Methodology

We used regressions to analyse the relationships between our dependent and independent variables. Table 7.6 provides the zero order correlations among the dependent and independent variables, reporting polychoric correlations for the categorical dependent variables and tetrachoric correlations between the binary independent variables.

The correlations reveal, in line with our expectations and Table 7.3, that there is a higher correlation between the dependent variables 'investment during the crisis' and 'following on from the crisis' than with 'investment before the crisis' (both with respect to T2 and T3). Among the independent variables, the highest overlap exists between in-house R&D and bought-in R&D ($r=0.63$; $P<0.01$). Previous studies have shown that internal and bought-in R&D activities are complementing strategies, rather than substitutes (Cassiman and Veugelers, 2006). A high overlap also exists between 'international collaboration' and 'investing in companies located abroad' ($r=0.65$; $P<0.01$), and both these variables and 'operating in international markets' ($r=0.54$; $P<0.01$ and $r=0.53$; $P<0.01$ respectively), suggesting that these variables taken together might be indicative of an international orientation of firms.[6] The variables in the category 'types of innovation' are mutually exclusive groups, and this is why the tetrachoric correlations return a value of -1. Competing on cost is our base comparison group in the regressions.

It is a limitation of our dependent variables that we do not have continuous data and so we cannot use the classic linear model. The dependent variables are categorical variables that take the following categories: 1 = decrease in innovation-related investment; 2 = innovation investment maintained; 3 = increase in innovation-related investment.

We report the results from two estimation models: a logistic regression model and a multinomial logistic regression model. The logistic regression predicting

Table 7.6 Correlations among the dependent and independent variables

Dependent variables	1	2	3
Investment in innovation-related activity			
1 Investment before the crisis	1.00		
2 During the crisis	0.28	1.00	
3 Following on from the crisis	0.21	0.44	1.00

Independent variables	1	2	3	4	5	6	7	8	9	10	11	12	13	14	15	16	17	18	19	
Characteristics of the innovating firms																				
1 Newly established	1.00																			
2 Small enterprise (base group)	0.09	1.00																		
3 Medium enterprise	0.02	-1.00	1.00																	
4 Large enterprise	-0.13	-1.00	-1.00	1.00																
5 Low innovation intensity (base)	-0.03	0.05	-0.02	-0.05	1.00															
6 High innovation intensity	0.03	-0.05	0.02	0.05	-1.00	1.00														
Types of knowledge source																				
7 In-house R&D	-0.03	-0.29	0.03	0.31	-0.28	0.28	1.00													
8 Bought-in R&D	-0.02	-0.31	0.01	0.33	-0.15	0.15	0.63	1.00												
9 Link with other firms	0.08	-0.15	-0.01	0.19	-0.28	0.28	0.45	0.37	1.00											
10 Links with the knowledge base	0.02	-0.25	0.01	0.27	-0.25	0.25	0.53	0.51	0.58	1.00										
11 International collaboration	-0.06	-0.19	-0.02	0.23	-0.25	0.25	0.41	0.36	0.47	0.37	1.00									
12 Investment in companies abroad	-0.06	-0.25	-0.09	0.34	-0.16	0.16	0.38	0.35	0.39	0.29	0.65	1.00								
Types of innovation																				
13 Enterprise competes on innovations	-0.01	-0.02	0.01	0.02	-0.20	0.20	0.21	0.18	0.18	0.17	0.13	0.13	1.00							
14 Competes on improvements	0.05	-0.06	0.03	0.04	0.03	-0.03	0.04	0.00	0.09	0.05	0.04	-0.07	-1.00	1.00						
15 Competes on business models	-0.04	0.01	-0.04	0.03	-0.05	0.05	0.05	0.06	0.13	0.08	0.06	0.12	-1.00	-1.00	1.00					
16 Competes on cost (base group)	-0.02	0.02	0.00	-0.03	0.14	-0.14	-0.14	-0.17	-0.15	-0.20	-0.14	-0.11	-1.00	-1.00	-1.00	1.00				
Characteristics of the market																				
17 IPRs	-0.05	-0.24	-0.06	0.31	-0.26	0.26	0.53	0.44	0.39	0.39	0.38	0.36	0.19	0.05	0.00	-0.18	1.00			
18 Technological opportunities	0.00	-0.18	0.00	0.21	-0.31	0.31	0.39	0.32	0.48	0.43	0.30	0.28	0.18	0.07	0.08	-0.19	0.31	1.00		
19 Market opportunities	0.03	-0.16	0.02	0.18	-0.27	0.27	0.35	0.35	0.28	0.31	0.41	0.29	0.18	0.04	0.13	-0.16	0.33	0.50	1.00	
20 International market	-0.02	-0.23	0.01	0.26	-0.17	0.17	0.35	0.26	0.26	0.22	0.54	0.53	0.11	0.02	0.01	-0.05	0.36	0.22	0.37	1.00

Source: Authors' elaboration on the Innobarometer, European Commission (2009a).

Note
Polychoric correlations between the dependent variables, and tetrachoric correlations between the independent variables, are reported. The variables Compete on innovations, improvements, business models and cost are mutually exclusive, and thus yield a tetrachoric correlation of –1.

increased innovation investment compared to both the remaining outcomes taken together (decreased and maintained) is presented because the interpretation of the coefficients is easier; however, the model ignores that the firm is presented with three choices – to increase, decrease or maintain investment. The latter is picked up by the multinomial logistic regression. Based on one multinomial logistic regression, three sets of coefficients are reported: the first set of coefficients compares the choice to increase investment with maintained investment; the second set compares increase with decrease in investment; and the third set compares the effects of the independent variables on maintaining investment compared with decreasing investment. We now turn to the presentation of the empirical results.

Results

Two models are presented in this section. The first – logistic regression – reports coefficients that are indicative of the probability to increase innovation investment if the independent variables – all dummies – take a value of 1, i.e. the characteristic such as 'newly established' is met. It is reported in Table 7.7.

Before the crisis (column T1 in Table 7.7), and with respect to the 'characteristics of the innovating firms', the coefficients suggest that firms are more likely to increase innovation investment if they exhibit high innovation intensity (our proxy for stock of investment). The coefficient $b = 0.97$ ($P < 0.01$) is the largest coefficient in the column T1. Size and age are not significantly associated with increased investment, but the positive sign of the coefficients is in line with technological accumulation patterns (as per Table 7.1). During the crisis (T2), 'large size' is negatively associated with increased investment, meaning that small firms (our base group) are statistically more likely to increase investment compared with the group of large firms. The coefficient $b = -0.64$ ($P < 0.01$) is the most influential coefficient in the column T2. Following on from the crisis (T3), new entrants are more likely to increase investment ($b = 0.27$; $P < 0.10$). Both patterns, small firms in T2 and new entrants in T3, lean towards the creative destruction hypothesis (as per Table 7.1).

In relation to 'types of knowledge source', our second category of independent variables, there are positive and significant coefficients for 'in-house R&D' and 'bought-in R&D' before the crisis supporting accumulation of technology before the crisis. 'In-house R&D' is not significant during the crisis, but is positively associated with increased investment following on from the crisis, while 'bought-in R&D' is not significant in either T2 or T3 and the sign of the coefficients are negative. 'Link with other firms' as well as 'international collaboration' is significant throughout, and irrespectively of the time period (T1, T2 or T3). We use 'link with other firms' as a proxy for access to applied knowledge that we thought less closely linked to accumulation compared with generic knowledge (proxied by 'links with universities and research institutes', which remains insignificant throughout). Thus, the collaboration variables do not suggest a change in pattern from before the crisis to during the crisis. Finally,

Table 7.7 Factors explaining the choice to increase innovation investment compared to maintaining or decreasing investment (combined) over time

Dependent variable: increase in innovation-related investment	Before the crisis	During the crisis	Following on from the crisis
Estimation method: logistic	(T1)	(T2)	(T3)
Characteristics of the innovating firms			
Newly established	−0.19 (0.13)	−0.12 (0.20)	0.27* (0.16)
Medium enterprise	0.13 (0.08)	−0.13 (0.13)	0.10 (0.11)
Large enterprise	0.12 (0.09)	−0.64*** (0.16)	−0.15 (0.13)
High innovation intensity	0.97*** (0.08)	0.20* (0.12)	0.01 (0.10)
Types of knowledge source			
In-house R&D	0.33*** (0.08)	0.21 (0.14)	0.20* (0.12)
Bought-in R&D	0.26*** (0.09)	−0.08 (0.13)	−0.07 (0.11)
Link with other firms	0.36*** (0.08)	0.33** (0.15)	0.23* (0.12)
Links with the knowledge base	0.07 (0.08)	0.15 (0.13)	0.15 (0.11)
International collaboration	0.30*** (0.09)	0.38*** (0.13)	0.35*** (0.11)
Investment in companies abroad	−0.02 (0.13)	−0.05 (0.19)	−0.33** (0.17)
Types of innovation			
Enterprise competes on innovations	0.29*** (0.10)	0.36** (0.15)	0.58*** (0.13)
Enterprise competes on improvements	0.24** (0.10)	0.22 (0.16)	0.61*** (0.13)
Enterprise competes on business models	0.14 (0.11)	0.15 (0.17)	0.52*** (0.15)
Characteristics of the market			
IPRs	0.27** (0.11)	0.32** (0.15)	0.16 (0.13)
Technological opportunities	0.20*** (0.08)	0.04 (0.12)	0.07 (0.11)
Market opportunities	0.16** (0.08)	0.40*** (0.13)	0.17 (0.11)
International market	−0.16* (0.08)	−0.02 (0.13)	0.00 (0.11)
Industry dummies	Included	Included	Included
Country dummies	Included	Included	Included
Number of observations	3959	3886	3890
Wald Chi^2 (64)	524***	150***	179***
Pseudo R^2	0.11	0.07	0.06

Notes
Robust standard errors are reported in brackets under the logistic regression coefficients.
*** $P<0.01$, ** $P<0.05$, * $P<0.10$

firms that invested in companies abroad appear less likely to increase innovation investment following on from the crisis (no effect before then in columns T1 and T2). This variable, albeit restricted to the time period starting 2006, might capture if a firm was part of a larger, multinational company. Interpreted that way, the finding is closer to a destruction hypothesis. From our theoretical point of departure, the drop in significance of in-house and bought-in R&D during and following on from the crisis lends some support for the destruction hypothesis. But the findings in this category are less clear with respect to applied and generic knowledge sources, as the coefficients are consistent across our three time periods.

Our proxies for 'types of innovation' reveal that, throughout the three periods, firms that increase investment in innovation are less likely to compete on cost than they are to compete on innovations (confirming similar results previously reported by Bogliacino and Pianta, 2010b). Firms competing on cost are also less likely to increase investment compared with firms that compete on improvements before and following on from the crisis, but not during the crisis. The size of the coefficients increases over the three time periods, which indicates that firms that compete on costs are increasingly less likely to increase innovation-related investment – specifically in T3, where the coefficients (compete on innovation, improvements and business model contrasted with competing on costs) have the strongest impact in the regression model. The sole significance of competing on innovation during the crisis, coupled with the increase in negative impact of 'competing on cost', is perhaps less indicative of accumulation as it is of destruction in T2 and T3.

With respect to 'characteristics of the market', our final category of independent variables, the coefficients in Table 7.7 for IPRs are positive and significant both before and during the crisis (but not following on from the crisis, T3). The coefficients for 'market opportunities', too, are positive and significant in T1 and increasing in terms of the size effect in T2 (during the crisis). 'Technological opportunities', however, are positively and significantly associated with increased investment only before the crisis. Strong 'IPRs' lean towards the accumulation hypothesis both before and during the crisis.

In Table 7.8, a pattern consistent with that in Table 7.7, but with greater detail with respect to the differences in the choices to maintain investment and decreasing investment, is reported. Table 7.8(a–c) contains one regression model for T1, T2 and T3 respectively, but three sets of coefficients are reported: (1) the first set of coefficients contrasts increase in innovation investment against maintaining of investment; (2) the second set contrasts increase in innovation investment against decrease in investment; and (c) the third set contrasts maintaining investment against decrease in investment.

One caveat that Table 7.8 reveals, and which cannot be seen in Table 7.7, is that firms that maintain investment, as opposed to both increase (Table 7.8a) and decrease investment (Table 7.8c), report lower innovation intensity during the crisis. Thus, reacting to the crisis by either increasing or decreasing innovation-related investment are the two choices made by the more innovative firms.

Another caveat taken from Table 7.8 is related to large firms. Before the crisis, large firms are more likely to increase investment (as opposed to decrease investment – Table 7.8b) and more likely to maintain investment (as opposed to decrease investment – Table 7.8c). In contrast, during the crisis large firms are less likely to increase investment as opposed to both the alternative choices – to maintain or decrease investment (Tables 7.8a and b). This, in line with the findings reported in Table 7.7, suggests that the role of small firms in innovation during a crisis is greater (1) than before the crisis and (2) compared with large firms during the crisis, supporting the destruction hypothesis.

Table 7.8a Factors explaining the discrete choices to increase, maintain, or decrease innovation-related investment over time

Dependent variable: increase in innovation investment (base group: maintain)	Before the crisis	During the crisis	Following on from the crisis
Estimation method: multinomial logistic	(T1)	(T2)	(T3)
Characteristics of the innovating firms			
Newly established	–0.19 (0.15)	–0.14 (0.50)	0.22 (0.19)
Medium enterprise	0.13 (0.15)	–0.18 (0.17)	0.06 (0.60)
Large enterprise	0.06 (0.56)	–0.67*** (0.00)	–0.21 (0.11)
High innovation intensity	0.99*** (0.00)	0.30** (0.02)	0.15 (0.16)
Types of knowledge source			
In-house R&D	0.39*** (0.00)	0.23 (0.10)	0.18 (0.14)
Bought-in R&D	0.23*** (0.01)	–0.09 (0.53)	–0.06 (0.62)
Link with other firms	0.42*** (0.00)	0.37** (0.01)	0.28** (0.02)
Links with the knowledge base	0.05 (0.55)	0.17 (0.19)	0.11 (0.36)
International collaboration	0.33*** (0.00)	0.41*** (0.00)	0.36*** (0.00)
Investment in companies abroad	–0.00 (0.98)	–0.04 (0.83)	–0.27 (0.13)
Types of innovation			
Enterprise competes on innovations	0.25** (0.01)	0.22 (0.16)	0.39*** (0.00)
Enterprise competes on improvements	0.21** (0.04)	0.07 (0.64)	0.47*** (0.00)
Enterprise competes on business models	0.14 (0.19)	0.08 (0.65)	0.43*** (0.00)
Characteristics of the market			
IPRs	0.32*** (0.00)	0.34** (0.03)	0.11 (0.43)
Technological opportunities	0.18** (0.03)	0.07 (0.57)	0.10 (0.35)
Market opportunities	0.13 (0.11)	0.39*** (0.00)	0.16 (0.16)
International market	–0.15* (0.09)	0.02 (0.86)	0.06 (0.61)
Industry dummies	Included	Included	Included
Country dummies	Included	Included	Included
Number of observations	3959	3886	3890
Wald Chi^2 (64)	652***	431***	419***
Pseudo R^2	0.10	0.07	0.06

Notes
Robust standard errors are reported in brackets under the multinomial logistic regression coefficients.
*** $P<0.01$, ** $P<0.05$, * $P<0.10$.

Finally, comparing the choices increase and decrease in investment in the time period following on from the crisis, Table 7.8b reports (as Table 7.7 before) newly established firms as more likely to increase investment. Among the remaining coefficients of the same set of coefficients, Table 7.8b also reports that firms with low innovation intensity (stock) increase investment in T3. But, among the same set of coefficients, 'in-house R&D' and 'links with the knowledge base' as well as 'IPRs' are significant, providing a mixed picture with some characteristics closer to creative destruction ('newly established' and 'low

Table 7.8b Factors explaining the choice to increase, maintain or decrease innovation investment over time

Dependent variable: increase in innovation investment (base group: decrease)	Before the crisis	During the crisis	Following on from the crisis
Estimation method: multinomial logistic	(T1)	(T2)	(T3)
Characteristics of the innovating firms			
Newly established	−0.16 (0.43)	−0.09 (0.68)	0.35** (0.05)
Medium enterprise	0.16 (0.23)	−0.01 (0.95)	0.16 (0.20)
Large enterprise	0.40** (0.01)	−0.54*** (0.00)	−0.04 (0.79)
High innovation intensity	0.91*** (0.00)	−0.02 (0.86)	−0.22* (0.06)
Types of knowledge sources			
In-house R&D	0.04 (0.79)	0.15 (0.33)	0.25* (0.05)
Bought-in R&D	0.34** (0.02)	−0.07 (0.66)	−0.09 (0.45)
Link with other firms	0.10 (0.45)	0.23 (0.15)	0.14 (0.29)
Links with the knowledge base	0.13 (0.35)	0.10 (0.51)	0.21* (0.09)
International collaboration	0.21 (0.14)	0.32** (0.04)	0.33*** (0.01)
Investment in companies abroad	−0.11 (0.58)	−0.06 (0.77)	−0.43** (0.02)
Types of innovations			
Enterprise competes on innovations	0.45*** (0.00)	0.71*** (0.00)	0.89*** (0.00)
Enterprise competes on improvements	0.36** (0.02)	0.55*** (0.00)	0.83*** (0.00)
Enterprise competes on business models	0.11 (0.51)	0.29 (0.13)	0.63*** (0.00)
Characteristics of the market			
IPRs	0.05 (0.76)	0.28* (0.10)	0.26* (0.08)
Technological opportunities	0.31** (0.02)	−0.04 (0.79)	−0.00 (1.00)
Market opportunities	0.27** (0.04)	0.45*** (0.00)	0.20 (0.10)
International market	−0.22* (0.09)	−0.15 (0.30)	−0.10 (0.41)
Industry dummies	Included	Included	Included
Country dummies	Included	Included	Included
Number of observations	3959	3886	3890
Wald Chi² (64)	652***	431***	419***
Pseudo R²	0.10	0.07	0.06

Notes
Robust standard errors are reported in brackets under the multinomial logistic regression coefficients.
*** $P<0.01$, ** $P<0.05$, * $P<0.10$

innovation intensity') and others closer to accumulation ('in-house R&D', 'links with the knowledge base' and 'IPRs'). Thus, while we might have expected the patterns between T2 and T3 to be highly similar but different from T1, increased investment is not necessarily done by firms with the exact same characteristics and environments across T2 and T3, and some of the patterns dominant (significant coefficients) in T1 re-emerge in T3.

Table 7.8c Factors explaining the choice to increase, maintain or decrease innovation investment over time

Dependent variable: maintained innovation investment (base group: decrease)	Before the crisis	During the crisis	Following on from the crisis
Estimation method: multinomial logistic	(T1)	(T2)	(T3)
Characteristics of the innovating firms			
Newly established	0.03 (0.88)	0.05 (0.74)	0.13 (0.32)
Medium enterprise	0.03 (0.80)	0.17* (0.07)	0.10 (0.26)
Large enterprise	0.34** (0.02)	0.13 (0.21)	0.18* (0.07)
High innovation intensity	−0.08 (0.55)	−0.32*** (0.00)	−0.37*** (0.00)
Types of knowledge source			
In-house R&D	−0.36*** (0.01)	−0.08 (0.40)	0.07 (0.42)
Bought-in R&D	0.11 (0.44)	0.02 (0.84)	−0.04 (0.70)
Link with other firms	−0.31** (0.02)	−0.13 (0.16)	−0.14 (0.11)
Links with the knowledge base	0.08 (0.56)	−0.08 (0.42)	0.11 (0.23)
International collaboration	−0.12 (0.40)	−0.09 (0.40)	−0.03 (0.78)
Investment in companies abroad	−0.11 (0.59)	−0.02 (0.88)	−0.16 (0.23)
Types of innovation			
Enterprise competes on innovations	0.20 (0.20)	0.50*** (0.00)	0.50*** (0.00)
Enterprise competes on improvements	0.15 (0.33)	0.48*** (0.00)	0.36*** (0.00)
Enterprise competes on business models	−0.03 (0.83)	0.21* (0.07)	0.19* (0.08)
Characteristics of the market			
IPRs	−0.27 (0.13)	−0.05 (0.66)	0.15 (0.20)
Technological opportunities	0.12 (0.33)	−0.11 (0.23)	−0.10 (0.22)
Market opportunities	0.14 (0.26)	0.06 (0.53)	0.04 (0.62)
International market	−0.07 (0.58)	−0.17* (0.06)	−0.16* (0.06)
Industry dummies	Included	Included	Included
Country dummies	Included	Included	Included
Number of observations	3959	3886	3890
Wald Chi2 (64)	652***	431***	419***
Pseudo R2	0.10	0.07	0.06

Notes
Robust standard errors are reported in brackets under the multinomial logistic regression coefficients.
*** $P<0.01$, ** $P<0.05$, * $P<0.10$.

Discussion

The aim of this chapter was to investigate whether the current economic downturn is significantly affecting the composition of innovating firms. During major recessions, the economic landscape is characterized by huge uncertainties about the direction of technological change, demand conditions, and new market opportunities. The first significant result at the aggregate level is that the crisis has substantially reduced the number of firms willing to increase their innovation investment, from 38 per cent to 9 per cent. There is no doubt that the crisis has brought, at least in its initial stage, 'destruction' in innovation investment. But the anatomy of these 9 per cent of firms that are still expanding their innovation investment can provide some insights to check if the gales of destruction are also bringing something creative.

We used two well-established, ideal typical models – creative destruction and creative accumulation – to frame our results (as summarized in Table 7.1). It has been assumed that there is a clear-cut division, according to which in regular times the model of creative accumulation will prevail, while in times of crisis the model of creative destruction will affirm itself. We are well aware that a clear-cut division between the two models does not exist. We recognize that both patterns of innovation co-exist and are likely also to be technology- and industry-specific (as tested empirically by Malerba and Orsenigo, 1995). However, our data suggest that during a depression firms' innovation behaviour is closer to creative destruction, while before a depression there is an overall landscape of creative accumulation.

More specifically, two hypotheses have been tested against the data: (1) that in periods of economic expansion firms which are already innovating are the most important drivers of the increase in innovation investment, supporting the technological accumulation hypothesis; and (2) that economic crises generate turbulence and newcomers are eager to spend more to innovate, confirming the creative destruction hypothesis.

The results support our argument. The identikit of the innovators has in fact changed considerably. Before an economic downturn, firms expanding their innovation are: (1) well-established; (2) engaged in formal research activities, both internally and bought-in; (3) exploit strong appropriability conditions; and (4) involved in collaboration with suppliers and customers. During an economic downturn, the few firms that are 'swimming against the stream' by increasing their innovation investment are: (1) smaller than before; (2) collaborating with other businesses; (3) exploring new market opportunities; (4) using methods of technological appropriation; and (5) less likely to compete on costs. Last, but certainly not least, it also seems that younger firms are more likely to increase innovation investment after the crisis. While before the crisis technological opportunities have a positive impact on investment, during and after the crisis this is no longer true. On the contrary, in response to the crisis firms are more likely to explore innovative solutions by looking at opportunities in new markets.

This witnesses an important change in the drivers of innovation as a result of the economic downturn. Since innovation is less based on local searching and cumulative processes, and less based on R&D activities within large firms, we conclude that the relative importance of behaviours is changing from creative accumulation to creative destruction in the snapshot of the business cycle that the Innobarometer makes it possible to observe. The fact that firms exhibit a more 'explorative' attitude, vis-à-vis an 'exploitative' attitude, is consistent with the situation of greater uncertainty that they face.

During the crisis, both formal R&D and technological opportunities stop playing a significant role in explaining companies' willingness to expand innovation. This might be interpreted as the result of a decline of technological opportunities in established sectors, which is typical during recessions characterized by technological discontinuities (Perez, 2002). Also, contrary to the previous period, innovation is driven by fresh opportunities in new markets.

It could not be taken for granted that during a period of sustained growth firms' behaviour leans towards accumulative patterns of innovation. During economic upswings firms have access to greater financial resources, and thus might be seen to be more likely to explore radical and risky solutions. Similarly, it can conceivably be maintained that during a depression large established firms are better equipped to manage a situation of fall in demand and lack of financial supply in the market. However, we show that this is not the case. The number of firms declaring an increase their innovation expenditure has dropped dramatically as a result of the crisis. It seems that what matters is not large size and internal R&D, but flexibility, collaborative arrangements and exploration of new markets.

8 Innovation in the manufacturing and service sectors

Impact and firms' strategies

Introduction: the increasing role of service innovation

The previous chapter shows how the innovation environment has shifted from one of creative accumulation prior to the crisis to one of creative destruction as a result of the crisis. This chapter investigates the innovation behaviour of the firm taking a different perspective. Are there important differences between the manufacturing sector and the service sector? Further, different strategies are pursued at the level of the firm in terms of types of innovation (i.e. product and process innovation, service innovation, organizational innovation). Which are the strategies more conducive to innovation during the crisis? Thus two different research questions arise in this analysis. The first takes a customary perspective in which differences in the innovation behaviour of the firm are analysed in the manufacturing sector vis-à-vis the service sector. In the second, the focus is on the very nature of the innovation strategies.

We know, for instance, that the introduction of new services is also playing an increasingly important role in manufacturing firms. In addition, innovation forms such as organizational innovation and marketing innovation can play a role both in manufacturing and in service firms (Evangelista and Vezzani, 2010; Tether and Tajar, 2008). Third, a combination of product with service innovation can also be a key strategy within a combined approach of product and service (Howells, 2004).

The relationship between technical change, innovation and economic development, largely discussed in Chapter 2, has been addressed within an economic system mainly characterized by the prominent role of the manufacturing sector. Within this context, innovation is that referring to technological innovation, which is the application of scientific novelties and technological developments to produce new products and to introduce new production processes. Here, R&D is regarded as the most relevant activity and the main source of innovation and competitiveness of the firm. However, the role of services has been dramatically increased over recent years, and today they play a prominent part in terms of share of output and employment in most advanced countries. The service sector has also been recognized as a key source of innovation and productivity (OECD, 2005a). In this respect, research on innovation has devoted increasing attention to the nature of the innovation activity in the service sector (Gallouj and Djellal, 2010; Gallouj and Savona, 2009).

The increasing importance of innovation activity that does not involve technological improvements has been largely recognized over the past decade (Arundel *et al.*, 2008). In the latest edition of the *Oslo Manual* (OECD, 2005b), innovation is defined as 'the implementation of a new or significantly improved product (good or service), or process, a new marketing method, or a new organizational method in business practices, workplace organization or external relations'.

Technology also plays an increasing role in the service sector. The firm-oriented business sector is characterized by an intensive use of knowledge and highly skilled human resources. Also, recent data regarding R&D expenditure of firms in the service sector show that the idea that the service sector is a mere user of technology is no longer true. High levels of R&D expenditure can be found mainly in the *knowledge-intensive* service sector, such as computer services and R&D services (Miles, 2005). Recent studies also point to the role played by services in terms of internationalization and innovation (Castellacci, 2010; Frenz *et al.*, 2005).

A fundamental step forward in analysing the role of service innovation has been the growing availability of data at the level of the firm, mainly by means of the Community Innovation Survey (CIS) and, more recently, the Innobarometer Survey. This has occurred in conjunction with a progressive shift of the empirical analysis regarding the patterns and strategies of innovation toward the firm level (Srholec and Verspagen, 2008). Along this line, recent empirical research has investigated the patterns of service innovation, as well as the impact of service innovation on productivity and economic performance (Abreu *et al.*, 2010; Cainelli *et al.*, 2006; Evangelista, 2000), while another strand of literature has explored the specific importance of non-technological innovation in the service sector (Filippetti, 2011; Hollenstein, 2003; Tether and Tajar, 2008).

The effects of the crisis on the manufacturing sector and the service sector

We have repeatedly argued that huge recessions are characterized by major technological discontinuities. According to the neo-Schumpeterian argument, economic depressions go hand in hand with radical technological innovation and structural change. Thus, structural change is an intrinsic feature of economic change and development. Over recent decades, most industrialized countries have experienced a secular trend of the service sector that has largely surpassed the manufacturing sector in advanced countries in terms of share of output and creation of employment. This section looks briefly at the effects of the current economic downturn on this trend.

Figure 8.1 shows the dynamic of the added value of the service sector and manufacturing sector in terms of share of GDP regarding the European countries in the past five years, while Figure 8.2 reports the relative variation rates.

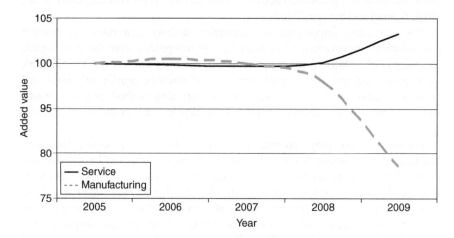

Figure 8.1 Added value in the service sector and manufacturing sector in the European Union, share of GDP, 2005–2009 (base year=2005).

Note
Authors' elaboration on Eurostat data.

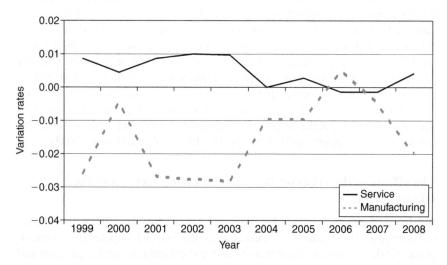

Figure 8.2 Added value in the service sector and manufacturing sector in the European Union, variation rates, 1998–2009.

Note
Authors' elaboration on Eurostat data.

It clearly appears that the circumstances of the economic downturn cannot be said to be neutral. Rather, we can claim that the gap between the manufacturing and service sectors in terms of share of added value is increasing as a result of the current economic crisis.

This is also reflected in terms of employment. Figure 8.3 reports the dynamic of the number of workers regarding the manufacturing sector and service sector in the US, EU27 and OECD countries. The drop in workers employed in the manufacturing sector is substantially larger that the moderate slowdown experienced in the service sector.

The first impression we can draw is that the crisis is exerting a non-neutral effect in the manufacturing sector in opposition to the service sector. Does this align with innovation strategies at the level of the firm? The rest of the chapter attempts to respond to this question.

The impact of the crisis, types of innovation and innovation strategies

The impact of the crisis and types of innovation

As usual, the Innobarometer Survey (European Commission, 2009b) is employed at the firm level (see the data section in Chapter 3 for a detailed description). Here, we only report some additional descriptive statistics that are relevant for this chapter's analysis (see Tables A8.1 and A8.2 in the Appendix to this chapter).

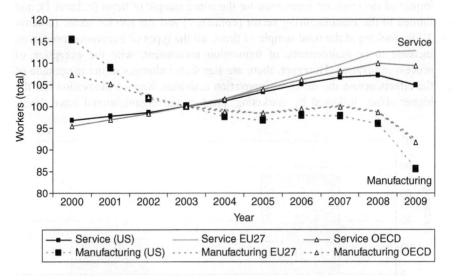

Figure 8.3 Workers in the manufacturing sector and services sector, US, EU27, and OECD – total, 2000–2009, (base year=2003).

Note
Authors' elaboration on OECD Stat data.

Dependent variable. In order to estimate the impact of the crisis on innovation investment of a firm across the types of innovation a logit model is employed. The dependent variable – inno2009 – is a categorical variable assuming a value equal to 1 where the firm reported having maintained *or* increased its innovation investment *as a direct result of the economic downturn,* and a value equal to 0 if the firm reported having decreased it. Figure 8.4 shows the percentages for the variable. This section's aim is to investigate the role played by different innovation types and innovation strategies in relation to firms which reported increasing or maintaining investment in response to the crisis; that is, inno2009 = 1.

Independent variables. The independent variables included in the model are the types of innovation activity carried out by the firm (in the three-year period 2006–2008). Five different types of innovation (non-mutually excludable) are identified by means of categorical variables (1/0 type): (1) product innovation; (2) process innovation; (3) service innovation; (4) marketing innovation; and (5) organizational innovation (see Table 8.1 for descriptive statistics).

Control variables. Four dummies at the firm level are also included: (1) a variable indicating whether the firm operates in international markets; (2) three variables accounting for the size of the firm as measured by the number of workers; (3) a variable controlling for the firm age; and (4) three variables accounting for innovation intensity, as measured in terms of share of turnover dedicated to innovation activity. Finally, dummies accounting for the industry and for the country have been included, as is customary in this type of analysis.

Table 8.2 show the robust estimates of three logit models estimating the impact of the crisis on innovation for the entire sample of firms (column 1), and limited to the manufacturing sector (column 2) and the service sector (column 3). By looking at the total sample of firms, all the types of innovation predict an increase in or maintenance of innovation investment, with the exception of process innovation. However, there are significant changes in the magnitude of the effects across the different innovation activities. Service innovation has the higher effect, followed by marketing, product and organizational innovations.

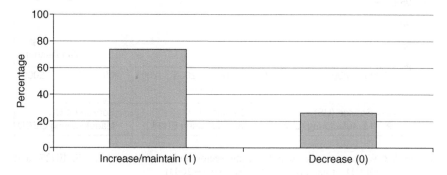

Figure 8.4 Share of firms increasing or maintaining, and those decreasing, innovation investment in response to the crisis.

Table 8.1 Descriptive statistics and correlation between independent variables

Variable	Obs.	Mean	Product innovation	Process innovation	Service innovation	Marketing innovation	Organizational innovation
Product innovation	4693	0.56	1.00				
Process innovation	4876	0.57	0.32	1.00			
Service innovation	4895	0.52	0.21	0.30	1.00		
Marketing innovation	4913	0.49	0.25	0.31	0.29	1.00	
Organizational innovation	4991	0.54	0.21	0.36	0.30	0.38	1.00

Table 8.2 The impact of the crisis and types of innovation activity

Dependent variable: investment in innovation during the crisis	Total sample	Manufacturing only	Service only
Product innovation	0.29** (0.14)	0.75*** (0.28)	0.10 (0.19)
Process innovation	0.19 (0.14)	0.25 (0.25)	0.13 (0.19)
Service innovation	0.74*** (0.14)	1.02*** (0.22)	0.60*** (0.21)
Marketing innovation	0.39*** (0.14)	0.23 (0.23)	0.50** (0.20)
Organizational innovation	0.29** (0.14)	0.13 (0.23)	0.43** (0.20)
Control variables			
International markets	0.25* (0.13)	0.63** (0.26)	0.11 (0.17)
Small firms	0.22 (0.14)	0.41* (0.24)	0.28 (0.19)
Medium–large firms	−0.32** (0.16)	−0.44* (0.26)	−0.16 (0.23)
New established firms (2001)	−0.27 (0.22)	−0.91** (0.45)	−0.12 (0.29)
Innovation intensity (between 25% and 50% of turnover)	0.26* (0.13)	0.13 (0.22)	0.43** (0.18)
Innovation intensity (more than 50% of turnover)	0.64** (0.25)	0.81* (0.42)	0.62* (0.36)
Country dummy	included	included	included
Industry dummy (NACE 2-digit)	included	included	included
Observations	3476	1367	1738

Notes
Robust standard errors in parentheses.
Levels of significance: *** $P<0.01$, ** $P<0.05$, * $P<0.1$.

Looking at column 2, the picture changes substantially; here, service innovation and product innovation are the only significant coefficients. The situation changes again when looking at column 3; here, product innovation is no longer significant, while service innovation is still the type of innovation showing the larger coefficient, followed by marketing innovation and organizational innovation. These results suggest that there are some patterns in the way firms react in the manufacturing and service sector, depending on their types of innovation. Further, this evidence seems to suggest the presence of complex innovation strategies in which firms combine different types of innovation activities.

The impact of the crisis and innovation strategies

Table 8.3 reports the relative importance of four different innovation strategies for the entire sample, and relative to the manufacturing and service sectors. The first strategy is a *pure technology* strategy, as defined by firms that are devoted solely to product innovation and/or process innovation. The second identified strategy – *combined strategy* – refers to firms that carry out both product *and* service innovation. The third strategy – *soft strategy* – identifies firms that carry out service innovation, marketing innovation and organizational innovation at the same time. Finally, the fourth strategy – *multifaceted strategy* – is that addressing those companies that are involved in all the five types of innovation activity. Note that the five strategies are mutually exclusive. While the

Table 8.3 Innovation strategies

Innovation strategies	Total sample %	Manufacturing %	Services %
Pure technology	12	33	–
Combined	11	9	13
Soft	7	3	9
Multifaceted	16	14	18

Note
The four innovation strategies are mutually exclusive.

multifaceted strategy is the widest spread among the firms, one can observe some differences across the sectors. Specifically, the *pure technology* strategy is prominent in the manufacturing sector, while the *combined strategy* is relatively more important in the service sector, along with the *soft strategy*.

Similarly to Table 8.2, Table 8.4 exhibits the robust estimates of three logit models using the four identified strategies as independent variables. Overall, the *pure technology* strategy does not arise as significant across the three models. By contrast, the *multifaceted strategy* is positive and significant in all the three cases. With regard to the other two strategies, the *combined strategy* is the most prominent strategy in the manufacturing sub-sample, while the *soft strategy* is the most relevant strategy regarding the service sub-sample.

Table 8.4 The impact of the crisis and the innovation strategy of the firm

Dependent variable: investment in innovation during the crisis	Total sample	Manufacturing only	Service only
Innovation strategy			
Pure technology	−0.36 (0.24)	−0.43 (0.27)	n.a.
Combined	0.94*** (0.16)	1.10*** (0.28)	0.75*** (0.23)
Soft	1.13*** (0.19)	0.34 (0.52)	1.19*** (0.24)
Multifaceted	1.06*** (0.15)	0.98*** (0.25)	1.15*** (0.20)
Control variables			
International markets	0.22* (0.12)	0.45** (0.23)	0.09 (0.16)
Small firms	0.09 (0.13)	0.22 (0.22)	0.13 (0.18)
Medium–large firms	−0.39** (0.15)	−0.47* (0.24)	−0.31 (0.22)
Newly established firms (2001)	−0.10 (0.20)	−0.53 (0.38)	0.05 (0.26)
Innovation intensity (between 25% and 50% of turnover)	0.28** (0.12)	0.23 (0.20)	0.34* (0.17)
Innovation intensity (more than 50% of turnover)	0.68*** (0.24)	0.91** (0.40)	0.63* (0.33)
Industry dummies	included	included	included
Country dummies	included	included	included
Observations	3972	1528	2043

Notes
Robust standard errors in parentheses.
Levels of significance: *** $P<0.01$, ** $P<0.05$, * $P<0.1$.
Reference variables: Large firms; innovation intensity (below 25% of turnover).

Concluding remarks

This chapter has examined the innovation behaviours of the firm during the crisis, focusing on the types of innovation and innovation strategies, taking a comparative perspective between the manufacturing sector and the service sector. We have shown that the crisis is exerting a different impact on the service sector in opposition to the manufacturing sector. Specifically, the negative effect has been less prominent in the former vis-à-vis the latter. This, at least in the observed period of the crisis, is bringing about a widening of the gap between the manufacturing and the service sector in terms of relative added values and number of workers.

We then investigated whether, at the level of the firm, there are also relevant differences in terms of types of innovation and innovation strategies. Based on our empirical results, we can draw the following conclusions:

- Overall, firms involved in service innovation tend to be more likely to invest in innovation during the crisis, *both* in the manufacturing sector and in the service sector
- Within the manufacturing sector, service innovation and product innovation are the best predictors of innovation investment. Regarding the service sector, marketing and organizational innovation are more prominent, along with service innovation.
- Interesting results also arise in terms of innovation strategy. Specifically, a strategy combining product and service innovation is the most important in the manufacturing sector. With regard to the service sector, the firms carrying out innovation in services coupled with organization and marketing innovation are those mainly associated with innovation investment during the crisis;
- Finally, firms involved in all the types of innovation tend to be more innovative during the crisis, regardless of the sector.

The importance of the *combined strategy* regarding the manufacturing sector suggests that service innovation is also key in the manufacturing sector, as suggested by the 'synthesis' stream of literature. It also implies that the presence of an innovative manufacturing sector can be an important driver for innovation in the service sector. On the other hand, the major importance of non-technological forms of innovation in the service sector suggests the presence of some specificities in the innovation patterns, as also suggested by the literature.

Appendix

Table A8.1 Distribution of the sample across sectors

Activity	Classificazione Ocse	Numerosity	%	% cumulate
Manufacturing sector	High and medium high tech	513	10.90	10.90
	Low and medium low tech	1406	29.90	40.80
Services sector	Knowledge intensive service	922	19.60	60.40
	Less knowledge intensive service	1863	39.60	100.00
	Total	4704		
	Non innovative firms	328		
	Sectors not classified	202		
	Total	5234		

Table A8.2 Distribution of the innovative firms according to size and sectors

Activity	Size				Total	%
	20–49	50–249	250–499	More than 500		
High and medium high tech	165	164	116	68	513	10.91
Low and medium low tech	601	433	287	85	1406	29.89
Knowledge intensive service	372	287	178	85	922	19.60
Less knowledge intensive service	982	542	234	105	1863	39.60
Other sectors					530	
Total	*2120*	*1426*	*815*	*343*	*4704*	*100.00*

9 Is 'slack' good for innovation in times of crisis?[1]

Introduction

In organizational theory, the capacity of an organization to absorb environmental variations is a central feature of organizational effectiveness. In this respect, the concept of 'slack' has been developed. That is, 'the ability to adapt to dramatic shift of discontinuities in the environment is frequently linked to the absorption mechanism termed organizational slack' (Bourgeois, 1981). Slack has also been considered in relation to innovation. It has been argued that slack is necessary for firms to innovate, as it allows them to engage in search and experimentation (Levinthal and March, 1981; March, 1981). This makes slack an ideal candidate when investigating the innovation behaviour of the firm during a crisis. In fact, a major recession can be represented as a big shock in the economic environment that brings about major discontinuities in the market, demand and technology. This chapter addresses empirically the following question: *Is slack good for innovation during an economic crisis?*

Slack has been generally defined as 'the pool of resources in an organization that is in excess of the minimum necessary to produce a given level of organizational output' (Nohria and Gulati, 1996). Slack resources refer to unused capacity, redundant employees, and unnecessary capital expenditures. Slack has been also criticized, as it represents a form of inefficiency of the firm, especially when firms are facing an increasing global competitive environment (Jensen, 1986, 1993). Hence, a specific tension can arise, as organizations risk undermining their innovation capabilities if they reduce slack. This has led scholars to investigate empirically whether slack facilitates or inhibits innovation (Greve, 2003; Nohria and Gulati, 1996, 1997).

In principle, both organizational and financial slack can be good for innovation during a crisis. Severe depressions are characterized by a substantial drop in the aggregated demand. This results in a plunge in sales and financial resources for the firm. As we know from the literature, innovation is usually financed by means of internal resources (Hall, 2002; Hall and Lerner, 2010), and thus is heavily dependent on the dynamic of the profit (Cainelli *et al.*, 2006). In addition, during a recession firms are more likely to face credit rationing and an increase in the cost of external financial capital. It might therefore be expected that in the face of a huge recession, firms which have larger financial resources can take advantage of this situation by investing more in innovation. We refer to this circumstance as *financial slack*.

The second form of slack regards the role played by searching and uncertainty. The other relevant feature that characterizes a major economic downturn is the high degree of uncertainty in the economic system. As suggested by the Schumpeterian literature (Freeman *et al.*, 1982; Perez, 2002; Schumpeter, 1939), these periods are characterized by major shift from old to new markets, industries and technological systems. This increases the role and scope for *searching* activity in organizations, both to cope with and to take advantage of the major discontinuities that arise. We might, then, expect that firms which have an organizational structure with higher searching capabilities are more likely to be innovative during an economic downturn. We define this circumstance as *organizational slack*.

To summarize, the theory – supported by some empirical evidence – predicts that slack is necessary for organizations to innovate. We advance the hypothesis that this is increasingly significant during a major depression, when the availability of financial resources and searching capabilities increases in importance and scope. This chapter aims to test this hypothesis empirically. The rest of the chapter is organized as follows. The next section introduces the debate in the organization theory and innovation theory. We then explain how we operationalized these two types of slack, and illustrate our empirical strategy. The results of the empirical analysis are presented in the next section, before being discussed in the last section.

Setting the scene: slack and innovation

According to the behavioural theory of the firm proposed by Cyert and March (1963), slack is important within an organization to address goal conflict between political coalitions. Developing on this first insight, scholars have argued that slack is vital for innovation for two reasons: slack leads to relaxation of control, and slack represents funds whose use may be approved even in cases of uncertainty (Nohria and Gulati, 1996). Thus, slack encourages experimentation within organizations pursuing innovative projects (Bourgeois, 1981).

Developing innovation is a form of organizational search. This has been emphasized both by the organizational and behavioural theory of the firm, and by the evolutionary theory of innovation. The former underlines the organizational processes for performance evaluation, search and decision-making, and how these affect the evolution of the organization. Here, innovation development refers to the 'search stage'. Within this framework, organizations with excess resources engage in slack research – that is, search for 'innovation that would not be approved in the face of scarcity' (Cyert and March, 1963). As March (1981) put it, 'slack protects individuals and groups, who pursue change for personal of professional reasons, from normal organizational controls. As a result, it has been argued that one of the ways in which organizations search when successful is through slack' (p. 573).

The engagement in searching along a variety of experimental solutions is also at the core of the evolutionary theorizing of the firm (Dosi, 1988; Nelson and Winter, 1982, 2002). In the evolutionary framework, economic agents have an imperfect understanding of the world in which they operate – due either to lack of information about it, or, more fundamentally, to an imprecise knowledge of its structure (Dosi *et al.*, 1996). In this context, searching activity is related to learning, which in turn allows the firm to innovate over time (Amendola and Bruno, 1990). Also in this case, searching and learning are framed within the organizational structure, namely within the concept of *organizational routines*. The latter represent behavioural procedures and decisional rules that firms develop to cope with changes in the market, and which are firm-specific and depend upon its past experience and activity (Dosi *et al.*, 2002; Nelson and Winter, 1982).[2]

The second form of slack we are concerned about here is that of *financial slack*. The latter pertains to financial reserves that an organization can maintain in the form of cash or financial instruments. The relationship between finance, innovation and R&D has been explored since the contribution of Schumpeter (1911 (1934)) describing the fundamental role played by the banking system in allowing the entrepreneur to enter the market with an innovation (see the discussion in Chapter 1). Later, two influential contributions, by Nelson (1959) and Arrow (1962), stressed the difficulties for firm to engage in R&D activity because of the presence of spillover effect, thus calling for the intervention of the State. The main problem resides in the specific nature of innovation activities with respect to other forms of investment. Innovation is a very risky activity, as its outcome is uncertain and (eventually) yields returns in the medium to long term.

One issue that has been explored in the literature is that of the type of financing related to innovation investment (for reviews, see Hall and Lerner, 2010, and O'Sullivan, 2005). One of the implications of the well-known Modigliani–Miller (1958) argument is that a firm choosing the optimal levels of investment should be indifferent to its capital structure, and should face the same price for investment and R&D investment on the margin. With respect to innovation, three main lines of arguments have been developed regarding why there might be a gap between the external and internal costs of capital: (1) asymmetric information between inventor and investor; (2) moral hazard; and (3) tax considerations (Hall, 2002; Hall and Lerner, 2010). On the basis of theory and empirical evidence, Hall and Lerner (2010) have drawn two conclusions. First, small and start-up firms in the R&D-intensive industry face a higher cost of capital than their larger competitors, and firms in other industries. Second, large R&D firms prefer to use internally generated funds for financing investment. These arguments parallel those made in a survey on finance and innovation by O'Sullivan (2005), where she also claims that R&D-intensive firms are more inclined to rely on internal funds to finance their investment.

The second relevant form of financial slack is that not directly related to innovation activity. As Greve (2003) explains, these types of financial reserves are not directed to the development of innovations, but they may affect decisions to continue or discontinue R&D projects. The lack of financial slack may be particularly damaging for innovations whose funding is at risk when the outcome is not yet clear enough or because of the ambiguous signals that they generate (Garud and Van de Ven, 1992). In other words, an excess of financial resources would facilitate the firm in engaging in risky and uncertain activity – such as innovation. This is the case regardless of the fact that these resources are specifically devoted to innovation activity. Here, the emphasis is on the general wealth of the firm: a situation of financial scarcity would in fact reduce the willingness of the management to allocate resources to innovation. A case in point is the reaction of the *chaebol* in South Korea during the 1997 crisis, as documented in Keller and Samuels (2003). They report that the crisis has exerted a significant influence over industrial R&D activities. The large *chaebol* reduced their R&D activities by about 13 per cent during the year following the onset of the crisis, in order to cope with short-term liquidity problems.

Table 9.1 summarizes the main arguments discussed in this section. Concerning organizational slack, organizational theory insists upon the internal incentives and capability of the organization to engage in innovation-driven searching activities. The evolutionary theory of innovation has stressed the importance of searching and learning processes being embedded in the organizational routine of the firm. This allows the firm to cope with external changes through innovating over time. As far as financial slack is concerned, the theory of innovation underlines the prominent role played by internal funds for the firm to finance innovation activity, while organizational theory emphasizes the importance of an excess of financial resources within the firm to encourage the decision to innovate. The next section illustrates how we measured and operationalized financial and organizational slack in our data.

Table 9.1 Organizational slack and financial slack in theory

	Organizational slack	*Financial slack*
Organizational theory	Slack leads to relaxation of control, and represents funds whose use may be approved even in case of uncertainty.	An excess of financial resources would facilitate the firm's decision to engage in risky and uncertain activity.
	Slack encourages experimentation within organizations pursuing innovative projects.	
Innovation theory	Searching and learning along a variety of experimental solutions leads to innovation.	Firms tend to rely on internal funds to finance their investment.
	Embedded in organizational routines.	

How do we measure organizational and financial slack

In 'slack' research, innovation has been measured both using the innovation count approach (i.e. by counting the number of innovations introduced by the firm) and by relying on secondary data about R&D expenditure of the company (Greve, 2003; Nohria and Gulati, 1996, 1997). We employ a measure of innovation investment of the firm, where innovation should be regarded in a broad sense, including R&D, industrial design, organizational innovation, the acquisition of machinery and so on. In this sense, this measure should be intended more in terms of innovation behaviour of the firm, rather than a direct measure of innovation. That is, here we are mainly concerned with the behaviour of the firm in terms of innovation as a response to a substantial change in the environment as a result of the crisis.

It is difficult to measure slack directly, because it can be deployed in several ways and forms. In many cases slack has been measured by using antecedents of slack as indicators, such as financial data at the level of the firm (Bourgeois, 1981; Davis and Stout, 1992; Majumdar and Venkataraman, 1993), and also at the subunit level of the firm (Nohria and Gulati, 1996). Drawing on the Innobarometer Survey (European Commission, 2009b), we picked several variables proxying for both organizational and financial slack.

In order to proxy organizational slack, we referred to several variables pointing to deliberate efforts of the firm directed to reinforcing the searching capabilities of the organizational structure aiming to develop innovation. Table 9.2 reports the variables and the related questions of the Innobarometer. All these variables are categorical variables of the type 1/0. Five variables have been taken in order to proxy organizational slack: organizational innovation, mechanisms for employees to submit new ideas, the creation of cross-functional teams to develop innovative projects, participation in Internet-based discussion forums related to innovation, and team-working capacity to support innovation. All these cases witness an effort of the firm to intervene in the organizational structure of the firm in order to encourage and reinforce searching activities aiming to develop innovation.

One single variable has been taken to proxy the level of slack financial resources that are present in the firm at the onset of the economic downturn, as summarized by the dynamic of profits of the previous three years. We have divided the firms in the sample into three groups depending on their turnover dynamic: decrease, small decrease or small increase, and substantial increase. Here, the idea is that firms with an increase in turnover of more than 10 per cent in the previous period are those with financial slack.

Along with slack, we have also tried to capture the intensity of innovation of the firm. The rationale for taking into account the innovation intensity of the firm is that innovation presents persistence to a relevant extent. Empirical studies have shown that innovative firms are more likely to keep on innovating with respect to non-innovative firms (Cefis and Orsenigo, 2001; Geroski *et al.*, 1997). Table 9.3 shows the variables proxying for innovation intensity of the firm,

Table 9.2 Variables and questions addressing organizational and financial slack

Type of slack	Name of the variable	Question in the Innobarometer Survey
Organizational slack	ORG_INNO	Has your company introduced new or significantly improved organizational structures (e.g. knowledge management, workplace organization or external relations)?
	IDEA	Since 2006, has your company started or increased internal mechanisms for employees to submit innovative ideas?
	TEAM	Since 2006, has your company started or increased the creation of cross-functional or cross-departmental teams on innovation projects?
	FORUM	Since 2006, has your company created or participated in Internet-based discussion forums to support its innovative activities?
	TEAM2	Since 2006, has your company targeted any of the following competences in its training or recruitment activities to support innovation, namely team-working capacity?
Financial slack	TURNlow	Firm whose turnover decreased by more than 5% from 2006 to 2008
	TURNmid	Firm whose turnover decreased by less than 5% or increased less than 10% from 2006 to 2008
	TURNhi	Firm whose turnover increased by more than 10% from 2006 to 2008

Table 9.3 Variables addressing innovation intensity

INNOhi	Please think of the total amount spent by your firm in 2008 on all innovative activities. What percentage does this represent of your total 2008 turnover: more than 5%?
INNOlow	Please think of the total amount spent by your firm in 2008 on all innovative activities. What percentage does this represent of your total 2008 turnover: less than 5%?
INNOincrease	Compared to 2006, has the total amount spent by your firm spent on all innovation activities in 2008 increased (adjusted for inflation)?
INNNOstay	Compared to 2006, has the total amount spent by your firm spent on all innovation activities in 2008 stayed approximately the same (adjusted for inflation)?
INNOdecrease	Compared to 2006, has the total amount spent by your firm on all innovation activities in 2008 decreased (adjusted for inflation)?

similarly to Table 9.1. The variables address the level of innovation expenditures as a share of the turnover, as well as the dynamic of innovation investment of the firm in the period preceding the crisis.

Empirical strategy and findings

The strategy followed in the empirical analysis of this chapter is the following. We first carried out a multiple correspondence analysis to group firms according to the variables described above proxying organizational slack, financial slack, and innovation intensity. By means of an ordered logit model, we then estimated to what extent the groups of firm identified in the correspondence analysis are inclined to invest in innovation in response to the crisis.

The multiple correspondence analysis

We were interested in whether underlying patterns exist in how the firms answered these questions, and we therefore used multiple correspondence analysis (a statistical technique equivalent to principal components analysis for categorical data) to examine the data. In more detail, correspondence analysis is a descriptive exploratory statistical technique designed to analyse two-way or multi-way tables containing some measure of correspondence between the rows and columns. The extraction of dimensions in (multiple) correspondence analysis is similar to the identification of components in principal components analysis, or factors in factor analysis. In this analysis it is common to use only the first two or three dimensions, as these capture the greatest deviation from statistical independence in the data. See Greenacre (1984) for a comprehensive description of the method.

For this analysis, the eight variables addressing slack (see Table 9.2) and the five variables related to innovation investment (see Table 9.3) were employed. The analysis was carried out employing the indicator matrix method with a standard normalization.[3] As is customary in this type of analysis, we decided to confine our attention to a small number of dimensions. Specifically, we focussed on the first three dimensions, as they seem to capture meaningful strategies of the firm in this context as explained in the following. In terms of variation explained, dimension 1, dimension 2 and dimension 3 account for 20 per cent, 13 per cent and 11 per cent, respectively, of the total variation (Table 9.4). Figure 9.2 indicates the importance of the variables relative to dimensions 1, 2 and 3 (see also the dimensions' coordinates in Table A9.1 of the Appendix). Two other categorical variables have been included in this summary: SME and LARGE, indicating small and medium firms respectively (with less than 249 employees), and large firms (with more than 250 employees). These variables are only descriptive, and do not affect the results of the correspondence analysis.

The first dimension shows high figures (i.e. variables assuming a value equal to 1) for the following variables: INNOhigh, INNOincrease, and all the five organizational slack variables. In terms of firm size, it is positively associated to

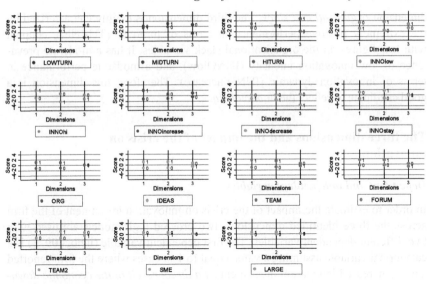

Standard normalization
Supplementary (passive) variables: SME LARGE

Figure 9.1 Multiple correspondence analysis (indicator matrix method).

Table 9.4 Revealed dimensions from two multiple correspondence analyses (Bart matrix method and indicator matrix method)

Dimension	Principal inertia	%	Cumulative percentage
1	0.1981	19.81	19.81
2	0.1298	12.98	32.79
3	0.1136	11.36	44.15
4	0.1004	10.04	54.19
5	0.0967	9.67	63.86
6	0.0698	6.98	70.84
7	0.0695	6.95	77.79
8	0.0573	5.73	83.52
9	0.0515	5.15	88.67
10	0.0477	4.77	93.45
11	0.0351	3.51	96.95
12	0.0233	2.33	99.28
13	0.0072	0.72	100
Total	1	100.00	

large firms, and negatively associated to SMEs. We thus call this dimension *innovative& organizational slack*. The second dimension is characterized by high figures for all the organizational slack variables, and for large firms in opposition to SMEs. It also performs very low on innovation intensity (INNOlow), and conservatively in terms of innovation dynamic (INNOstay). Therefore, we name this dimension *organizational slack.* The third dimension is mainly characterized by the extremely positive performance in terms of turnover (TURNhi), coupled with low figures on the organizational slack variables. It has a moderate prevalence of low innovation intensity (INNOlow), and a moderate performance in terms of innovation dynamic (INNOincrease). Therefore, this dimension is a good candidate to reflect the *financial slack.*

The three dimensions and the impact of the crisis on innovation

Dependent and independent variables

In order to estimate the impact of the crisis on innovation investment of the firm across the three identified dimensions, two ordered logit models are used with two different dependent variables. The first dependent variable (inno2009_3) is a categorical variable assuming a value equal to 1 in cases where the firm reported having increased innovation investment *as a direct result of the economic downturn,* a value equal to 0 in cases where it reported having maintained innovation investment, and a value equal to –1 in cases where it reported having decreased innovation investment. The second variable (forecast_3) takes the same values (1, 0 and –1) depending on innovation investment but in relation to what the firm is expected to do in the coming months. Figure 9.2 shows the percentage figures of the two variables. The independent variables included in the model are the three dimensions identified in the multiple correspondence analysis: *innovation&organizational slack, organizational slack* and *financial slack.* These are continuous variables (see Table 9.5 for descriptive statistics).

Control variable

Three dummies at the firm level are also included: a variable accounting for the size, a variable indicating whether the firm carries out internal R&D activity, and

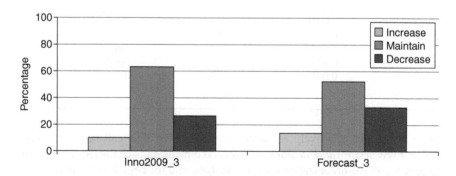

Figure 9.2 Percentage of firms increasing, maintaining, and decreasing innovation investment during the crisis and following on from the crisis.

Table 9.5 Descriptive statistics and pairwise correlations among the independent variables

Variable	Obs	Mean	Std.	TURNlow	TURNmid	TURNhi	INNOlow	INNOhi	INNOincrease	INNOdecrease	INNOstay	ORG	IDEAS	TEAM	FORUM	TEAM2
TURNlow	5234	0.13	0.33	1.00												
TURNmid	5234	0.18	0.39	-0.18	1.00											
TURNhi	5234	0.42	0.49	-0.32	-0.40	1.00										
INNOlow	5234	0.56	0.50	0.00	0.05	0.02	1.00									
INNOhi	5234	0.26	0.44	0.02	-0.04	0.11	-0.68	1.00								
INNOincrease	5234	0.38	0.49	-0.11	0.00	0.22	-0.14	0.27	1.00							
INNOdecrease	5234	0.09	0.29	0.21	0.08	-0.09	0.08	-0.02	-0.25	1.00						
INNOstay	5234	0.42	0.49	-0.01	0.01	-0.10	0.26	-0.14	-0.67	-0.27	1.00					
ORG	5234	0.52	0.50	-0.08	-0.01	0.10	-0.03	0.10	0.21	-0.05	-0.07	1.00				
IDEAS	5234	0.49	0.50	-0.03	0.01	0.05	-0.05	0.13	0.16	-0.05	-0.06	0.30	1.00			
TEAM	5234	0.42	0.49	-0.07	0.00	0.07	-0.07	0.12	0.18	-0.06	-0.07	0.28	0.37	1.00		
FORUM	5234	0.16	0.37	-0.02	0.00	0.03	-0.05	0.10	0.08	-0.03	-0.02	0.12	0.16	0.18	1.00	
TEAM2	5234	0.56	0.50	-0.06	0.03	0.02	-0.06	0.11	0.14	-0.03	-0.06	0.26	0.33	0.35	0.15	1.00

a variable indicating whether the firm operates in international markets. In principle, the circumstances accounted for by these three variables can affect the firm's decision in terms of innovation investment during a major recession. As far as size is concerned, large firms can be better equipped to face a recession thanks to their larger financial resources and capital markets, as well as a larger spectrum of markets in which they sell their products and services. The circumstance that the firm carries out internal R&D activity can also take a part here, because R&D activities are usually more long-term and structural in nature, as they imply investment in fixed capital, machinery and dedicated labs. This might lead the firm not to reduce innovation investment even during hard times. Finally, international markets can play a role in both directions. One the one hand, relying on different markets can make the firm less dependent on domestic fall in the demand. On the other hand, firms heavily exposed to international trade can bear substantial consequences depending on their reference markets (see also the results in Chapter 3).

Finally, three other variables have been included. The variable gdp0910 is a variable at the country level that accounts for the drop in the gross domestic product in the period between the third term 2008 and the first term 2009. This should control for the impact of the crisis on the macroeconomic environment of each country, which can exert an important role on the behaviour of the firm. Finally, dummies accounting for the industry and for the country have been included, as is customary in this type of analysis.

The results

Table 9.6 shows the robust estimates of six ordered logit models: the first three columns refer to the inno2009_3 variable, while the other three refer to the forecast_3 variable. Looking at the first column, it can be seen that the three dimensions show positive and significant coefficients, but with different magnitudes. The greatest is that related to *financial slack* (0.29), followed by *innovation&organizational slack* (0.26) and *organizational slack* (0.13), all significant at the 0.01 level. The model in the second column also includes the variable INTRD, which reports the circumstance that the firm carries out internal activities of R&D. This variable is positive and significant, and moderately reduces the magnitude of the first dimension and the second dimension. Two of the interaction effects added up in the third column are significant but with a negligible negative sign, and do not alter the results significantly.

A slightly different picture arises from the second model addressing the forecasting of innovation investment. In this case, all the three dimensions are still positive and significant, and the differences among them are less marked. In this case, the larger coefficient is that of *innovation&organizational slack* (0.14), followed by *organizational slack* (0.14) and *financial slack* (0.12). Here, the addition of the internal R&D variable is positive and significant (0.16) and significantly reduces the coefficient mainly of the first two dimensions, which nonetheless still remain significant at the 0.01 level. In this case, the interaction

Table 9.6 Robust logit estimation (dependent variables: innovation investment in response to the crisis, current and forecast)

Variables	(1) inno2009_3	(2) inno2009_3	(3) inno2009_3	(4) forecast_3	(5) forecast_3	(6) forecast_3
Dimensions						
dim 1: innovation and organizational slack	0.263*** (0.033)	0.255*** (0.033)	0.240*** (0.036)	0.144*** (0.036)	0.126*** (0.031)	0.126*** (0.034)
dim 2: organizational slack	0.126*** (0.034)	0.120*** (0.035)	0.107*** (0.035)	0.139*** (0.035)	0.124*** (0.032)	0.121*** (0.033)
dim 3: financial slack	0.291*** (0.033)	0.292*** (0.034)	0.278*** (0.035)	0.125*** (0.035)	0.121*** (0.032)	0.121*** (0.032)
internal R&D activity (INTRD)		0.039 (0.075)			0.159** (0.070)	0.159** (0.070)
Interactions						
d1*d2			-0.070 (0.047)		0.015 (0.042)	0.014 (0.044)
d1*d3			-0.073** (0.037)		0.012 (0.033)	0.003 (0.034)
d2*d3			-0.086** (0.037)		-0.005 (0.033)	-0.014 (0.034)
Control variables						
Large firms	-0.272*** (0.072)	-0.292*** (0.075)	-0.266*** (0.072)	-0.026 (0.067)	-0.027 (0.066)	-0.045 (0.069)
Internationalized firms	-0.077 (0.070)	-0.076 (0.072)	-0.075 (0.070)	-0.058 (0.067)	-0.058 (0.067)	-0.051 (0.070)
GDP drop (first term 2009)	0.111*** (0.019)	0.104*** (0.020)	0.111*** (0.019)	0.070*** (0.018)	0.070*** (0.018)	0.071*** (0.018)
Industry dummies (NACE 2-digit)	included	included	included	included	included	included
Country dummies	included	included	included	included	included	included
Observations	4431	4431	4431	4452	4452	4452

Note
Robust standard errors in parentheses; *** $P<0.01$, ** $P<0.05$, * $P<0.1$; reference variables: small and medium firms.

effects are not relevant and do not affect the results of the other variables. The coefficients of the control variables show mixed results. In the first three models large firms seem to be more affected by the crisis, while this is not the case for the forecasting case. The circumstance of being internationalized does not seem to affect the innovation behaviour of the firm in either of the two cases. As expected, in both cases the drop in gross domestic product exerts a negative effect on the decisions of the firm – that is, the lower the magnitude of the drop, the higher the likelihood of investing in innovation.

Discussion

The crucial issue of the relationship between the organization and its environment has been addressed in several guises. When addressing organization change, organizational theory usually assumes that change is taken in response to the environment, and that in turn organizations shape their environment (March, 1981). The evolutionary theory of innovation, which emphasizes the co-evolution of organization and the environment, takes the environment simultaneously as endogenous and exogenous (Amendola and Bruno, 1990; Nelson and Winter, 1982; Tsoukas and Knudsen, 2003). This chapter takes a short-term perspective by assuming that firms' behaviour is substantially affected as a result of an exogenous shock such as the current economic downturn. We then tried to discover whether the circumstance of having some form of slack affects the behaviour of the firm. Overall, our findings lend support to the hypothesis, proposed in the introduction, claiming that slack can play a role when firms face a severe recession.

The environment that characterizes a severe recession is by all means a particular one. Three main features shape the environment during a major recession: (1) the drop in the demand; (2) increased uncertainty brought about by technological and market discontinuity; and (3) a lack of financial resources both within and outside the firm. The immediate direct consequence for the firm is that of a drop in the expected profits and current cash flows. Second, there is the need to re-define its strategy in terms of innovation plans and markets. In principle, a major crisis represents a good opportunity for firm to gain market share and to enter new markets. In these cases, innovation plays a key role. However, at the same time the particular environment also provides important constraints to the firm, in terms of a lack of financial resources and increased uncertainty.

As we have stressed in this volume, the number of firms that have reported maintaining or even increasing innovation investment as a direct result of the crisis is remarkable, even if there is also a substantial share of firms reducing their innovation investment. It is hence legitimate to ask whether there are some specific features of the firm that are more conducive to innovation during a crisis. We believe that the relationship between slack and innovation is particularly appropriate in a 'crisis' environment. First, the availability of larger financial resources can be a crucial issue in the case of a recession. Second, in such an environment characterized by uncertainty and technological discontinuities, the capability of the firm for searching over a major spectrum of opportunities represents a key resource.

We have operationalized the two concepts of *financial slack* and *organizational slack* in order to investigate their role on the innovation behaviour of the firm during a crisis. Specifically, three dimensions have been identified in our sample by means of a multiple correspondence analysis. The three dimensions have interesting features: the first summarizes very innovative firms that also present organizational slack; the second identifies organizational slack, while the third identifies financial slack. Overall, slack seems to be important in every respect. However, some differences have emerged. Three main conclusions can be summarized from our findings:

1   Slack matters! There is little doubt that firms showing some form of slack, both organizational and financial, are more likely to carry out innovation during the crisis.
2   Specifically, the circumstance of having internal financial resources from the three-year period before the crisis seems to be the most important factor.
3   Being a strong innovator before the crisis, with organizational slack, predicts innovation during the crisis. This does not seem to depend on the fact that some specific innovation activities, such as R&D, are structural in nature.

In line with the results shown in Chapter 3, innovation shows persistency to some extent. In Chapter 6, we demonstrated that there has been a significant shift with respect to prior to the crisis in the innovation environment; namely, from creative accumulation to creative destruction. We argued that the identikit of the innovator during the crisis has also changed. This chapter's evidence seems to qualify these results, providing a micro explanation for both the degree of persistency in innovation and the rise of new innovators in response to the crisis.

The persistent innovators are those firms characterized by high innovation performance prior to the crisis, and *organizational slack.* In this case, the availability of financial resources does not seem to be a necessary condition for the firm to keep on innovating. On the other side, the *new* innovators are firms characterized by financial slack and, to a lesser extent, organizational slack. The circumstance of having larger financial resources, or an organizational structure that is particularly oriented towards searching activity both within and outside the firm, makes the firm more likely to invest in innovation in response to the crisis, regardless of whether it was an innovator before the crisis. We can conclude by saying that if, in principle, innovation in times of crisis can be a wise strategy for the firm, the circumstances of having organizational and financial slack seem to be the conditions that allow this to be put into practice.

Appendix

Table A9.1 Multiple correspondence analysis statisics and dimensions coordinates

Variables	Categories	mass	distance	inertia	dimension1	dimension2	dimension3
TURNlow	0	0.067	0.378	0.010	0.168	0.214	0.584
	1	0.010	2.644	0.067	−1.177	−1.495	−4.080
TURNmid	0	0.063	0.472	0.014	0.085	−0.230	0.600
	1	0.014	2.119	0.063	−0.382	1.033	−2.695
TURNhi	0	0.044	0.854	0.032	−0.609	0.103	−1.959
	1	0.032	1.171	0.044	0.835	−0.142	2.687
INNOlow	0	0.034	1.134	0.043	1.201	−1.747	−0.849
	1	0.043	0.882	0.034	−0.934	1.359	0.661
INNOhi	0	0.057	0.598	0.020	−0.754	0.779	0.373
	1	0.020	1.671	0.057	2.105	−2.175	−1.042
INNOincrease	0	0.048	0.782	0.029	−1.187	0.590	−0.500
	1	0.029	1.279	0.048	1.942	−0.966	0.819
INNOdecrease	0	0.070	0.315	0.007	0.117	0.168	0.363
	1	0.007	3.176	0.070	−1.180	−1.695	−3.666
INNOstay	0	0.044	0.854	0.032	0.947	−1.198	−0.094
	1	0.032	1.171	0.044	−1.298	1.643	0.129
ORG	0	0.037	1.035	0.040	−1.154	−1.041	0.103
	1	0.040	0.967	0.037	1.078	0.973	−0.096
IDEAS	0	0.040	0.972	0.037	−1.155	−1.147	0.536
	1	0.037	1.029	0.040	1.222	1.213	−0.568
TEAM	0	0.044	0.856	0.033	−1.059	−0.999	0.373
	1	0.033	1.168	0.044	1.446	1.363	−0.509
FORUM	0	0.064	0.440	0.012	−0.302	−0.284	0.158
	1	0.012	2.273	0.064	1.560	1.467	−0.816
TEAM2	0	0.034	1.119	0.043	−1.237	−1.302	0.709
	1	0.043	0.894	0.034	0.988	1.040	−0.566
SME	0	0.553	0.539	0.007			
	1	−0.212	−0.207	−0.003			
LARGE	0	−0.212	−0.207	−0.003			
	1	0.553	0.539	0.007			

Conclusions

This book's empirical analysis has focused on the effect of the 2008–2009 crisis on innovation investment of firms in European countries. It is divided into two parts, the first addressing the role played by country-specific factors in affecting innovation investment of the firm, and the second investigating firm-level factors. Overall, interesting findings have emerged at both levels. There is no doubt that there are country-specific factors which have influenced innovation investment of the firm during the recession. In particular, Chapter 4 emphasizes the role of the characteristics of National Systems of Innovation – e.g. human capital and knowledge, the financial sector and industrial specialization. In Chapter 5, we show that systematic differences of innovation investment are associated to different labour market institution, skills, and human capital provisions. Along with the importance attached to country-specific factors affecting the innovation behaviour of the firm, we have also demonstrated a good deal of heterogeneity across firms. This is in line with a large part of innovation research which has emphasized the need to explore the patterns of innovation at the micro level. As already stated, this book could not examine the dynamic of the industries, which certainly represents a key topic for future research. In the light of our evidence, in what follows we discuss some policy recommendations, and speculate about future directions in the innovation studies.

Schumpeterian policy for recovering

Is it possible for policy to counteract the reduction of innovation expenditure that generally occurs during a crisis? An interesting example is that provided by the case of South Korea in the 1997 crisis, as reported in Keller and Samuels (2003). In that case, the large *chaebol* reduced their R&D expenditures by about 13 per cent in the year following the onset of the crisis. By contrast, the government remarkably increased its R&D budget, raising its share in total R&D from 23 per cent in 1997 to 27 per cent in 1998. Interestingly, the downsizing of R&D by the *chaebol*, coupled with the intervention of the government, led to an increase in technology-based small firms in South Korea. The long-term effects of these measures were striking. In 1997, SME spending accounted for just 12 per cent of total business R&D, but by 2006 this figure had increased to 24 per cent (OECD, 2009).

This parallels what happened in Finland during the crisis in 1990. As the OECD (2009a) reports;

> Most public expenditures were cut almost across the board, and some taxes were raised. The main exception to this was R&D spending, which was *increased* rather than *cut*. In particular, the counter-cyclical support of TEKES (the largest Finnish Funding Agency for Technology and Innovation) proved very important in reducing the depth and length of the downturn in business R&D, which helped lay the ground for a strong rebound. The government decision to complement macroeconomic stabilization measures with sustained investment in infrastructure, education and incentives for structural change helped put the Finnish economy on a stronger, more knowledge-intensive, growth path following the crisis.

Even though is not easy for governments to devote attention and resources to innovation policy during a major recession, these examples from the past show that this should be done. However, when it comes to innovation, a Schumpeterian approach to policy is more suitable (Antonelli, 2009) – meaning that policies for recovery should not treat all the markets, industries and firms in the same fashion. As discussed in Chapter 2, neo-Schumpeterian research has demonstrated that over time, and during different technological breakthroughs, different industries have taken the lead towards recovery. Furthermore, in line with this research, we have shown that, as a result of the current crisis, the identikit of the innovator has changed. Identifying the characteristics of innovators during the turmoil, as we have tried to do here, can shed some light on how policy instruments interact with technological accumulation and creative destruction.

In the light of empirical evidence, we can put forward the following points as key targets for policy for recovery: education, skills, new and small firms, incentives to innovation not limited to R&D, and EU policy for New Member States. Chapters 5 and 6 have both, by and large, confirmed that in the knowledge economy human capital is the key resource, not only during ordinary times but also and particularly during a recession. Countries with both a flexible labour market and rigid employment security show a good performance in innovation if their institution arrangements in the labour market are coupled with high levels of skills and higher education of the labour force. This supports the case for designing labour market policies which take into full account the presence of complementarities with education and training policies. In brief, workers are better 'protected' when they are also highly valuable in terms of what they can do within the firm, and what they know.

Public incentives to promote innovation can be directed either towards supporting the already existing R&D infrastructures, or towards fostering new entrants. In which group of firms will the Bill Gates and Steve Jobs, Larry Page and Sergey Brin of the next generation be found? From our evidence, we can argue that during a recession: (1) different types of innovation activity other than R&D play a role; and (2) some of the firms which were not strong innovators prior to the crisis are now increasing their innovation investment. The former finding suggests that other forms of innovation, such as innovation in services, becomes more important in comparison to prior to the crisis. Furthermore, we have observed during the crisis a shift towards the importance of exploring new markets, instead of exploring along technological opportunities. This suggests directing public incentives not only towards R&D activity, but also to other forms of innovation activity and in the service sector. The second finding reveals the contribution that *new innovators* can make, thus calling for policy promoting young, small, existing firms and new entrants.

Finally, our results reinforce the idea that specific innovation policies should be considered in the overall cohesion strategy of the EU. With the polarization of the generation of knowledge and innovation across the EU, a few countries are responsible for the bulk of innovation and knowledge production. The technology gap provides a fundamental potentiality for lagging-behind countries to catch up, and in fact some of them have already benefited from this. However, we have pointed out the presence of a general fragility, as the effects of the crisis have shown. The emerging countries, though, are also those most vulnerable to external shocks, and those that have most reduced their innovative investment as a direct consequence of the economic crisis. This casts some doubt on the structural nature of the observed convergence process in innovation capabilities. EU innovation policies aimed at enhancing the mechanisms underlying the diffusion of knowledge and the circulation of human resources seem totally justified, since they will facilitate the catching up of laggard and more fragile areas, and increase the potential innovative output of Europe.

Towards a broadening of innovation activity

In this last section of the book, we discuss briefly the effect of the crisis on the evolution of innovation. As argued in Chapter 2, innovation activity has been substantially changing over recent decades, as a result of the shift towards the services and the rise of new key industries such as the software industry and the Internet industry. Today, among the top innovators in the world we find companies like *Google, Facebook* and *Apple*, which are far from being leaders in technological development and science. Our evidence shows that during a crisis the innovators are those that tend to look for new opportunities in new markets. One could speculate that this is reinforcing the importance of (relatively) new types of innovation activities that imply the exploration of new markets and new business models.

Firms that carry out service innovations tend to be more likely to continue to invest during the crisis. We suspect that the crisis is reinforcing the shift from the manufacturing to the service industries. We wonder if this is a general rule or is something associated to the current phase of capitalist development, where the manufacturing sector, the core generator of *technological* innovations, is progressively accounting for lower shares of income and employment, while, to the contrary, the service sector is gaining share and is more likely to compete through *non-technological* innovations and by new business models. We can speculate that, if the economic recession is reinforcing the shift from manufacturing to services, it would not be surprising that the firms increasing their innovation investment are more likely to be driven by searching for new business lines and business models than by technological opportunities.

These innovative activities are less based on formal R&D activity and on science. Innovation strategies seem to be playing an increasing role, and they are more likely to be firm-specific, thus less easy to grasp at a more aggregated level such as industry- and the country-levels. All in all, this calls for an afterthought in the innovation studies along the following directions. First, a new, broader definition of innovation, able to capture the process of change in both manufacturing and services, is needed, along with the necessity to pay more attention to these new forms of innovation and the relative strategies underlying them. Second, new empirical evidence is also needed. Here, case studies might be paramount in pointing out new problems, raising new questions and opening up new avenues of research. Third, it is clear that traditional forms of innovation measurement, such as R&D expenditures and patents, are not able to capture innovation in this form. Innovation surveys can make a substantial contribution, but they have to be amended in order to take into full account the broadening of innovation activity.

For many years, Schumpeterian economics has concentrated on the *technological* dimension of innovation, which is typical of the manufacturing industries, and has somehow denied the *non-technological* dimension, which is more common when innovating in services. Times are ready to use a wider understanding of innovation, similar to that which was pioneered by Schumpeter himself a century ago in the first edition of the *Theory of Economic Development*.

Notes

Introduction

1 There have also been several special issues dealing with the crisis; among others, see the *Cambridge Journal of Economics* (2009), 33(4); the *Oxford Review of Economic Policy*'s 'The Financial Crisis Collection', at www.oxfordjournals.org/subject/social_sciences/financialcrisis.html; and the *Technological Forecasting and Social Change* special issue on the financial crisis, forthcoming.

1 At the root of the crisis: some proposed explanations

1 The term was coined by Paul McCulley in 1998, to describe the 1998 Russian financial crisis. A Minsky moment is a situation in which investors who have borrowed too much are forced to sell even good assets to pay back their loans.

2 This occurred through the 'originate and distribute' banking model, in which loans are pooled, tranched, and then resold via securitization. This led to a substantial decline in the lending standard. Banks did so this creating 'structured' products, the so-called 'collateralized debt obligations' (CDO).

3 Available at www.ecb.int/stats/money/surveys/sme/html/index.en.html.

4 For example, in the 1990s Internet-related investments were estimated to account for between 70 and 75 per cent of all venture capital investment (O'Sullivan, 2005).

2 Technological change, patterns of innovation, and economic development: the contribution of neo-Schumpeterian research

1 Other strands of literature have provided insights for the understanding of business cycles, such as the Keynesian and New Keynesian theory, the Rational Expectations model, and Real Business Cycle model, among others (Knoop, 2004).

2 Andrew Tylecote (Tylecote, 1992) also recognizes the important role played at the beginning of the 20th century by Van Gelderen, who 'has had very little credit for his work as he made the obvious mistake of writing only in Dutch, and the less obvious one of writing during an upswing' (p. 11); see also Freeman *et al.*, 1982; Kleinknecht, 1987.

3 Schumpeter clearly distinguishes innovations from inventions, the main difference being that the former is strictly an economic phenomenon, while scientific and technological advancement play a secondary role.

4 Schumpeter is not interested in identifying the points of equilibrium of the system, as he believes that an economic system will never be in this state. He is, rather, interested in the forces that *dynamically* tend to bring the system towards the equilibrium.

5 Schumpeter did not see innovation activity as the only single cause or prime mover accounting for all the economic fluctuations in general. He rather puts its analysis at

the centre of this analysis, as he believes it is a fundamental force of economic development.

6 In this book Schumpeter also discusses at greater detail the statistical methodology. A crucial aspect of his empirical work, similarly to Kondratieff's, is in fact the methodology used to tackle time series – specifically, those time series characterized by a secular trends which were central to their argument (for a detailed analysis of this issue, see Reijnders 1990).

7 The process of creative destruction is widely described in Schumpeter's *Theory of Economics Development* (Schumpeter, 1911 (1934)), although the term itself was used for the first time in his *Capitalism, Socialism and Democracy* (Schumpeter, 1942). Paradoxically, the book that introduced the term 'creative destruction ' vindicated instead the importance of creative accumulation.

8 Interestingly, Mensch briefly observed the important role that energy-saving technology might have played in terms of basic innovations. This is today again a very timely issue (Perez, 2009b).

9 On these issues see, among others, Brusoni and Prencipe, 2001; Iansiti and Levien, 2004; Langlois, 2002, 2003; Langlois and Robertson, 1992; Pavitt, 2005; Sanchez and Mahoney, 1996; Sturgeon, 2002.

10 The venture capital industry began in the US in 1946 with the founding of American Research and Development for the finance of new ventures.

3 The role of the rules: National Systems of Innovation and labour market institutions

1 It should be noted that the same concept has been more recently applied within nations at the regional level (see Howells, 1999; Iammarino, 2005; Rodriguez-Pose and Crescenzi, 2008, among others).

2 Interestingly, this parallels a statement about the role played by institutions in the long recession that has taken place in Japan since the beginning of the 1990s. In Keller and Samuels (2003) one can read about the Japanese innovation system, which 'is not designed to encourage bold new conceptualizing, *radical* departures from the prevailing orthodoxy [...]. Instead, Japanese organizations are geared to operate on the basis of caution, conservatism, and *incremental* change' (p. 52, our emphasis).

4 Is the crisis hampering innovation convergence in Europe?

1 For a preliminary attempt, see European Commission 2009a.

2 In the smallest EU countries, Cyprus, Malta and Luxembourg, the sample consisted of seventy enterprises; in non-EU countries, Switzerland and Norway, the sample size was 100. The industry sectors included are: aerospace, defence, construction equipment, apparel, automotive, building fixtures, equipment, business services, chemical products, communications equipment, construction materials, distribution services, energy, entertainment, financial services, fishing products, footwear, furniture, heavy construction services, heavy machinery, hospitality and tourism, information technology, jewellery and precious metals, leather products, lighting and electrical equipment, lumber and wood manufacturers, medical devices, metal manufacturing, oil and gas products and services, chapter, (bio)pharmaceuticals, plastics, power generation & transmission, processed food, publishing and printing, sport and child goods, textiles, transportation and logistics, utility.

3 A detailed description of the survey, including the sampling and data collection methods, can be found in a methodological report by the European Commission, 2009b.

4 The interviews were conducted between 1 and 9 April 2009, and thus the question relates to the period starting October 2008 and ending March 2009.

5 The Innobarometer survey reports a lower number of non-innovation active firms compared with similar datasets, and specifically the Community Innovation Surveys. The following factors might contribute: (1) a difference in the industrial composition – 'the enterprises interviewed in Innobarometer were sampled from sectors that are likely to be innovative' (EC, 2009), and (2) the Innobarometer includes firms with twenty or more employees while the Community Innovation Survey includes enterprises with ten and more employees.

6 Both the Innobarometer and EIS reports can be find on the web site: www.proinno-europe.eu/index.cfm?fuseaction=page.display&topicID=51&parentID=48.

7 See Cantwell and Iammarino, 2003; Cappellen *et al.*, 2003; Maurseth, 2001; Moreno *et al.*, 2005; Paci and Usai, 2009; Rodriguez-Pose, 1999; among others.

8 We are grateful to an anonymous referee for this point. This is related to the growing literature dealing with regional innovation systems (see Iammarino 2005; Rodríguez-Pose and Crescenzi, 2008) and localized technical change (see Antonelli, 2001).

9 For more structural analysis see Keyat *et al.*, 2004 and Palan and Schmeiderberg, 2010.

10 For some review studies and methodological assessments see Bazo *et al.*, 1999; Lorenz and Lundvall, 2006; Petrakos and Artelaris, 2009; Quah, 1996.

11 Malta and Cyprus have been excluded from the analysis of the chapter due to a lack of data.

12 The fact that the 'Innovators' dimension is not significant may be due to the circumstance that, relative to this indicator, data are taken from the Community Innovation Survey, which are available only for two years.

13 This EU10, including Bulgaria, the Czech Republic, Estonia, Hungary, Latvia, Lithuania, Poland, Romania, Slovakia and Slovenia. We exclude from the analysis Cyprus and Malta.

14 For a comparison between the EU and US, see Crescenzi *et al.*, 2007; Dosi *et al.*, 2006.

15 As is well known, activity rates are higher than in Europe – a fact that should be borne in mind when analysing the drivers of US competitiveness compared to the EU.

16 For an investigation of the convergence within the United States, see Barro, 1991. For studies which consider the European and United States experiences similarly in terms of market integration, see Sala-i-Martin and Sachs, 1991.

5 National Systems of Innovation, Structure, and Demand

1 Both Cyprus and Malta have been excluded from the analysis.

2 We also tried to take 1 whether the drop in domestic demand or export is higher than the third quartile, but we prefer the current choice because it allows us to include more countries.

3 This point suggests that there can be differences across the countries depending on the different structure and organization of the labour market, as explored in the next chapter.

6 Varieties of capitalism and the impact of the crisis

1 This chapter has been written by Andrea Filippetti and Frederick Guy.

2 The OECD indicators of employment protection measure the procedures and costs involved in dismissing individuals or groups of workers and the procedures involved in hiring workers on fixed-term or temporary work agency contracts (see www.oecd.org/employment/protection).

7 The shift of the innovation environment: from creative accumulation to creative destruction

1 This chapter has been prepared together with Marion Frenz.
2 The processes of creative destruction is widely described in Schumpeter's *Theory of Economics Development* (Schumpeter, 1911 (1934)), although the term itself was used for the first time in his *Capitalism, Socialism and Democracy* (Schumpeter, 1942). Paradoxically, the book which introduced the term 'creative destruction' vindicated instead the importance of creative accumulation. See also the discussion in Chapter 2.
3 Also assuming constant demand and fixed technologies, but here the emphasis is on the role played by appropriability.
4 The interviews were conducted between 1 and 9 April 2009, and, thus, the question relates to the period starting October 2008 ending with March 2009.
5 The dataset has a fourth category – innovation-related expenditure above 50 per cent of turnover – but less than 1 per cent of firms fell into this group, and this is why we merged it with the next smaller band.
6 In order to address an issue of multicollinearity between these variables, we have computed all regressions (1) without the variable international collaborations and (2) without the variable 'operating in international markets'. The findings remained unchanged. Results are not published, but are available upon request from the authors.

9 Is slack good for innovation in times of crisis?

1 We are indebted to Keld Laursen for having suggested we address this stream of literature in relation to innovation during a crisis.
2 It is worth stressing that the recent Open Innovation paradigm also pertains to the way firms go about organizing a search for new ideas outside their boundaries (Chesbrough, 2003; Laursen and Salter, 2005).
3 We decided to choose this method with respect to the default Bart matrix method because in the former case the variation explained is more evenly distributed across the first three dimensions. However, the results are robust across the different methodologies.

References

Abreu, M., Grinevich, V., Kitson, M. and Savona, M. (2010) 'Policies to enhance the hidden innovation in services: evidences and lessons from the UK', *Service Industries Journal*, 30: 99–118.

Adam, C. and Vines, D. (2009) 'Remarking on macroeconomic policy after the global financial crisis: a balance-sheet approach', *Oxford Review of Economic Policy*, 25: 507–52.

Aiken, L. and West, S. (1991) *Multiple Regression: Testing and Interpreting Interactions*, London: Sage.

Akkermans, D., Castaldi, C. and Los, B. (2009) 'Do "liberal market economies" really innovate more radically than "coordinated market economies"? Hall and Soskice reconsidered', *Research Policy*, 38: 181–91.

Amendola, M. and Bruno, S. (1990) 'The behaviour of the innovative firm: relations to the environment', *Research Policy*, 19: 419–33.

Antonelli, C. (1997) 'The economics of path-dependence in industrial organization', *International Journal of Industrial Organization*, 15: 643–75.

Antonelli, C. (2001) The Microeconomics of Technological Change, Oxford: Oxford University Press.

Antonelli, C. (2009) 'Appunti per una lettura schumpeteriana della crisi e implicazioni di politica economica', Bureau of Research in Innovation, Complexity and Knowledge, Collegio Carlo Alberto. WP series, University of Turin.

Archibugi, D. (2001) 'Pavitt's taxonomy sixteen years on: a review article', *Economics of Innovation and New Technology*, 3: 415–25.

Archibugi, D. and Coco, A. (2005a) 'Is Europe becoming the most dynamic knowledge economy in the world?' *Journal on Common Market Studies*, 43: 433–59.

Archibugi, D. and Coco, A. (2005b) 'Measuring technological capabilities at the country level: a survey and a menu for choice', *Research Policy*, 34: 175–94.

Archibugi, D., Howells, J. and Michie, J. (1999) *Innovation Policy in a Global Economy*, Cambridge: Cambridge University Press.

Archibugi, D. and Iammarino, S. (1999) 'The policy implications of the globalisation of innovation', *Research Policy*, 28: 317–36.

Archibugi, D. and Michie, J. (eds) (1997) *Technology, Globalisation and Economic Performance*, Cambridge: Cambridge University Press.

Archibugi, D. and Pianta, M. (1992) *The Technological Specialization of Advanced Countries*, Dordrecht: Kluwer Academic Publishers.

Arrow, K. (1962) Economic welfare and the allocation of resources for invention. In Nelson, R. R. (ed.), *The Rate and Direction of the Inventive Activity: Economic and Social Factors*. Princeton, NJ: Princeton University Press.

Arundel, A., Bordoy, C. and Kanerva, M. (2008) 'Neglected innovators: how do innovative firms that do not perform R&D innovate?' INNO-Metrics Thematic Paper.

Balconi, M. and Brusoni, S. (2010) 'In defence of the linear model: An essay', *Research Policy*, 39: 1–13.

Barro, R. J. (1991) 'Economic growth in a cross section of countries', *Quarterly Journal of Economics*, 106: 407–44.

Barro, R. J. and Sala-i-Martin, X. (2005) *Economic Growth*, New York, NY: McGraw Hill.

Bazo-Lopez, E., Vayà, E., Mora, A. J. and Surinach, J. (1999) 'Regional economic dynamics and convergence in the European Union', *Annals of Regional Science*, 33: 343–70.

Bell, M. and Pavitt, K. (1993) 'Technological accumulation and industrial growth: contrasts between developed and developing countries', *Industrial and Corporate Change*, 2: 157–210.

Bogliacino, F. and Pianta, M. (2009) 'Innovation performance in Europe: a long term perspective', EIS Thematic Paper.

Bogliacino, F. and Pianta, M. (2010a) 'Innovation and employment. A reinvestigation using revised Pavitt classes', *Research Policy*, 39: 799–809.

Bogliacino, F. and Pianta, M. (2010b) 'Profits, R&D and innovation. A model and a test', Working Paper, available at: http://works.bepress.com/mario_pianta/1.

Boldrin, M., Casanova, F., Pischke, J. and Puga, D. (2001) 'Inequality and convergence in Europe's regions: reconsidering European regional policies', *Economic Policy*, 32: 207–53.

Borras, S. (2003) *The Innovation Policy of the EU*, Cheltenham: Edward Elgar.

Bourgeois, L. J. (1981) 'On the measurement of organizational slack', *Academy of Management Review*, 6: 29–39.

Breschi, S., Malerba, F. and Orsenigo, L. (2000) 'Technological regimes and Schumpeterian patterns of innovation', *Economic Journal*, 110: 388–410.

Brouwer, E. and Kleinknecht, A. (1999) 'Keynes-plus? Effective demand and changes in firm-level R&D: an empirical note', *Cambridge Journal of Economics*, 23: 385–91.

Brunnermeier, M. K. (2009) 'Deciphering the liquidity and credit crunch 2007–2008', *Journal of Economic Perspectives*, 23: 77–100.

Brusoni, S. and Prencipe, A. (2001) 'Unpacking the Black Box of Modularity: technologies, products and organizations', *Industrial and Corporate Change*, 10: 179–205.

Cainelli, G., Evangelista, R. and Savona, M. (2006) 'Innovation and economic performance in services: a firm-level analysis', *Cambridge Journal of Economics*, 30: 435–58.

Cantwell, J. and Iammarino, S. (2003) *Multinational Enterprises and European Regional Systems of Innovation*, London: Routledge.

Cappelen, A., Fagerberg, J. and Verspagen, B. (1999) Lack of regional convergence. In Fagerberg, J. *et al.* (eds), *Lack of Regional Convergence*. Cheltenham: Edward Elgar.

Cassidy, J. (2008) 'The Minsky moment', *The New Yorker*, February, 4, 2008.

Cassiman, B. and Veugelers, R. (2006) 'In search of complementarity in innovation strategy: internal R&D and external knowledge acquisition', *Management Science*, 52: 68–82.

Castellacci, F. (2008) 'Technology clubs, technology gaps and growth trajectories', *Structural Change and Economic Dynamics*, 19: 301–14.

Castellacci, F. (2010) 'The internationalization of firms in the service industries: channels, determinants and sectoral patterns', *Technological Forecasting & Social Change*, 77: 500–13.

Cefis, E. and Orsenigo, L. (2001) 'The persistence of innovative activities. a cross-country and cross-sectors comparative analysis', *Research Policy*, 30: 1139–58.

Chandler, A. D. (1977) *The Visible Hand: The Managerial Revolution in American Business*, Cambridge, MA: Belknap Press.

Chandler, A. D. (1990) *Scale and Scope. The Dynamic of Industrial Capitalism*, Cambridge, MA: Harvard University Press.

Chesbrough, H. W. (2003) *Open Innovation: the New Imperative for Creating and Profiting from Technology*, Boston, MA: Harvard Business School Press.

Chesbrough, H., Vanhaverbeke, W. and West, J. (eds) (2008) *Open Innovation. Researching a New Paradigm*. Oxford: Oxford University Press.

Christensen, C. M. (1997) *The Innovator's Dilemma*, New York, NY: HarperBusiness Edition.

Christensen, C. M. and Rosenbloom, R. S. (1995) 'Explaining the attacker's advantage: technological paradigms, organizational dynamics, and the value network', *Research Policy*, 24: 233–57.

Cipolla, C. (1966) *Guns, Sails and Empires: Technological Innovation and the Early Phases of European Expansion, 1400–1700*, New York, NY: Pantheon Books.

Cohen, W. (1995) Empirical studies of innovative activity. In Stoneman, P. (ed.), *Empirical Studies of Innovative Activity*, Oxford: Basil Blackwell.

Cohen, W. M. and Levinthal, D. A. (1989) 'Innovation and learning: the two faces of R&D', *Economic Journal*, 99: 569–96.

Coriat, B. and Dosi, G. (2000) The institutional embeddedness of economic change. An appraisal of the 'Evolutionary' and 'Regulationist' research programmes. In Dosi, G. (ed.), *Innovation, Organization and Economic Dynamics*, Cheltenham: Edward Elgar.

Coriat, B. and Weinstein, O. (2002) 'Organizations, firms and institutions in the generation of innovation', *Research Policy*, 31: 273–90.

Cornelius, B. (2005) 'The institutionalization of venture capital', *Technovation*, 25: 599–608.

Crescenzi, R., Rodriguez-Pose, A. and Storper, M. (2007) 'The territorial dynamics of innovation: a Europe–United States comparative analysis', *Journal of Economic Geography*, 7: 673–709.

Crotty, J. (2009) 'Structural causes of the global financial crisis: a critical assessment of the "new financial architecture"', *Cambridge Journal of Economics*, 33: 563–80.

Crouch, C., Finegold, D. and Sako, M. (1999) *Are Skills the Answer? The Political Economy of Skill Creation in Advanced Industrial Countries*, Oxford: Oxford University Press.

Culpepper, P. (2001) Employers, public policy, and the politics of decentralized cooperation in France and Germany. In Hall, P. A. and Soskice, D. (eds), *Varieties of Capitalism: The Institutional Foundations of Comparative Advantage*, Oxford: Oxford University Press.

Cyert, R. M. and March, J. G. (1963) *A Behavioural Theory of the Firm*, New York, NY: Prentice-Hall.

Davis, G. F. and Stout, K. (1992) 'Organization theory and the market for corporate control: a dynamic analysis of the characteristics of large takeover targets, 1980–1990', *Administrative Science Quarterly*, 37: 605–33.

Davis, L. E. and North, D. C. (1971) *Institutional Change and American Economic Growth*, Cambridge: Cambridge University Press.

Dooley, M., Folkerts-Landau, D. and Garber, M. (2005) 'Savings glut and interest rates: the missing link to Europe ', Working Paper 11520, NBER.

Dosi, G. (1982) 'Technological paradigms and technological trajectories', *Research Policy*, 11: 147–62.

Dosi, G. (1984a) Technological paradigms and technological trajectories. In Freeman, C. (ed.), *Technological Paradigms and Technological Trajectories*, London: Frances Pinter.

Dosi, G. (1984b) *Technical Change and Industrial Transformation*, London: The Mac-Millan Press.

Dosi, G. (1988) 'Sources, procedures and microeconomic effects of innovation', *Journal of Economic Literature*, 26: 1120–71.

Dosi, G. (1997) 'Opportunities, incentives and the collective patterns of technological change', *Economic Journal*, 107: 1530–47.

Dosi, G., Marengo, L. and Fagiolo, L. (1996) 'Learning in evolutionary environments', LEM Working Paper.

Dosi, G., Nelson, R. and Winter, S. G. (eds) (2002) *The Nature and Dynamics of Organizational Learning*, Oxford: Oxford University Press.

Dosi, G., LLerena, P. and Labini, M. S. (2006) 'The relationship between science, technologies and their industrial exploitation: an illustration through the myths and realities of the so-called European Paradox', *Research Policy*, 35: 1450–64.

Easterly, W. (2002) *The Elusive Quest for Growth*, Cambridge, MA: The MIT Press.

Edquist, C. (1997) Systems of innovation approach: their emergence and characteristics In Edquist, C. (ed.), *Systems of Innovation: Technologies, Institutions and Organizations*, London: Frances Pinter.

Edquist, C. and Lundvall, B. A. (1993) Comparing the Danish and Swedish systems of innovations. In Nelson, R. R. (ed.), *National Innovation Systems*, Oxford: Oxford University Press.

Estevez-Abe, M., Iversen, T. and Soskice, D. (2001) Social protection and the formation of skills: a reinterpretation of the Welfare State. In Hall, B. and Soskice, D. (eds), *Varieties of Capitalism: The Institutional Foundations of Comparative Advantage*, Oxford: Oxford University Press.

European Commission (2009a) *European Innovation Scoreboard 2008. Comparative Analysis of Innovation Performance*, Brussels: European Commission, DG Enterprise.

European Commission (2009b) *Innobarometer 2009*, Brussels: DG Enterprise and Industry.

European Commission (2009c) 'Shared commitment for employment', *Communication of the European Commission – Employment, Social Affairs & Inclusion*.

European Commission (2010a) *The 2008 EU Survey on R&D Investment Business Trends*, Brussels, Joint Research Centre – IPTS.

European Commission (2010b) *European Innovation Scoreboard 2009*, Brussels: DG Enterprise and Industry.

Evangelista, R. (1999) *Knowledge and Investment. The Sources of Innovation in Industry*, Cheltenham, UK: Edward Elgar Publishing.

Evangelista, R. (2000) 'Sectoral patterns of technological change in services', *Economics of Innovation and New Technology*, 9: 183–221.

Evangelista, R. and Vezzani, A. (2010) 'The economic impact of technological and organizational innovations. A firm-level analysis', *Research Policy*, 39: 1253–63.

Fagerberg, J. (1988) 'International competitiveness', *Economic Journal*, 98: 355–74.

Fagerberg, J. (1994) 'Technology and international differences in growth rates', *Journal of Economic Literature*, 32: 1147–75.

Fagerberg, J. and Godinho, M. M. (2005) Innovation and catching-up. In Fagerberg, J., *et al.* (eds), *The Oxford Handbook of Innovation*, Oxford: Oxford University Press.

Fagerberg, J. and Srholec, M. (2008) 'National innovation systems, capabilities and economic development', *Research Policy*, 37: 1417–35.

Fagerberg, J. and Verspagen, B. (1996) 'Heading for divergence? Regional growth in Europe reconsidered', *Journal of Common Market Studies*, 34: 431–48.

Fagerberg, J., Verspagen, B. and Caniels, M. (1997) 'Technology, growth and unemployment across European regions', *Regional Studies*, 31: 457–66.

Fagerberg, J., Srholec, M. and Knell, M. (2007) 'The competitiveness of nations: why some countries prosper while others fall behind', *World Development*, 35: 1595–620.

Fagerberg, J., Mowery, D. and Verspagen, B. (2009) *Innovation, Path Dependency, and Policy: The Norwegian Case*, Oxford: Oxford University Press.

Faruqee, H., Scott, A. and Tamirisa, N. (2009) 'In search of a smoking gun: macroeconomic policies and the crisis', *Oxford Review of Economic Policy*, 25: 553–80.

Ferguson, N. (2008) *The Ascent of Money: A Financial History of the World*, London: Penguin Books.

Field, A. (2003) 'The most technologically progressive decade of the century', *American Economic Review*, 93: 1399–413.

Filippetti, A. (2011) 'Innovation modes and design as a source of innovation: a firm-level analysis ', *European Journal of Innovation Management*, 14: 5–26.

Filippetti, A. and Peyrache, A. (2010) 'Productivity growth and catch up in Europe: a new perspective on total factor productivity differences', SSRN Working Paper.

Filippetti, A. and Peyrache, A. (2011) 'The patterns of technological capabilities of countries: a dual approach using composite indicator & data envelopment analysis', *World Development* (forthcoming).

Filippetti, A., Frenz, M. and Ietto-Gillies, G. (2011) 'Are innovation and internationalization related? An analysis of European countries', *Industry and Innovation*, 18 (forthcoming).

Freeman, C. (1987) *Technology Policy and Economic Performance: Lessons from Japan*, London: Frances Pinter.

Freeman, C. (1994) 'The economics of technical change', *Cambridge Journal of Economics*, 18: 463–514.

Freeman, C. (1995) 'The "National Systems of Innovation" in historical perpective', *Cambridge Journal of Economics*, 19: 5–24.

Freeman, C. and Louca, F. (2001) *As Time Goes By: From the Industrial Revolution to the Information Revolution*, Oxford: Oxford University Press.

Freeman, C. and Soete, L. (1997) *The Economics of Industrial Innovation*, Cambridge, MA: The MIT Press.

Freeman, C. and Soete, L. (2007) Science, technology and innovation indicators: the twenty-first century challenges. In Freeman, C. and Soete, L. (eds), *Science, Technology and Innovation Indicators in a Changing World: Responding to Policy Needs*. Paris, OECD.

Freeman, C., Clark, J. and Soete, L. (1982) *Unemployment and Technical Innovation*, London: Frances Pinter.

Frenz, M. and Ietto-Gillies, G. (2009) 'The impact on innovation performance of different sources of knowledge: evidence from the UK Community Innovation Survey', *Research Policy*, 38: 1125–35.

Frenz, M., Girardone, C. and Ietto-Gillies, G. (2005) 'Multinationality matters in innovation. The case of the UK financial services', *Industry and Innovation*, 12: 65–92.

Friedrich, R. (1982) 'In defense of multiplicative terms in multiple regression equations', *American Journal of Political Science*, 26: 797–833.

Galbraith, K. (1952) *American Capitalism: The concept of countervailing power*, Boston, MA: Houghton-Mifflin.

Galbraith, K. (1954) *The Great Crash 1929*, London: Penguin Group.

Gallouj, F. and Djellal, F. (2010) *The Handbook of Innovation and Services*, Cheltenham: Edward Elgar.

Gallouj, F. and Savona, M. (2009) 'Innovation in services. A review of the debate and a research agenda', *Journal of Evolutionary Economics*, 19: 149–72.

Garud, R. and Van de Ven, A. (1992) 'An empirical evaluation of the internal corporate venturing process', *Strategic Management Journal*, 15: 365–85.

Geroski, P. A. and Walters, C. F. (1995) 'Innovative activity over the business cycle', *The Economic Journal*, 105: 916–28.

Geroski, P. A., Van Reenen, J. and Walters, C. F. (1997) 'How persistently do firms innovate?' *Research Policy*, 26: 33–48.

Gompers, P. A. and Lerner, J. (1999) *The Venture Capital Cycle*, Cambridge, MA: The MIT Press.

Grandstrand, O., Patel, P. and Pavitt, K. (1997) 'Multi-technology corporations: why they have "distributed" rather than "distinctive core" competences', *California Management Review*, 39: 52–71.

Greenacre, M. J. (1984) *Greenacre, M.J., 1984. Theory and Applications of Correspondence Analysis*, London: Academic Press.

Greve, H. R. (2003) 'A behavioural theory of R&D expenditures and innovations: evidence from shipbuilding', *Academy of Management Journal*, 46: 685–702.

Griffith, R., Redding, S. and Van Reenen, J. (2004) 'Mapping the two faces of R&D: productivity growth in a panel of OECD countries', *Review of Economic and Statistics*, 86: 883–95.

Grossman, G. M. and Helpman, E. (1991) *Innovation and Growth in the Global Economy*, Cambridge, MA: The MIT Press.

Hall, B. (2002) 'The financing of research and development', *Oxford Review of Economic Policy*, 18: 35–51.

Hall, B. (2007) 'Patents and patent policy', *Oxford Review of Economic Policy*, 23: 568–87.

Hall, B. and Lerner, J. (2010) The financing of R&D and innovation. In Hall, B. and Rosenberg, N. (eds), *Handbook of the Economics of Innovation*, Oxford: North-Holland.

Hall, P. A. and Gingerich, D. (2004) 'Varieties of capitalism and institutional complementarities in the macro-economy', Discussion Paper 04/05, Cologne: Max Plank Institute.

Hall, P. A. and Soskice, D. (2001) *Varieties of Capitalism: The Institutional Foundations of Comparative Advantage*, Oxford: Oxford University Press.

Hanckè, B. (2009) *Debating Varieties of Capitalism*, Oxford: Oxford University Press.

Henderson, R. M. and Clark, K. B. (1990) 'Architectural innovation: the reconfiguration of existing product technologies and the failure of established firms', *Administrative Science Quarterly*, 35: 9–30.

Hodgson, G. M. (2006) 'What are institutions?' *Journal of Economic Issues*, 15: 1–25.

Hodson, D. and Quaglia, L. (2009) 'European perspective on the global financial crisis: Introduction', *Journal of Common Market Studies*, 47: 939–53.

Holbrook, D., Cohen, W., Hounsell, D. and Klepper, S. (2000) 'The nature, sources, and consequences of firms' differences in the early history of the semiconductor industry', *Strategic Management Journal*, 21: 1017–41.

Hollenstein, H. (2003) 'Innovation modes in the Swiss service sector: a cluster analysis based on firm-level data', *Research Policy*, 32: 845–63.

Howells, J. (1999) Regional systems of innovation? In Archibugi, D. *et al.* (eds), *Regional Systems of Innovation?* Cambridge: Cambridge University Press.

Howells, J. (2004) 'Innovation, consumption and services: encapsulation and the combinatorial role of services', *Service Industries Journal*, 24: 19–36.

Iammarino, S. (2005) 'An evolutionary integrated view of Regional Systems of Innovation: concepts, measures and historical perspectives', *European Planning Studies*, 13: 497–519.

Iansiti, M. and Levien, R. (2004) *The Keystone Advantage*, Boston, MA: Harvard Business School Press.

Ibrahim, D. M. (2010) 'Financing the next Silicon Valley', *Washington University Law Review*, 87: 717–62.

Jagannathan, R., Kapoor, M. and Schaumburg, E. (2009) 'Why are we in a recession?' NBER Working Paper 15404.

Jensen, M. C. (1986) 'Agency costs of free cash flow, corporate finance, and takeovers', *American Economic Review*, 76: 323–29.

Jensen, M. C. (1993) 'The modern industrial revolution, exit, and the failure of internal control systems', *Journal of Finance*, 48: 831–80.

Johnson, D. M. (2010) 'High-tech indicators: assessing the competitiveness of selected European countries', *Technology Analysis & Strategic Management*, 22: 277–96.

Johnson, S. and Kwak, J. (2010) *13 Bankers. The Wall Street Takeover and the Next Financial Meltdown*, New York, NY: Pantheon Books.

Jungmittag, A. (2004) 'Innovations, technological specialization and economic growth in the EU', *International Economics and Economic Policy*, 1: 247–73.

Kejak, M., Seiter, S. and Vávra, D. (2004) 'Accession trajectories and convergence: endogenous growth perspective'. *Structural Change and Economic Dynamics*, 15: 13–46.

Keller, W. W. and Samuels, R. J. (eds) (2003) *Crisis and Innovation in Asian Technology*, Cambridge University Press: Cambridge.

Kerr, W. R., Lerner, J. and Schoar, A. (2010) 'The consequences of entrepreneurial finance: a regression discontinuity analysis', Harvard Business School Working Paper 10–086.

Kindleberger, C. P. and Aliber, A. (2005) *Maniacs, Panics, and Crashes*, Hokoben, NJ: John Wiley & Sons, Inc.

Kleinknecht, A. (1987) *Innovation Patterns in Crisis and Prosperity: Schumpeter's Long Cycle Reconsidered*, London: Macmillan.

Kleinknecht, A. and Verspagen, B. (1990) 'Demand and innovation: Schmookler reexamined', *Research Policy*, 19: 387–94.

Klepper, S. and Simons, K. L. (2000) 'Dominance by birthright: entry of prior radio producers and competitive ramifications in the US television receiver industry', *Strategic Management Journal*, 21: 997–1016.

Kline, S. J. and Rosenberg, N. (1986) An overview of innovation. In Landau, R. and Rosenberg, N. (eds), *An Overview of Innovation*, Washington, DC: National Academy Press.

Knoop, T. A. (2004) *Recessions and Depressions*, London: Praeger.

Knoop, T. A. (2008) *Modern Financial Macroeconomics. Panics, Crashes, and Crises*, Malden, MA: Blackwell Publishing.

Kok, W. (2003) *The Kok Report: Making a Success of Enlargement*, Florence: prepared by the Robert Schuman Centre for Advanced Studies at the European University Institute.

Kondratieff, N. D. and Stolper, W. F. (1935) 'The long waves in economic life', *Review of Economics and Statistics*, 17: 105–15.

Kondratiev, N. D. (1979) 'The major economic cycles', *Review* (first published in 1925), 11: 519–62.

Krammer, S. M. S. (2009) 'Drivers of national innovation in transition: evidence from a panel of Eastern European countries', *Research Policy*, 38: 845–60.

Krugman, P. (1991) *Geography and Trade*, Cambridge, MA: The MIT Press.

Kuhn, T. (1962) *The Structure of Scientific Revolution*, Chicago, IL: The University of Chicago Press.

Kuznets, S. (1940) 'Schumpeter's business cycle', *American Economic Review*, 30: 257–71.

Kuznets, S. S. (1969) *Modern Economic Growth: Rate, Structure, and Spread*, New Haven, CT: Yale University Press.

Lall, S. (1992) 'Technological capabilities and industrialization', *World Development*, 20: 165–86.

Landes, D. (1969) *The Unbound Prometheus*, Cambridge: Cambridge University Press.

Landes, D. (1998) *The Wealth and Poverty of Nations*, London: Abacus.

Langlois, R. N. (2002) 'Modularity in technology and organization', *Journal of Economic Behaviour & Organization*, 49: 19–37.

Langlois, R. N. (2003) 'The vanishing hand: the changing dynamics of industrial capitalism', *Industrial and Corporate Change*, 12: 351–85.

Langlois, R. N. and Robertson, P. L. (1992) 'Networks and innovation in a modular system: lessons from the microcomputer and stereo component industries', *Research Policy*, 21: 297–313.

Laursen, K. (2000) *Trade, Specialisation, Technology and Economic Growth*, Cheltenham: Edward Elgar.

Laursen, K. and Salter, A. (2005) 'Open for innovation: the role of openness in explaining innovation performance among the UK manufacturing firms', *Strategic Management Journal*, 27: 131–50.

Leonard-Barton, D. (1992) 'Core capabilities and core rigidities: a paradox in managing new product development', *Strategic Management Journal*, 13: 111–26.

Leonardi, R. (1995) *Convergence, Cohesion and Integration in the European Union*, London: Macmillan.

Lerner, J. (1999) 'The government as venture capitalist: the long-run effects of SBIR program', *Journal of Business*, 72: 285–318.

Levinthal, D. A. and March, J. G. (1981) 'A model of adaptive organizational search', *Journal of Economic Behaviour & Organization*, 2: 307–33.

Levinthal, D. A. and March, J. G. (1993) 'The myopia of learning', *Strategic Management Journal*, 14: 95–112.

Lorenz, E. and Lundvall, B. A. (eds) (2006) *How Europe's Economies Learn.* Oxford: Oxford University Press.

Louca, F. and Mendonca, S. (1999) 'Steady change: The 200 largest US manufacturing firms in the twentieth century', Working Paper 14/99, CISEP-ISEG, UTL, Lisbon.

Lundvall, B. A. (1992) *National Systems of Innovation*, London: Pinter Publishing.

Lundvall, B. A. (1999) Technology policy in the learning economy. In Archibugi, D. *et al.* (eds), *Innovation Policy in a Global Economy*, Cambridge: Cambridge University Press.

Lundvall, B. A. and Borras, S. (2005) Science, technology, and innovation policy. In Fagerberg, J. *et al.* (eds), *The Oxford Handbook of Innovation*, Oxford: Oxford University Press.

Lundvall, B. A., Johnson, B., Andersen, E. S. and Dalum, B. (2002) 'National systems of production, innovation and competence building', *Research Policy*, 31: 213–31.

Majumdar, S. K. and Venkataraman, S. (1993) 'New technology adoption in US telecommunications: the role of competitive pressures and firm-level inducements', *Research Policy*, 41: 521–36.

Malerba, F. (2004) Sectoral systems of innovation: basic concepts. In Malerba, F. (ed.), *Sectoral Systems of Innovation: Basic Concepts*, Cambridge: Cambridge University Press.

Malerba, F. and Orsenigo, L. (1995) 'Schumpeterian patterns of innovation', *Cambridge Journal of Economics*, 19: 47–65.

Manca, A. R., Governatori, M. and Mascherini, M. (2010) *Towards a Set of Composite Indicators on Flexicurity: a Comprehensive Approach*, Brussels: ISPRA – Joint Research Centre, European Commission.

March, J. (1991) 'Exploration and exploitation in organizational learning', *Organization Science*, 2: 71–87.

March, J. G. (1981) 'Footnotes to organizational change', *Administrative Science Quarterly*, 26: 563–77.

Markit (2009) Markit Credit Conditions Survey, London: Markit.

Martin (2001) 'EMU versus the regions? Regional convergence and divergence in Euroland', *Journal of Economic Geography*, 1: 51–80.

Massini, S., Lewin, A. Y., Numagami, T. and Pettigrew, A. M. (2002) 'The evolution of organizational routines among large Western and Japanese firms', *Research Policy*, 31: 1333–48.

Maurseth, P. B. (2001) 'Convergence, geography and technology', *Structural Change and Economic Dynamics*, 12: 247–76.

Meliciani, V. (2001) *Technology, Trade and Growth in OECD Countries*, London: Routledge.

Mensch, G. O. (1979) *Stalemate in Technology: Innovations Overcome the Depression*, Cambridge, MA: Ballinger Publishing Company.

Methé, D., Swaminathan, A. and Mitchell, W. (1996) 'The underemphasized role of established firms as the sources of major innovations', *Industrial and Corporate Change*, 5: 1181–203.

Miles, I. (2005) Innovation in services. In Fagerberg, J. *et al.* (eds), *The Oxford Handbook of Innovation*. Oxford: Oxford University Press.

Minsky, H. P. (1975) *John Maynard Keynes*, New York, NY: Columbia University Press.

Minsky, H. P. (1986) *Stabilizing an Unstable Economy*, London: Yale University Press.

Modigliani, F. and Miller, M. H. (1958) 'The cost of capital, corporation finance and the theory of investment', *American Economic Review*, 48: 261–97.

Mokyr, J. (1992) *The Lever of Riches: Technological Creativity and Economic Progress*, Oxford: Oxford University Press.

Mokyr, J. (2002) *The Gifts of Athena. Historical Origins of the Knowledge Economy*, Princeton, NJ: Princeton University Press.

Moreno, R., Paci, R. and Usai, S. (2005) 'Spatial spillovers and innovation activity in European regions', *Environment and Planning*, 37, 1793–812.

Mowery, D. C. and Rosenberg, N. (1989) *Technology and the Pursuit of Economic Growth*, Cambridge: Cambridge University Press.

Myrdal, G. (1957) *Economic Theory and Underdeveloped Regions*, London: Duckworth.

Nelson, R. (1993) *National Systems of Innovation*, Oxford: Oxford University Press.

Nelson, R. (2001) 'Making sense of institutions as a factor shaping economic performance', *Journal of Economic Behaviour & Organization*, 44: 31–54.

Nelson, R. and Winter, S. (1982) *An Evolutionary Theory of Economic Change*, Cambridge, MA: Harvard University Press.

Nelson, R. and Winter, S. G. (2002) 'Evolutionary theorizing in economics', *Journal of Economic Perspectives*, 16: 23–46.

Nelson, R. R. (1959) 'The simple economics of basic scientific research', *Journal of Political Economy*, 67: 297–306.

Neven, D. and Gouymte, C. (2008) 'Regional convergence in the European Community', *Journal of Common Market Studies*, 33: 47–65.

Nohria, N. and Gulati, R. (1996) 'Is slack good for innovation?' *Academy of Management Journal*, 39: 1245–64.

Nohria, N. and Gulati, R. (1997) 'What is the optimum amount of organizational slack? A study of the relationship between slack and innovation in multinational firms', *European Management Journal*, 15: 603–11.

North, D. C. (1990) *Institutions, Institutional Change and Economic Performance*, Cambridge: Cambridge University Press.

North, D. C. (2005) *Understanding the Process of Economic Change*, Princeton, NJ: Princeton University Press.

OECD (2005a) *Growth in Service. Fostering Employment, Productivity and Innovation*, Paris: OECD.

OECD (2005b) *Oslo Manual. Guidelines for Collecting and Interpreting Innovation Data*, Paris: OECD.

OECD (2009a) *Policy Responses to the Economic Crisis: Investing in Innovation for Long-Term Growth*, OECD.

OECD (2009b) *Green Growth: Overcoming the Crisis and Beyond*, OECD.

O'Sullivan, M. (2005) Finance and innovation. In Fagerberg, J. *et al.* (eds), *The Oxford Handbook of Innovation.* Oxford, UK: Oxford University Press.

Paci, R. and Usai, S. (2009) 'Knowledge flows across European regions', *Annals of Regional Science*, 43, 669–90.

Palan, N. and Schmiedeberg, C. (2010) 'Structural convergence of European countries'. *Structural Change and Economic Dynamics*, doi:10.1016/j.strueco.2010.01.001.

Patel, P. and Pavitt, K. (1994) 'Uneven (and divergent) technological accumulation among advanced countries: evidence and a framework of explanation', *Industrial and Corporate Change*, 3: 759–87.

Patel, P. and Pavitt, K. (1997) 'The technological competences of the world's largest firms: complex and path-dependent, but not much variety', *Research Policy*, 26: 141–56.

Pavitt, K. (1984) 'Sectoral patterns of technological change: towards a taxonomy and a theory', *Research Policy*, 13: 343–73.

Pavitt, K. (1987) 'The objectives of technology policy', *Science and Public Policy*, 14: 182–88.

Pavitt, K. (1988) International patterns of technological accumulation. In Hood, N. and Vahlne, J. E. (eds), *International Patterns of Technological Accumulation*, London: Croom Helm.

Pavitt, K. (2005) Innovation processes. In Fagerberg, J. *et al.* (eds), *The Oxford Handbook of Innovation.* Oxford: Oxford University Press.

Pavitt, K. and Patel, P. (1988) 'The international distribution and determinants of technological activities', *Oxford Review of Economic Policy*, 4: 35–55.

Perez, C. (2002) *Technological Revolutions and Financial Capital: The Dynamics of Bubbles and Golden Ages*, Cheltenham: Edward Elgar.

Perez, C. (2009a) 'The double bubble at the turn of the century: technological roots and structural implications', *Cambridge Journal of Economics*, 33: 779–805.

Perez, C. (2009b) 'After crisis: creative construction', *Open Democracy*, 5 March 2009.

Perez, C. (2010) 'Technological revolutions and techno-economic paradigms', *Cambridge Journal of Economics*, 34: 185–202.

Perez, C. and Soete, L. (1988) Catching up in technology: entry barriers and windows of opportunity. In Dosi, G. *et al.* (eds), *Technical Change and Economic Theory*, London: Pinter Publisher.

Petrakos, G. and Artelaris, P. (2009) 'European regional convergence revisited: a weighted least squares approach', *Growth and Change*, 40: 314–31.

Pianta, M. (2001) Innovation, demand and employment. In Petit, P. and Soete, L. (eds), *Technology and the Future of European Employment*, Cheltenham: Elgar.

Pianta, M. (2004) Innovation and Employment. In Fagerberg, J. *et al.* (eds), *The Oxford Handbook of Innovation*, Oxford, UK: Oxford University Press.

Piore, M. J. and Sabel, C. (1984) *The Second Industrial Divide. Possibilities for Prosperity*, New York, NY: Basic Books.

Piscitello, L. (2004) 'Corporate diversification, coherence and economic performance', *Industrial and Corporate Change*, 13: 757–87.

Piva, M. and Vivarelli, M. (2007) 'Is demand-pulled innovation equally important in different groups of firms?' *Cambridge Journal of Economics*, 31: 691–710.

Polanyi, M. (1966) *The Tacit Dimension*, New York, NY: Doubleday.

Quah, D. T., (1996) 'Empirics for economic growth and convergence', *European Economic Review*, 4: 1353–75.

Rabe-Hesketh, S. and Skrondal, A. (2004) *Generalized Latent Variable Modelling*, Boca Raton, FL: Chapman & Hall.

Reijnders, J. (1990) *Long Waves in Economic Development*, Aldershot: Edward Elgar.

Rodriguez-Pose, A. (1999) 'Innovation prone and innovation averse societies: economic performance in Europe', *Growth and Change*, 30: 75–105.

Rodriguez-Pose, A. and Crescenzi, R. (2008) 'Research and development, spillovers, innovation systems, and the genesis of regional growth in Europe', *Regional Studies*, 42: 51–67.

Rodrik, D. (2007) *One Economics Many Recipes*, Princeton, NJ: Princeton University Press.

Romer, P. (1986) 'Increasing returns and long run growth', *Journal of Political Economy*, 94: 1002–37.

Rosenberg, N. (1982) *Inside the Black Box: Technology and Economics*, Cambridge: Cambridge University Press.

Roubini, N. and Mihm, S. (2010) *Crisis Economics: A Crash Course in the Future of Finance*, New York, NY: Penguin Press.

Ruttan, V. W. (1997) 'Induced innovation, evolutionary theory and path dependence: Sources of technical change', *Economic Journal*, 107: 1520–29.

Sala-i-Martin, X. and Sachs, J. (1991) 'Fiscal federalism and optimum currency areas: evidence for Europe from the US', National Bureau of Economic Research, Working Paper 3855.

Sanchez, R. and Mahoney, J. (1996) 'Modularity, flexibility, and knowledge management in product and organization design', *Strategic Management Journal*, 17: 63–76.

Santarelli, E. (1995) *Finance and Technological Change: Theory and Evidence*, London: Macmillan.

Scherer, F. M. (1982) 'Demand-pull and technological invention: Schmookler revisited', *Journal of Industrial Economics*, 30: 225–37.

Scherer, F. M. (1992) 'Schumpeter and plausible capitalism', *Journal of Economic Literature*, 30: 1416–33.

Scherer, F. M. (2000) 'Technology policy for a world of skew-distributed outcomes', *Research Policy*, 29: 559–66.

Schmookler, J. (1962) 'Economic cources of inventive activity', *Journal of Economic History*, March: 1–20.

Schmookler, J. (1966) *Invention and Economic Growth*, Cambridge, MA: Harvard University Press.

Schumpeter, J. A. (1911 (1934)) *The Theory of Economic Development*, Cambridge, MA: Harvard University Press.

Schumpeter, J. A. (1939) *Business Cycle: A Theoretical, Historical and Statistical Analysis of the Capitalist Process*, New York, NY: McGraw-Hill.

Schumpeter, J. A. (1942) *Capitalism, Socialism and Democracy*, New York, NY: Harper.

Simonetti, R. (1996) 'Technical change and firm growth: 'creative destruction' in the Fortune List, 1963–1987', *Open Discussion Papers in Economics*, 13.

Solow, R. (1956) 'A contribution to the theory of economic growth', *Quarterly Journal of Economics*, 70: 65–94.

Srholec, M. and Verspagen, B. (2008) 'The Voyage of the Beagle in innovation system land. Exploration on sectors, innovation, heterogeneity and selection', UNU-Merit Working Paper.

Sturgeon, T. J. (2002) 'Modular production networks: a new American model of industrial organization', *Industrial and Corporate Change*, 11: 451–96.

Sylos Labini, P. (1962) *Oligopoly and Technical Progress*, Boston, MA: Harvard University Press.

Teece, D. J., Rumelt, R., Dosi, G. and Winter, S. (1994) 'Understanding corporate coherence: theory and evidence', *Journal of Economic Behaviour & Organization*, 23: 1–30.

Tether, B. and Tajar, A. (2008) 'The organizational-cooperation mode of innovation and its prominence amongst European service firms', *Research Policy*, 37: 720–39.

The Economist (2008) 'The invasion of the sovereign-wealth funds. the biggest worry about rich Arab and Asian states buying up Wall Street is the potential backlash', 17 January 2008.

Tsoukas, H. and Knudsen, C. (2003) *The Oxford Handbook of Organization Theory*, Oxford: Oxford University Press.

Tushman, M. L. and Anderson, P. (1986) 'Technological discontinuities and organizational environments', *Administrative Science Quarterly*, 31: 439–65.

Tushman, M., Smith, W. K., Wood, R. C., Westerman, G. and O'Reilly, C. (2004) 'Innovation streams and ambidextrous organization design', HBS Working Paper.

Tylecote, A. (1992) *The Long Wave in the World Economy: The Present Crisis in Historical Perspective*, London: Routledge.

Van Duijn, J. J. (1983) *The Long Wave in Economic Life*, London: George Allen & Unwin.

Veblen, T. (2008 (1899)) *The Theory of the Leisure Class*, Oxford: Oxford University Press.

Verspagen, B. (2005) Innovation and economic growth. In Fagerberg, J. *et al.* (eds), *The Oxford Handbook of Innovation*, Oxford, UK: Oxford University Press.

von Hippel, E. (1998) *The Sources of Innovation*, New York, NY: Oxford University Press.

von Hippel, E. (2005) *Democritizing Innovation*, Cambridge, MA: The MIT Press.

Von Tunzelmann, N. and Nassehi, S. (2004) 'Technology policy, European Union enlargement, and economic, social and political sustainability', *Science and Public Policy*, 31: 475–83.

Wade, R. (2009) 'From global imbalances to global reorganisations', *Cambridge Journal of Economics*, 33: 539–62.

Wonglimpiyarat, J. (2006) 'The dynamic economic engine at Silicon Valley and US government programmes in financing innovation', *Technovation*, 26: 1081–89.

Zimmermann, K. (1995) 'Tackling the European migration problem', *Journal of Economic Perspectives*, 9: 52–71.

Zimmermann, K. (2005) 'European labour mobility: challenges and potentials, *De Economist*, 127: 425–50.

Zizmond, E. and Novak, M. (2007) 'Controversies of technology convergence within the European Union', *Industrial Management & Data System*, 107: 618–35.

Index

Evangelista 91, 136–7
Evolutionary 43, 46, 114, 147, 148, 149, 158

Facebook 163
Fagerberg 44–6, 56, 60, 81, 98
Faruqee 15
Federal Reserve 11
Ferguson 2, 16–17
Field 97
Filippetti 44, 61–2, 91, 98, 137
fixed capital 34, 156
flexicurity 51, 96–8, 100, 105, 108, 124
Freeman 3, 25–6, 29, 32–5, 39–43, 45–6, 79, 82, 97, 115, 147, 165
Frenz 91, 137
Friedrich 87

Galbraith 2, 11, 119
Gallouj 137
Garud 149
Geroski 40, 43, 47, 83, 90, 115, 150
Google 163
Grandstrand 39, 90, 116, 119
Greve 146, 148, 150
Griffith 56
Grossman 60

Hall 5, 28, 36, 38–9, 43–5, 48–9, 51, 79, 81, 97, 104, 114–15, 146, 148
Hanckè 45, 48–9
Henderson 39, 113, 115, 118
Hodgson 42, 55
Holbrook 115
Hollenstein 137
Howells 136, 166

Iammarino 44, 56, 166–7
Iansiti 39, 119, 166
IBM 4, 163
Ietto-Gillies 91
inertia 32, 39, 115, 118
Innovation policy 44, 56, 72, 93, 162
institutions 4–5, 17, 32, 42, 44–52, 55, 75, 79–82, 97–102, 106, 118, 123
internationalization 86, 91, 137
internet 18, 35, 150–1, 163, 165

Kleinknecht 43, 82, 156
Knudsen 158

learning 34, 39, 46, 51, 69, 76, 80–2, 88, 93–4, 113, 115, 148–9
Lerner 36, 43, 146, 148

Levien 39, 119, 166
lock-in 99–100
Lundvall 34, 44–7, 55–6, 79–80, 97–8, 167

Mahoney 166
Malerba 38, 45, 114, 116, 118–19, 134
March 39, 59, 115, 118, 121, 146–7, 158
market structure 4, 27, 33, 38, 115, 119
Mowery 42
multinational corporations 93

Nassehi 56
national system of innovation 41–2, 46–7, 74, 79–80
North 9, 32, 42, 44–6, 48, 61, 79, 81, 104
Novak 61

O'Sullivan 27, 36, 43, 81, 148, 165
Oecd 9–10, 35, 73, 81, 83, 91–2, 98–9, 102, 136–7, 139, 161–2, 167
open innovation 45, 168, 171
organizational capabilities 38
Orsenigo 38, 40, 47, 90, 97, 114–16, 119, 134, 150

Paci 167
Palan 167
Patel 38–9, 47, 55, 90, 114, 119
patterns of innovation 3, 5, 22, 38, 47–8, 80–1, 93, 116, 134–5, 161, 165, 170
Pavitt 4, 34, 37–9, 44, 47, 55–6, 90, 92, 114, 116, 119, 166
Perez 3, 18, 27–8, 30–2, 42, 56, 92, 97, 113, 115, 135, 147, 166
Petrakos 167
Peyrache 61–2, 98
Pianta 43–4, 47, 83, 130, 169
Piore 34
Piscitello 116
Piva 83
Polanyi 74
Prencipe 166

Quaglia 55
Quah 167

Rabe-Hesketh 104
Reijnders 23, 166
Rodriguez-Pose 56, 74, 166–7
Rodrik 42, 44, 99
Romer 60
Rosenberg 42–3
Roubini 2, 11

For Product Safety Concerns and Information please contact our
EU representative GPSR@taylorandfrancis.com Taylor & Francis
Verlag GmbH, Kaufingerstraße 24, 80331 München, Germany